Classic Christianity

A Year of Timeless Devotions
Volume II Summer and Autumn

Based on the Writings of The Reverend L.A. Meade,
Revised and Edited by
Patricia Ediger and Cara Shelton

CROSSBOOKS
PUBLISHING

CrossBooks™
A Division of LifeWay
1663 Liberty Drive
Bloomington, IN 47403
www.crossbooks.com
Phone: 1-866-879-0502

First published by CrossBooks 10/26/2011

ISBN: 978-1-4627-0647-1 (sc)
ISBN: 978-1-4627-0648-8 (hc)
ISBN: 978-1-4627-1159-8 (e)

Library of Congress Control Number: 2011918655

Printed in the United States of America

Table of Contents

Summer

Autumn

Classic Christianity
A Year of Timeless Devotions

SUMMER
Daily Devotions for July, August, and September

Based on the Writings of
The Reverend L.A. Meade

Revised and Edited by
Patricia Ediger and Cara Shelton

Under the Tent

From Michigan to Florida, from South Carolina to the west coast, Lawrence Meade traveled to bring God's Word to those who needed to hear it. One day he went to get a permit to erect the tent for an upcoming revival and met the assistant to the city manager of Sanford, Florida, a young widow named Lillian Duley. She was a devoted Christian worker. Lawrence invited her to the revival. After a lengthy courtship, on June 25th, 1928, Lawrence and Lillian were married in the Meade Brothers' tent, with over 2,000 in attendance, in Sumter, South Carolina.

Lillian was a graceful addition to the work. She loved working with the children and the "young people," as the teens were known then. Traveling with Lawrence across the country, she worked tirelessly alongside him, two workers with one yoke. In state after state, she sang, played the piano, taught children's lessons and led young people's programs. She was truly in all things his helpmeet. In L.A.'s words she was "of inestimable value then and remain(ed) so after nearly 50 years."

In 1931, the congregation of a local church where the Meades had been holding meetings came to call. Their pastor's health had suddenly failed, forcing his retirement. The church was in a quandary, would the Rev. Meade help them out for three months? The three months lengthened to several years, the first pastorate he had held since those early days in Grand Ledge. After seeing the church back on its feet, the Meades once again headed out, for the fields were "white unto harvest," and God's call still led out onto the road.

It wasn't until 1941, when he was called to Pleasant Valley Baptist Church in Camarillo, California to replace Pastor Dawson, who entered WW II as a chaplain, that the Rev. Meade finally settled down. Although the form of his ministry changed, his fervor, drive, passion, and uncompromisingly Biblical views did not. His booming voice, so well-suited to huge tents and auditoriums, sang out to lead the hymns and to speak the truth in love for another twenty-five years.

Preface

Several years ago, as we helped our elderly mother move, we discovered a treasure in the rafters above her garage.

Our grandfather, the Reverend Lawrence A. Meade, was an internationally known evangelist and ordained minister who preached all over this nation for more than fifty years. We knew he spoke and taught with passion and fervor, sincerity and integrity to the Word. What we didn't know was that he wrote with the same power and honesty.

When we lifted the lids on the dusty boxes in the attic, we discovered words so fraught with meaning for today's world and for today's Christian that we were amazed. Could words this fresh really be over ninety years old? It seemed impossible, but it is so.

This treasure was a stewardship from God to us. We have felt deeply the responsibility to share these insights that others might benefit. And now, this stewardship passes to you, the reader. These devotions are not a fast-food meal, dear friend. They are a full course dinner to be savored and enjoyed over time. They are not flashy. The light that shines through them, however, is steady and unwavering. This is a book for those of us who want "more" of God. God bless you as you follow Him.

Patricia and Cara

Profit and Loss

Scripture Reading: Mark 8:34-38

Key Verse: ". . . what will it profit a man if he gains the whole world and loses his own soul?" Mark 8:36

Jesus was never interested in winning disciples whose loyalty was born of blindness or lack of understanding. When a young man came to Him all aflame with enthusiasm vowing, "I will follow you wherever you go," the Master wanted him to first count the cost of discipleship.

Some time ago a friend of mine gave himself the trouble of boarding the wrong train. He thought it was going to Washington D.C. when it really was going to Washington, North Carolina. When his mistake was discovered he had to get off and walk about a mile back to the station carrying two heavy cases. Not only that, but by taking the wrong train he had missed the right one. Our Lord urges that we count the cost, that we know where the train is going before we get on board.

"What will it profit a man if he gains the whole world and loses his own soul?" This text sounds a bit old fashioned. You have heard it quoted many times. But it has one word in it that is thoroughly up-to-date. In fact, this word is as much at home in our day as it was when it was uttered 2,000 years ago. That word is "profit."

Now, everyone is interested in profits of one kind or another, and rightly so. The tragedy is that so many have an eye for only one kind of profit, that which is of this earth.

Some years ago an enthusiastic young teacher sought to erect a high school building in the village where he was teaching. He invited some of the leading citizens of the town to a meeting. When he had outlined his plan, the wealthiest of the group said, "I am all for it if you will show me the dividends." By this he meant he wanted to be shown how it would pay him in dollars and cents. Of course the dividends would pay him in terms of better-trained boys and girls. But, teaching better citizens did not interest him in the least. He was only interested in profit measured in cash.

On the other hand, here is a lonely man in the heart of Africa. He has had one attack of fever after another. In addition, because he is suffering from scurvy his own teeth are dropping into his hand one by one. Why does David Livingstone not go home where he can keep his health? What is he seeking to gain? He is seeking the profit that comes from helping to heal the world's open sores. He is seeking profit for others rather than himself and by so doing he is being vastly enriched.

Jesus sums up these two kinds of profit in two words. He calls them "the world," and "the soul." To lose my soul is to lose my very self. It means the loss of all of my finest possibilities. It means the loss of companionship with God. The man who loses his soul loses all. He will lose all opportunity for peace with God and pardon for sin. He will lose Eternal life and all hope of it. For such there is absolutely no compensation. To save the soul is to come into a relationship with Jesus Christ and gain all these things.

My friends, you have just one life to invest. Where are you going to invest it? Will you put God first or yourself first? If you choose yourself and the world where are you going to carry your bags of wealth or your fame or popularity when your life on this earth is finished? What is your choice?

Dear Lord, by not making my choice I have already chosen great loss. I purposefully and deliberately choose You, understanding where this train of life is going and what it might cost. I may be asked to forsake some things of this world, but my profit through You will be so much greater. Thank You Father. Amen

Scripture Reading: Revelation Chapter 5

Key Verse: "And they sang a new song, saying: 'You are worthy to take the scroll, and to open its seals; for You were slain and have redeemed us to God by Your blood out of every tribe and tongue and people and nation, and have made us kings and priests to our God; and we shall reign on the earth.'"
Revelation 5:9

Ever since the morning stars sang together and the sons of God shouted for joy, music has been ordained of God for the expression of the soul's highest emotion of gladness and praise. God has given it a great place among both the earthly peoples and the celestial inhabitants.

The new song is a perpetual song because its source is in the inexhaustible resources of God. We sing it here in happy anticipation and we will sing it there in blessed realization. You see, that which will make heaven so happy is shared with earth. We practice it here so we may be better prepared in glory.

It is a song of gratitude. Gratitude is a part of the soul's wardrobe, a garment of praise. What a beautiful garment it is, and how few of us use it often enough.

And, this song commemorates the passing of the dark into light, the battle that was fought until victory. It sings of temptations overcome, afflictions endured, and persecutions suffered. The martyrs of all ages will lead the singing in blessed remembrance of Him who was faithful.

This song will not forget the manger and the incarnation. It will not overlook the cross where He took the sinner's blame. It will have a swelling note on the theme of resurrection, will vibrate on ascension glory, and resound with the trumpet-blast at the Savior's second coming.

When Düsseldorf held its famous musical convocation it lasted four days, but the new song whose rapturous notes John heard has hardly begun. Its song will be constantly swelling and rising higher and higher as the inhabitants increase. Yes, the new song is an unending song. It will honor Christ and celebrate His victory forever.

History tells us of the enthusiasm of the French soldiers in World War I as they swept through the city of Paris. Regiment by regiment they marched by singing "La Marsellaise." They sang of the hope of victory awaiting them. If such enthusiasm attended a hoped-for victory, what will be the enthusiasm of the singers of the new song when the gates and everlasting doors open and we lift up our heads for the King of Glory?

With graves empty and death, the last enemy, destroyed, Christ's conquering feet lead His hosts marching in. You know the enthusiasm a national anthem can create if you have ever witnessed an English assembly when the bands strike up "God Save the Queen." But, oh, what enthusiasm awaits our hearts when the new song begins to roll and echo and reverberate throughout heaven.

Oh, that your heart and mine might be made attuned here in preparation for a share in that celebration yonder! Oh, for the day when our voices rise with the celestial chorus to sing His praises, "Worthy is the Lamb who was slain to receive power and riches and wisdom, and strength and honor and glory and blessing! Blessing and honor and glory and power be to Him who sits on the throne, and to the Lamb, forever and ever!"

Praise Your Holy Name, my sweet Lord Jesus! Praise Your mighty power and Your mighty works! How I look forward to the day when, "every knee shall bow and every tongue confess that Jesus Christ is Lord." Halleluiah! Praise Your Name . . . Amen.

Scripture: Jonah Chapter 4

Key Verse: . . . 'Ah, Lord, was not this what I said when I was still in my country? Therefore I fled previously to Tarshish; for I know that You are a gracious and merciful God, slow to anger and abundant in lovingkindness, One who relents from doing harm.'" Jonah 4:2

The story of Jonah is one of the amazingly beautiful miracles of the Old Testament. It is so fragrant with the breath of inspiration that it is impossible to account for it except in terms of God. In no other book of the Old Testament are narrowness, intolerance, and selfishness more sharply rebuked. In no other book do we realize more compellingly the tender love of God, not only for His children, but for all His creatures as well.

Here we see that God cannot bear the thought of destroying Nineveh not only because of the six score thousand babies within its walls, but also because there is much cattle. We cannot read this book without realizing that as God's children we must be brotherly toward all men. Not only so, but we must not be needlessly unkind to any living thing.

The Book of Jonah is peculiar among the prophetic writings in that it contains no message delivered to the people of God by the prophet whose name it bears. The Book is a story, and the story is the message.

In order to discover the message of the book, we must sift the incidental from the essential in the story. The incidental things are the ship, the storm, the fish, the gourd, the wind, and Nineveh. The essential things are only the transactions between Jonah and God.

We note that Jonah's commission was from the Lord, "Arise and go to Nineveh that great city and cry against it." God spoke to Jonah in that day and Jonah recognized it. Jonah did not want to go to Nineveh. So Jonah attempted to 'resign' from God's service, ". . . Jonah arose to flee to Tarshish from the presence of the Lord. He went down to Joppa, and found a ship going to Tarshish; so he paid the fare, and went down into it, to go with them to Tarshish from the presence of the Lord." Jonah was fleeing from the appointment of God.

There was a ship ready to sail. It was going to the destination he wanted, as well. It seemed so much easier to Jonah to take a ship to Tarshish than to walk all the way to Nineveh. But if the latter would leave you in God's company, you are a fool to set sail.

Jonah thought he paid the fare. He was badly mistaken. This was no excursion fare, for there was much more to be paid. The most expensive trip any young man or woman takes is when he or she sails away from God. The sea may be calm at first. It may be a good ship and sociable company. Everything may seem quite agreeable at first, but that's the way surrender to temptation begins, with sunny skies and smooth sailing. But there is a storm coming and you will find yourself hopeless. Sunny skies and smooth sailing soon disappear in the sea of temptation. Ask those who have run from God. Ask the broken-hearted, those with ruined lives from fleeing God. Ask them, "What's the fare from Joppa to Tarshish?"

Listen, beloved, there are just two cities on your map today. There is Nineveh of Obedience or Tarshish of Disobedience. Which city are you headed for? Oh, you know what God wants you to do. Don't sail away. Rather, say with Samuel, "Here I am." Say with Isaiah, "Here I am, send me." And say with Paul, "Lord, what will You have me to do?"

Here I am, Lord. Send me. Use me. What will You have me to do? Amen.

July 4   Ask For the Old Paths

Scripture: Jeremiah 6: 16-20

Key Verse: ". . . Ask for the old paths, where the good way is, and walk in it; then you will find rest for your souls.'" Jeremiah 6:16

On any Fourth of July the great words of the Declaration of Independence ring like bells throughout the nation. Our forefathers had come to a crossroad in their lives and the life of this nation. From that famed intersection of history they formed the Continental Congress and out of that the Declaration of Independence, the birth certificate of our country.

There are many crossroads in history, and it is at these intersections of life God often speaks words of guidance. Let us consider one such episode in the Scriptures. One day the Lord appeared to Jeremiah the prophet and bade him stand at the crossroads where various types of humanity were surging by to see if he could not help influence them to do at least three things; ask for the old paths, walk in the old paths, and enjoy the rest that comes to those who seek and find the old paths.

One of the old paths is the corridor which leads back to the places of prayer and consecration. Our forefathers emphasized the devotional life. They prayed alone, in family circles, in little groups, and when they prayed revival fires broke out upon the nation. When the Federal Convention met in Philadelphia in 1787 for the purpose of framing the constitution, Benjamin Franklin introduced a resolution that the meetings should always be opened with prayer. We are a nation founded on prayer. Let us maintain this nation by going back to the old path.

We also need to ask for and seek the paths which lead to the inspired Word of God. This book contains the mind of God, the state of man, the way of salvation, the doom of sinners, and the joy of believers. Its doctrines are holy, its precepts are binding, its histories are true, and its decisions are immutable. Read it to be wise. Believe it to be safe. Practice it to be holy. It contains light to direct you, food to support you, and comfort to cheer you.

It is the traveler's map, the pilgrim's staff, the pilot's compass, the soldier's sword, and the Christian's charter. Christ is its grand subject, our good the design, and the glory of God its end. It should fill the memory, rule the heart, and guide the feet. Read it slowly, frequently, and prayerfully. It is a mine of wealth, a paradise of glory, and a river of pleasure. It involves the highest responsibility, will reward the greatest labor, and will condemn all who trifle with its contents.

The Lord spoke to the prophet and said that he must not only beseech the people to yearn and ask for the old paths, but also walk in them. It isn't enough to be hearers of the Word; we must be doers of it also. We must be more than signboards pointing the way. We must be pilgrims walking in the way.

Those who have asked for the old paths and walked in them have had the guidance and blessings of Almighty God, and more than that, they enjoy the greatest thing in life, soul rest, soul rest down here and eternal rest up there.

How best can we serve our country? By serving our God. By taking the old paths that formed this nation. The One who formed it will keep it, if when we stand at the intersection we choose to walk the old paths.

Almighty God, thank You for this nation. Bless it and guide our leaders. Be with our President and our congress. May their hearts be led to the old paths that our country might have peace. And Lord, let me choose rightly the old paths You have given. But, let my foundations be with You. Amen

July 5   Four Great Things

Scripture Reading: John Chapter 3

Key Verse: "For God so loved the world that He gave His only begotten Son, that whoever believes in Him should not perish but have everlasting life." John 3:16

Is that a groan I hear? Do I hear someone say, "Surely we're not going to study that text again?" Yes, we are. There is so much to learn from it we could study it many times and not fathom its riches. It has been called the key text of the Bible because, as a key, it unlocks the meaning and mystery of the Bible. It is the fulfilling of the prophets. It is the explanation of the Gospels and the Epistles. It is the essential of Christianity for all ages everywhere.

So, these things being true, let us proceed to study four facets of this verse: First A Great Fact, *God loves you*; Second A Great Gift, *He gave His Son for you*; Third A Great Promise, *that you should not perish*; Fourth A Great Result, *but have everlasting life.*

This text shows the fact: God loved, the object that He loved, the world, and the extent of His love, "So." The most stupendous truth in the universe is this fact, God is love. But why did He love us? Nicodemus sat talking to Jesus, and you and I with him would be willing to acknowledge that God created the whole world, that God governs the whole world and directs affairs, that God would finally judge the world. But to be told that God loved the world, it must have jarred upon his Jewish mind. And so with the unbelieving hearts of the children of men everywhere, they find it hard to believe that God loves them.

He does because it is His nature; it is as natural for God to love as for the sun to shine. This great burning sphere shines because it is its nature to shine. The sun is no respecter of bodies as he shines on the bald mountain, the verdant valley, the blossoming rosebud, and the dead tree. He shines on all things alike. So, God's nature and name is Love, and God is no respecter of persons in His love. He loves all men, the meanest and the best, the most abandoned sinner and the holiest saint. Perhaps even more so the sinner. Where does that doctrine come from? The life of Christ. "What man of you, having a hundred sheep, if he loses one of them, does not leave the ninety- nine in the wilderness, and go after the one which is lost?"

Does God's love save? If love could save no mother's boy would stagger into a drunkard's grave. If love could save then no good wife's husband would ever die on the gallows. Hear me, love can pity, love can help, love can suffer, love can die, but love cannot save. It cannot save. God so loved that He gave.

That is the Gift. He loved us so much He gave His Son. No other gift would do. He gave His best, His only, His masterpiece. It was the only way the promise could be fulfilled, the promise that we should not perish. Someone had to pay the penalty for sin. Justice demands it. Because God loves us He gave the gift of Jesus to take our place so we might not perish. Jesus perished for us.

Because of the fact that God loves us, and gave the gift of His Son to fulfill the promise that we would not perish, we have the result. He raised Jesus through the resurrection and by the resurrection purchased for us the same results, "For God so loved the world that He gave His only Son, that whoever believes in Him should not perish, but have everlasting life."

Father God, Your love is so universal, yet so personal. To think that the Almighty Lord loves ME is nearly unfathomable. Let my life be a reflection of my gratitude for Your unending love by loving others. Amen

The Meanest Word

Scripture Reading: I Corinthians Chapter 13

Key Verse: "Love . . . thinks no evil; does not rejoice in iniquity, but rejoices in the truth . . . ."

I Corinthians 13: 4-6

What is the meanest word because it is both cowardly and cruel? What is the word that has destroyed friendships, disrupted churches, devastated homes, engendered wars and strife, saddened and clouded the lives of men and women? What is the word that the devil first became in the Garden of Eden when he spoke against God? What is the word that has the lowest and softest sound and yet the loudest and noisiest echo? That word is "Whisperer."

". . . whisperer separates the best of friends;" recounts Proverbs 16: 28. The Whisperer speaks all languages, wears all kinds of clothing, is a citizen of all countries, belongs to all political parties, moves in all circles and is a member of all churches.

Nehemiah, the heroic builder of the walls of Jerusalem was a victim of the Whisperer. The leaders of the neighboring tribes tried in every way to prevent the building of the walls. Their first weapon was ridicule. Then they tried the threat of armed attack, but Nehemiah armed his men with swords so that he who worked with a trowel was also girded with a sword. Then they tried a futile attempt to trap Nehemiah into a supposedly friendly council where they could assassinate him. As a last resort, they tried to frighten him from his task by slander. They came to him with an open, unsealed letter, inferring that all knew what was in it. It read like this; "It is reported among the nations, and Geshem says, that you and the Jews plan to rebel; therefore, according to these rumors, you are rebuilding the wall, that you may be their king." There was not a more serious charge and dangerous rumor to be afloat. But Nehemiah, instead of being frightened by the report and the whispered slander, denied it and denounced it to these crafty heathen and asked God for strength to complete his task, "So, the wall was finished."

Now, all in the story are dead except Geshem. You will find him in ancient Jerusalem, and in New York, and even your town. He belongs to all nations and races. He has many aliases, among which are the following, "Have you heard? Do you think it could be true? Don't tell anyone but . . . . this is off the record but . . . ."

Yet, Geshem is hard to locate. His name never appears in the telephone book and he changes his address continually. Geshem, you see, is the symbol and sign of the Talebearer, the Defamer, the Detractor, the Slanderer, and the Whisperer.

Whoever listens with interest and delight to a slanderous tale is almost as guilty as the man who whispers the tale, and an old writer has said that both ought to be hanged, the Whisperer by his tongue and the Listener by the ear.

The Old Testament description of the Godly man still stands. ". . . who may abide in Your tabernacle? Who may dwell in Your holy hill? He who walks uprightly, and works righteousness, and speaks the truth in his heart; he who does not backbite with his tongue, nor does evil against his neighbor, nor does he take up a reproach against his friend . . . ."

A beautiful sketch of the Christian is in I Corinthians 13, the man who "thinks no evil, does not rejoice in iniquity . . . ." The mature Christian will always seek to feel another's woes and hide the faults he sees. Test your words. Are they true? Are they needful? And above all, are they kind?

Heavenly Father, please help me to speak only truth, love, and kindness of others. Amen.

Scripture Reading: Colossians Chapter 1

Key Verse: ". . . He is head of the body, the church, who is the beginning, the firstborn from the dead, that in all things He may have the preeminence. For it pleased the Father that in Him all the fullness (of the Godhead) should dwell." Colossians 1:18-19

What a Jesus Paul preached!

First, Paul preached a pre-existent Jesus. He was with God in the beginning, before the foundations of the earth were laid, or the cornerstone was fastened. The pre-existence of Jesus is so baffling a thought that we need to approach it in terms of time as well as eternity. Push your way back in history, from Lincoln at Gettysburg to Washington at Valley Forge, farther now, to the hush of Eden. Go farther still, before the mountains were brought forth or ever God had lighted the fires of millions of suns. Go on out in the vast timeless, fleckless eternity, into the solitudes of infinite being, Jesus of the Carpenter's shop in Nazareth was with God.

But Paul also preached a divine Jesus. He shared the divine nature and ". . . it pleased the Father that in Him all the fullness (of the Godhead) should dwell." He was the Word, the utterance of God, for "All things were created through Him and for Him. And He is before all things." Centuries ago the astronomers had counted 1,022 stars. But today, with telescopes and other helps to peer beyond the boundaries of the eyes, we have found undreamed of depths lighted by unthought-of suns. Millions, billions of them, hurry upon their measureless orbits. And the Carpenter of Nazareth made them all.

Paul also preached a humiliated Jesus. Men are not naturally inclined to give up their all. He was rich in the realm where gold is but paving dust, yet for our sakes He became poor that though His poverty we might become rich. Can you fathom the truth of it?

Paul preached a human Jesus. A mother held Him in her arms, and he was human in his hungers, desires and loves. But, where Plato guesses, Jesus affirms. Where great thinkers reason, Jesus illumines. Where Shakespeare's incomparable genius stands a dumb porter of the soul at the gates of infinite mystery, Jesus walks as Prince of the Realm, and says "I am the way, the truth, and the life."

And Paul preached an exalted Jesus. General Grant was so ill he could scarcely raise a glass of water, when up the avenue came the strains of a military band and the sound of striking feet. He understood it all. His old veterans were honoring their chief. Slowly, painfully, he raised himself from the bed and stood before the window, lifting his hand to his brow and letting it fall. It was his last military salute and the world said, "It was well done." But Jesus met our deadly enemy, sin and death, and alone He conquered them, and stooping His mighty shoulders He lifted us back to God. I and 10,000 times 10,000 cry, "Well done, my Savior and my God."

Lastly, Paul preached a returning, glorified Jesus. John the Divine saw Jesus riding a white horse, with a vesture dipped in blood, followed by the armies of Heaven and all His holy angels, before whom every knee shall bow and every tongue confess.

Today he is saying to His church as He said to Peter, "Do you love me more than these?" And if you do, you'll cry back, "Even so, come, Lord Jesus."

Gracious Jesus, thank You that You came in the form of a man to save me and teach me. From eternity past to eternity future You have been, are, and will be. Thank You that You gave Yourself for me. Amen.

July 8   What Do You Long for?

Scripture Reading: Matthew Chapter 5

Key Verse: "Blessed are those who hunger and thirst for righteousness, for they shall be filled." Matthew 5:6

If we were to put this beatitude in common English, I believe it would read, "Blessed are the men and women who long more than anything else to be Godly." We recognize in this beatitude a divergence from the others. This beatitude is not a benediction pronounced upon those who have attained to righteousness, but upon those who long for it. Evil is the absence of good as darkness is the absence of light. And just as darkness cannot be driven out of a room with a fan or a sword, but by turning on a light, so evil is banished by turning on goodness.

When we get a taste of the good life it arouses our appetite for more. Hence, the first three beatitudes lead to the fourth. "Blessed are those who hunger and thirst for righteousness, for they shall be filled." A mother was riding on the train with her four children. She did not try to interest the little ones; she only sought to control them. Her conversation was a mere series of exclamations, "No! Stop! Don't do that!" When one little fellow ran to the other end of the car she sent sister after him with this injunction, "Go see what Willie is doing and tell him to stop it." She assumed that everything he did was wrong and in that atmosphere she created, the assumption was pretty nearly correct.

Contrast her with the wise and patient mother. She restrains too, but she looks for good points to encourage, she awakens wholesome interests, she banks on the best and thereby she brings out the best. She gradually changes her children's attitude to a desire to obey and please her out of love. This also was Jesus' attitude. He sought to arouse a hunger and thirst after righteousness.

Have you ever been hungry? One has to have known the gnawing, aching pain of hunger if he is to catch the full intensity of Jesus' words in this Beatitude. And while hunger can be terrible, thirst can be far more so. Palestine was a dry country as well as a starved one. And when we read Jesus' words we must try to catch the force of those longings in that land of scarcity and thirst. He is not describing a mere vague preference for doing the right thing. He is depicting a longing which means the difference between life and death.

It is not enough for us to say that our heart is in the right place if our head and hands are in the wrong places. We must give intelligent devotion, and tactful service to the things which are of eternal import.

Righteousness is defined as conformity to the divine standard of right and justice.

The story of the Good Samaritan on the Jericho road illustrates the thought Jesus had in mind. It was not the thought when the Samaritan saw the wounded man, "Now I am a Samaritan and not in very good standing in this Jewish region, therefore I had better help this poor fellow." Nor was it, "My religion tells me I should help another in distress and to do so might merit me in the Day of Judgment." That would have been the story of the self-righteous Samaritan. The Good Samaritan, forgetting self, put the wounded man on his own beast, poured oil in his wounds, took him to the inn, paid the lodging bill and bade the innkeeper take care of him and send him any further expense account. His selflessness forms the story of the Good Samaritan. Why does this parable live on? It is righteousness redeemed by love into active goodness.

Dearest Father, may I not simply contain good intentions, but infused by Your love may they spring to life in deeds and actions in a hurting world. Amen.

July 9   What Do You Long For? II

Scripture Reading: Matthew Chapter 5

Key Verse: "Blessed are they who hunger and thirst for righteousness, for they shall be filled." Matthew 5:6

Jesus gave us love to supplement our laws, and love is never repealed. Our taste for fruit must be raised from the forbidden fruit to the fruit of the Spirit. When we taste love, joy, peace, longsuffering, gentleness, meekness, and temperance, we soon love the taste, for when we want physical things of this world we really long for the temporary feeling it gives us. The fruit of the Spirit is the end result of all our longings. When we realize this, then our desires have become identical with our needs.

To those who hunger and thirst after righteousness, the promise is that they shall be filled. Just as the prodigal in the far country of self indulgence was not satisfied with the husks that the swine ate, so it is with you and me today. We are not satisfied with the crumbs of life; we want to have something wonderful enough to live for. In that case, we need a purpose large enough to gather up our temporary interests into something which gives meaning and zest to the whole of life.

We must ask of our life and interests, "What do they add up to?" Our works must be of such a nature that when age forces us to retire, we can rejoice in the works which follow after us. And such is the satisfaction of those who hunger and thirst after righteousness. Being concerned for the Kingdom of God and His righteousness rather than for their own records, they are satisfied. They are filled with the satisfaction that they are in God's green pastures where the grazing is not limited. When we seek righteousness rather than our rights, we find a contentment and peace of mind which the world cannot know.

Now, when we learn a principal from the Master, we must examine the rest of Scripture to study it well, and the Scripture tells us that there is not one who is good, not a single one. Then how are we to make sense of this beatitude? Is righteousness something that can ever be attained if there is not even one who is good according to God's standards? No, we will never be completely righteous in this life. It is the righteousness of Christ we are to attain. He is the only perfect One and He is attainable. Our deeds are an overflow of a full heart of love for our Savior. He is the one who will complete our righteousness in time. He forgives our failings and makes up the difference in our righteousness.

In the words of the great Apostle Paul, we can sum up our message in these words. That I may "be found in Him, not having my own righteousness . . . but that which is through faith in Christ, the righteousness which is from God by faith." Those who hunger and thirst after righteousness shall be filled only by Him.

I once had a dream that I was standing before God. My clothes were dirty and I was ashamed. But the Father looked down upon me with compassion and I saw a tunic come down from heaven. It was red on the inside which I knew was the blood of Christ. I raised my arms to God and the tunic settled over me and I noticed that it was gleaming white on the outside and covered my own dirty clothes. I knew this was the righteousness of Christ. Now when I looked into the face of the Father I saw only love and approval because He no longer saw my sin and smudge, He saw the clean, new righteousness of Christ who covered my sin with His blood.

Dear Lord, Thank you that You are my righteousness for I keep falling down and never come close to perfection. It's all You. Amen.

July 10   When Jesus Wrote in the Sand

Scripture Reading: John 8:1-11

Key Verse: ". . . Jesus stooped down and wrote on the ground with His finger . . ." John 8:6

Jesus is teaching in the temple. Surrounded by a large group, suddenly he is interrupted by a commotion, a muffled cry, and sobs. In a moment a number of scribes and Pharisees appear dragging along with them a woman, her hair disheveled, her garments in disarray, fear stamped upon her face.

Pointing at her they demand, "Teacher, this woman was caught in adultery, in the very act. Now, Moses in the law, commanded us that such should be stoned. But what do You say?"

First, why did they bring the woman alone? Where was the other transgressor? Where was the man whose identity was as well known as the woman's? The world has moved very slowly toward a single standard of morality for men and women. In fact, only since the First World War has it been possible in Great Britain for a woman to bring suit against the husband on the ground of adultery.

No doubt these scribes were not greatly shocked at the sin this woman was guilty of. Morals were at low ebb. Moreover, the laws of Moses provided that both the man and woman be stoned. All the scribes and Pharisees had in mind was to put Jesus on the horns of a dilemma. Whatever his answer to them, they were certain He was trapped and would be discredited as a teacher and the Messiah.

But Jesus gave them a deep, profound and overwhelming answer which none of them had expected. The first thing that Jesus did was to stoop down and write on the ground with His finger. The silence was intense. Jesus continued to write. Then He said, "He who is without sin among you, let him throw a stone at her first." Having said that, Jesus began again to write.

In silence, each one of the accusers looked at the other, expecting that he would break the stillness and reach for the first stone. But each was convicted in his own conscience. The Scripture says that they went out one by one from the eldest even unto the last.

Jesus said to the woman, "Where are those accusers of yours? Has no one condemned you?" When she answered that none had, Jesus said to her, "Neither do I condemn you; go and sin no more."

We do not know what Jesus wrote in the sand. It was His only written sermon and it disappeared quickly under the feet of men, blown away by the wind. Did He write their sins, or did His manner and His powerful words speak the sermon? We know only that each man was convicted in his conscience, and with lowered countenance walked silently away.

Perhaps He wrote the words "Pity, compassion," for He was severe about sin, yet compassionate to the transgressor. The Scribe and Pharisee dared not condemn her and Jesus would not. Paul says, "There is therefore now no condemnation to those who are in Christ Jesus."

When we enter heaven perhaps the angels will greet us with some word of encouragement or congratulations. Yes, I think it might be true; perhaps an angel will say, "Enter and labor no more. Enter and suffer no more. Enter and fear no more." But above all the salutations that we shall hear would be the salutation of the angel who shall say to the redeemed souls as they pass in through the gates of Heaven, "Enter, and sin no more."

Lord, Father God, thank You for Your mercy and kindness. I accept Your loving forgiveness with my deepest gratitude. Amen

July 11   What We Know About Heaven

Scripture Reading: John Chapter 14

Key Verse: "And if I go and prepare a place for you, I will come again and receive you to Myself; that where I am, there you may be also." John 14:3

You will notice by the words of our text that not only is heaven a place, but a prepared place for a prepared people. Heaven is the mightiest reward that God holds out to those who will accept His Son. It is a joyous, noble, inspiring, and cheering doctrine which has encouraged the martyrs at the stake, and the bed-ridden saint tormented by the ailments of the flesh.

No matter how seemingly unconcerned about spiritual things, who does not think about and wonder about eternity? We ask ourselves the question, "After death, what?" Our faith and our Scriptures teach us that if we belong to God through Christ, heaven is waiting for us. And what is it like?

It is a prepared place. It is not accidental, incidental or hypothetical. It is built by God with definite, minute consideration for the welfare of His children. He is making every arrangement for their delight.

It is a populated place. John said he saw a great multitude out of every nation, kindred and tribe out of all the earth. So, thank God, there will be black and white, Catholic and Protestant, Baptists and Methodists, old and young, rich and poor, educated and uneducated, all bidden to the marriage feast.

All of us have friends who were dear to us here, our loved ones, flesh and blood whom God has called higher. They too are waiting to welcome us into that place of eternal bliss and fellowship. Open your Bible and see some of the things God says about Heaven.

Heaven is a place of fellowship with Jesus. John 14: 1-3 says ". . . where I am, there you may be also." It is a place of life. Revelation 21:4 declares, ". . . there shall be no more death . . . ." Heaven is a place of worship and praise. Revelation 5:12 states, "Worthy is the Lamb who was slain to receive power and riches and wisdom."

It is a place of happiness. Revelation 7:17 tells us, "For the Lamb who is in the midst of the throne will shepherd them . . . and God will wipe away every tear from their eyes." The Scriptures teach us that heaven is a place of knowledge. I Corinthians 13:12 proclaims, "Now I know in part, but then I shall know just as I also am known."

It is a place of comfort. Revelation 7:16 indicates, "They shall neither hunger anymore nor thirst anymore; the sun shall not strike them, nor any heat." Heaven is a place of health. As we see in Revelations 21:4, "There shall be no more pain." Some people are surprised to learn that heaven is a place of service. But, Revelation 22:3 shows us that ". . . there shall be no more curse, but the throne of God and of the Lamb shall be in it, and His servants shall serve Him." It is a place of rulership. Rev. 22:5 says, "And they shall reign forever and ever."

It is a perfect place. In heaven and only heaven, will the fatherhood of God and the brotherhood of man come to an endless realization.

Lastly, we can have the assurance that we are going there. If we are saved, we are sealed and sustained. That hope is based on the infallible, unchangeable and unshakable word of God. "Whoever confesses Me before men, him I will confess before My Father who is in heaven."

Lord God, thank You for the promise of heaven to all who submit to You as their Lord and Savior. I am humbled by this great hope. You have swung the door open, yet so many don't believe. I lift up to You _____ and pray that they will turn to You, live for You, and someday go to heaven with You. Amen.

Scripture Reading: Romans Chapter 13

Key Verse: "And do this, knowing the time, that now it is high time to awake out of sleep; for now our salvation is nearer than when we first believed." Romans 13:11

One of the most widely circulated cartoons of recent years depicts Uncle Sam kneeling at the mourner's bench with tears down his cheeks crying out, "God be merciful to me a sinner." Something has happened in America and in the world as a whole in recent years. We have drifted from our moorings. We have forgotten God, rejected His Son, spurned His Book, and have been dominated by a materialistic philosophy of life. It is high time for a change.

It is high time the church preached the gospel of Christ without apology. Our Lord is not a dead hero, but a living and mighty Redeemer. Let the church take her stand not in controversy, but with a holy passion to declare the glorious truth that Jesus, God's Son, is the Savior of the world. Our attitude must be "woe is me if I preach not the gospel and woe is you if you reject it."

It is high time men ceased offering the Word of God as a sort of optional panacea for the help of the world's ills. Half a gospel is no gospel at all. The message of Christ is not a salve to heal the wounds created by selfishness.

The Word of God fits no man-made social order. The gospel is not to be utilized, it is to be obeyed. We cannot adapt Jesus to our own selfish ideals, we must find His will, His way, and follow it.

It is high time we returned to solid Biblical terminology with its satisfying content; that speaks of sin and explains its meaning; that tells of salvation and of what it consists, that preaches of sanctification, justification, heaven and hell, and their reality. We simply must tell the truth in the face of the lies of this world. Only the truth of God has the power to set men free from the enslavement of sin.

It is high time we are interested in the individual souls of men and women. Our mechanical age is crushing the souls of men. People long for someone to really care about them. The world cares not, but Christ is interested in the individual. Men to Him are not "hands" but "souls."

Christ was not the proponent of mass evangelism, but an example of personal evangelism. He spent more time with twelve men than with the multitudes. We must gather folks to God one by one, for Christ died for the individual.

It is high time we heeded the warnings of the Bible for our time, and that we warn against conformity to the age. Should we not be warning our generation against the awful effects of crucifying the Son of God afresh by our carnal and sinful lives? And shall we not be ashamed to stand before the Shepherd of the Sheep, if we fail to warn the sinner of the awfulness of eternity without Him?

It is high time that we awoke out of our sleep and begin to work together, pray together, and live together for the honor and glory of God. Why should we not tell others of the exceeding sinfulness of sin and warn of its consequences? Why should not the dangers of indifference to the pleading of God be presented without apology? If men insist on playing the fool why should we not tell them the price of their folly? We should and we must do this, and we should begin today.

Oh Dear Shepherd of my Soul, I tend to be far too comfortable in this world. Give me boldness to speak the gospel. Replace the fear of man with true awe of you, my omnipotent, mighty God. Replace uncertainty with calm reliance on you, In Jesus' name, Amen.

July 13   The Church, the Offering, and the Testimony

Scripture Reading: Matthew Chapter 6

Key Verse: "But seek first the kingdom of God and His righteousness, and all these things shall be added to you." Matt. 6:33

Loyalty to God and His House is a hard choice in these breezy summer days. The beaches and mountains call to us to spend lazy weekends in the balmy air. No effort, no problems, only refreshment, rest, recreation, and laughter. Doesn't it sound wonderful? And it is. God has given us lovely nature and His beautiful world to enjoy. I think He is pleased when we do.

The Christian life is a balanced life. When we are employed, we would never think of forgoing our responsibilities for a day at the beach. Well, we might think about it. We might even take a rare day to indulge that temptation. But if we want to be successful in our work, we don't take the responsibilities of employment lightly.

As we balance our Christian life, we enjoy all the blessings and fun of fellowship and outings with our families, friends, and church family. But, let us not forget that the church is an altar, but it is also a halter, a halter to the enterprises of the Kingdom. When we begin neglecting our church we begin to slip and soon we go down and out. The people who have made the most useful Christians, best church-workers, and best soul-winners are those who are faithful to the church. If you are not missed at church, it may be that you aren't contributing the gifts God has given you to share, because you are a vital part of His plan for your fellowship.

Now, let us address the question of giving our offerings. God has provided that the church be sustained by the offerings of His people. He has a divine law of giving. It is not according to your good impulse or your good will but as the Lord has prospered us. Will you not pray with me today that we will measure up in our giving as God has measured

His love to us? Shall I give to the Lord that which costs me nothing? His love for us cost Him the life and suffering of His dear Son.

Next, let us think about our testimony of the gospel of Christ to others. Daniel 12:3 says, "Those who are wise shall shine like the brightness of the firmament. And those who turn many to righteousness like the stars forever and ever." One secret of the early church's power and glory was their love for soul winning.

Some person led Moody to Jesus. Was it worthwhile? Some person led Spurgeon to Christ. Was that worthwhile? Somebody led you to accept Jesus Christ. Was that worthwhile?

Oh beloved, when we get to heaven and see the great immortal company of the saints, and stand before the judgment seat of Christ to be rewarded for the deeds done in the body, then and only then will you be able to fully appreciate how truly worthwhile it was to be a child of God. The time, the labor of love, the tears and work, all were worthwhile.

It was worthwhile to have given your gifts to God's work. Every dollar you give bears eternal interest. Then you'll hear about the heathen that came to God because you gave.

To hear boy or girl, that neighbor or husband say, "I would not be here today if you had not thought it worthwhile to speak to me about Jesus." What a blessing. What could possibly compare?

"My Lord and My God, I want to start today to choose Your kingdom first. I want my life to count and make a real and eternal difference. Amen

July 14   A Challenge, A Crisis, An Opportunity

Suggested Reading: II Peter Chapter 3

Key Verses: "For a great and effective door is opened to me, and there are many adversaries." 1 Corinthians 16:9 and ". . . since all these things will be dissolved, what manner of persons ought you to be . . .?" II Peter 3:11

Never in all the magnificent history of Christianity and the church was Paul's challenging statement more true than now. The church of the Living God is facing an open door that should send a clarion call through the heart of every soldier of the Cross. It is a door of venture, and adventure, for Christ, and the souls of men. With yearning hearts, the peoples of the world are waiting with bated breath for someone to point the way out of the corruption and despair that sweeps across the affairs of a seemingly doomed earth. Science has failed, diplomacy has failed, and human schemes and reforms have failed. Church rulers, presidents, and dictators have stepped in, only to increase the tempo of the dance of doom.

This Old World is like a patient before whose bed the doctor stands and says, 'The outcome of this sickness depends now upon factors beyond my control. The crisis has come." A world crisis is upon us. It is either a turn for the worse or the better in man's relationship to his fellow man and to God. It is a dangerous time. But, a time of crisis is also a time of opportunity. Out of sickness can come health. Out of a world catastrophe can come progress.

World civilization is sick. Now, as in every generation, we know the soul that sins or the nation that sins shall die. We falter, we fail, and we fall, unless by the grace of God, the Lord Jesus Christ and His gospel is given the right of way in the hearts, souls, and activities of men. The prophet of that day saw the truth and cried, ". . . since all these things shall be dissolved, what manner of persons ought you to be?" Well, for one thing, certainly we ought to be persons of spiritual earnestness. We ought to love God with all our mind as well as heart, in times like these. We learned our lesson well when crises came in the Second World War. Take the rubber shortage for example. Scientists got busy. They worked day and night, to discover new supplies and sources, to the point that we even made a slogan for our resourcefulness, "The difficult we do immediately, the impossible takes a little longer."

But, what about our spiritual resourcefulness? We have the message the world needs. We have the panacea for all the world's ills. We know the only way out. Will we be content with the routine way of doing things? Shall we not rather rend our clothes, and don sackcloth and ashes at the thought that outside of the few connected with the families of the churches, the vast non-believing multitudes are increasing in number, godlessness, and indifference to sin? In view of all this, what manner of persons ought we to be? We ought to be persons of personal conviction, of imagination in spreading the gospel, of resourcefulness in finding open doors for our testimony and integrity as we live our lives before a watching world. For who has a worthier cause than we? Who ever had a nobler master than this Savior of ours? Who in all the annals of man's heroism had a more important task than the one laid before us? We must not retreat from the great Commission. "The difficult we do immediately, the impossible takes a little longer," ". . . for nothing is impossible with Christ."

Dear Lord, Please let me see the opportunities You bring to share Christ with my co-workers, with my neighbors, with the people I meet. In these days of despair, violence and fear, Jesus is the only One who can bring hope, peace and eternal life. Amen.

Scripture Reading: Matthew 22

*Key Verse: "What do you think about the Christ? Whose Son is
He . . .?" Matthew 22:42*

Everything depends on the answer to this question. Is He the meager human Jesus or is He the mighty Christ of the New Testament? If He was merely a peasant-prophet, however good, and well intentioned, then He sleeps forever. But if He is the Son of God, He is mightier than death, the risen Lord who pushed the end out of Joseph's tomb, waved His shroud in the teeth of the wind and proclaimed, "I am alive forevermore." He is the unique and solitary Son of God.

Who is He? I cannot explain Him on the basis of His earthly inheritance. There was nothing in that peasant family that would account for His unequaled life. I cannot explain Him on the basis of environment. He was born in a stable, lived and worked in an obscure, whitewashed carpenter shop, yet He rose above all traditions and all bigotry, all sectionalism and all sectarianism. No, in reverence, in adoration, in awe, and in mystery, I come back to read in the Word of God of the carpenter of Nazareth of whom it was written, that they called His name Jesus.

He is the Christ of the sinless life. The claim is made over and over again. He committed no sin. He was the Lamb without blemish, and was the very essence of purity, and sinlessness. So, Jesus stands today facing all of His critics in all of the centuries, on all of the continents asking, "Which of you convicts Me of sin?" Behold the blameless Son of God.

Behold likewise the Christ of the vicarious death. Vicarious means doing for another, doing for me that which I cannot do for myself. This is the message of His life, the message of His coming. Isaiah cried, "He was wounded for our transgressions, He was bruised for our iniquities; the chastisement for our peace was upon Him, and by His stripes we are healed." So Christ on the cross is not an example of how a good man can bear pain, but the Savior of the World doing vicariously by His death that which man cannot do for Himself.

The Christ of the victorious resurrection is our mighty Savior. It was He who said, "I am alive forevermore," and "because I live, you shall live also." The resurrection of Jesus Christ is the proof of our resurrection and the pattern of it.

He was the Christ not only of the supernatural birth and of the sinless life and of the vicarious death and of the victorious resurrection, but also of the endless life. For Hebrews says Christ has entered "into Heaven itself, now to appear in the presence of God for us." As He died to redeem us, so He lives to plead our cause. So, He is alive and men can find Him and call upon Him. He is not a myth, a memory, nor a bit of history. There's a Man in glory for you and me.

So let us be sure about our answer. It is the most important of questions. What do you think of Christ? Whose son is He?

He is the mind of God speaking out to man. He is the voice of God calling out to man. He is the heart of God throbbing out to man. He is the hand of God reaching out to man. He is the Person of God who put on the vestments of humanity and lived in a carpenter shop that He might take us back to God. So I say with Thomas, "My Lord and my God." I say with Peter, "You are the Christ, the Son of the living God."

Holy Lord My God, I worship and adore You. You are the Almighty One, the source of all life and the Holy Creator. I praise Your wonderful name and thank You for living and dying and living again for me, in the name of Jesus, Amen.

July 16   The Reward of Victory

Scripture Reading: Revelation Chapter 2

Key Verse: ". . . To him who overcomes I will give to eat from the tree of life . . . ." Revelation 2:7

The seven-fold promises which conclude the seven letters to the Asiatic churches are in substance one. We may say that the inmost meaning of them all is the gift of Christ Himself. Yet like the diamond that flashes multi-colored lights in many directions, so these blessed promises also sparkle with diversified rays of blessings. Oh that we might understand the glorious truths and the mighty challenge therein contained for all.

Today Christians suffer loss to their spiritual growth through neglect of the teaching of the New Testament as to the future life. We have allowed the glitter of this life (tinsel compared to the diamond of salvation) to blind us to the things which really satisfy and are eternal. We are thereby also deprived of a strong motive for action and a sure comfort in sorrow. Let us rather be guided in our thinking and planning and living by these truths and promises of the future.

Have you noticed that to every Church the Spirit of God writes in the terms of "To him that overcomes I will . . ."? It is evident that God believes in giving rewards to those of His people who are willing to wage a struggle in the Christian life to the very end. The struggle and time of training is a victorious one for it is designed to make us capable of the heavenly life. But the victor can only conquer one way, "This is the victory that overcomes the world, our faith."

If we trust in Christ we shall receive His power into our hearts, then we will be more than conquerors through Him who loves us. We will have overcome through Him. To those who overcome, Christ made the following promises of reward:

"To him who overcomes I will give to eat of the tree of life which is in the midst of the Paradise of God." Revelation 2:7

"He who overcomes shall not be hurt by the second death." Rev. 2:11

"To him who overcomes I will give some of the hidden manna to eat. And I will give him a white stone, and on the stone a new name written which no one knows except him who receives it." Rev. 2:17

"He who overcomes and keeps My works unto the end, to him I will give power over the nations." Rev. 2:26

"He who overcomes shall be clothed in white garments, and I will not blot out his name from the Book of Life; but I will confess his name before My Father and before His angels." Rev. 3:5

"He who overcomes, I will make him a pillar in the temple of My God, and he shall go out no more. I will write on him the name of My God and the name of the city of My God, the New Jerusalem, which comes down out of heaven from My God. And I will write on him My new name." Rev. 3:12

"To him who overcomes I will grant to sit with Me on My throne, as I also overcame and sat down with My Father on His throne." Rev. 3:21

When our trials are nearly unbearable, when circumstances threaten to overwhelm us, when we think we can bear the hardships that befall us no more, remember the promises before us and persevere in the power of the Spirit. He will give us no more than we can carry and the blessings now and in the future make this choice of the Christian life worth it all.

Dear Father, Help me to keep my eyes on Christ and His promises and blessings. Protect me from the draw of this flashy mortal life on my heart. I am so thankful my eternity is in Heaven and not in this brief school of life on earth. Amen

July 17   The Night of the Shipwreck

Scripture Reading: Acts Chapter 27

Key Verse: "Striking a place where two seas met, they ran the ship aground; and the prow stuck fast and remained immovable, but the stern was being broken up by the violence of the waves." Acts 27:41

A wreck is always a terrifying experience, whether train, automobile or airplane. Most terrible of all is a shipwreck, however, because of the prolonged strain of agony under which shipwrecked people suffer. Today, let's look a little closer at the experience of Paul, and then tomorrow perhaps we can draw some lessons from it.

It had been two weeks since that large ship had been tempted by the soft south winds to leave the harbor of Fair Havens, seeking to reach the port of Phoenix, a little farther along the coast of Crete. But she had scarcely cleared the headlands when the winds shifted. Up near Mt. Ida, the fabled abode of Zeus, the terror of the sea, a Euroclydon, had been watching and waiting for its deluded victims, and now he loosed upon this ship all his fury. When this hurricane broke over the ship and tossed it hither and yon like a cork, all they could do was to let her run before the sea and the wind. Day after day, and night after night, with no light of sun by day and no light of stars by night, the ship plunged and wallowed in the great deep.

Huddled on the deck, clinging in terror to mast or spar, drenched with the waves and cut with the winds, the two hundred and seventy-six souls on board waited for what most of them assuredly felt was certain death.

At length, at midnight on the fourteenth night, a cry went up from the lookout, "Breakers ahead, Breakers ahead!" And by the ominous sound of the crashing sea, they knew they neared some country. They were drifting rapidly towards a dangerous shore. Lifting his voice above the gale, the captain shouted, "Stern anchors down." And Paul records, ". . . they dropped four anchors from the stern and prayed for day to come."

Everything depended upon those four anchors. All through the night, those passengers prayed for dawn. What a night it must have been with the sky as black as ink and the great waves surging over the ship, submerging her stern as her prow rose toward the sky.

But at length, the dawn came. In front of them, they could see the huge gray cliffs. As the ship began to break up, the order was given for everyone to cast himself into the sea. So, here they came, one on a board, another clinging to part of a mast, all of them making towards shore out of the clutches of the angry sea. "And it was that they all escaped, all safe to land."

Now out of the storm and hurricane of that night, with its fears and despairs, its heroism and its faith, there are a number of truths which are of value to us who take this long and oftimes dangerous voyage of life. Life is a wonderful journey, with wonderful lands to visit and great discoveries to be made. But, there are also treacherous tides and currents, dangerous sands and shoals with cruel rocks and reefs along the way. Now we feel the allure of the beguiling South Wind, then sometimes we face the howling, raging Euroclydon. The Holy Spirit has preserved for our instruction, comfort, and warning, the story of this shipwreck. What can we learn from Paul's chronicle?

Dear Father, this amazing, harrowing tale does indeed reflect the times in life when we are unable to see any way out. Help me to remember that just because I cannot see the light, doesn't mean it isn't there. Amen.

Scripture Reading: Acts Chapter 28

Key Verse: "Then, Paul dwelt two whole years in his own rented house, and received all who came to him, preaching the kingdom of God and teaching the things which concern the Lord Jesus Christ with all confidence, no one forbidding him." Acts 28:30-31

What lessons can we find within Paul's detailed account of the shipwreck on Malta, which we considered yesterday? First, we should remember to beware the soft wind of temptation. Remember, Paul's ship already weathered one great storm on this journey and found itself at Fair Havens on the southern shore of the Island of Crete.

But a little farther distant on that island was a big town called Phoenix. The harbor at Phoenix was more commodious, the town was bigger, and there were more amusements for the sailors and possibly better prices for the merchants. So, when the south wind blew softly the captain said, "Let's go to Phoenix."

What happened to that ship is a parable of what happens to the lives and souls of many today, deceived by the soft winds of pleasure and prosperity. Don't forget the fact that after the south wind came the hurricane. It is always so. The soft winds of temptation lead straight into the hurricane of consequences.

It seems to me that the experience of that night for the 276 passengers is but the condition of this world today. The sea is tempestuous. The night is dark. The sun, moon and stars are obscured. The church and the Christians in it are drifting in shallow waters and there are hidden rocks upon which her bark may soon suffer shipwreck. It is time to do some real sounding, beloved, both personally and collectively.

Drifting through life is as perilous as drifting through a stormy sea. Suffice it to say that in the voyage of life the soul needs some anchors. In fact, while other things about a ship have changed in the intervening years between Paul's writing and our reading of this text, the need for good anchors remains. So too, human life has changed outwardly, but not inwardly. Life has the same perils, the same sorrows, and the same temptations.

As we have previously discovered, in "The Christian's Anchors," God has provided us with the four anchors of His Word, the assurance of the Deity of Christ, the precious cleansing of the Blood of Christ, and the hope of His return. These are truly our anchors and the light that shines in the dark night until the day dawns.

Perhaps the best lesson of all in this remarkable record, however, is the sure Sovereignty of God. The hurricane could destroy the ship, but not the Christians on it. Paul stood on that ship that night, God's man. On the land, in the sea, or in the air, a Christian is safe anywhere. His soul can suffer no harm.

I suppose they had a roll call that night and as they called the roll, how wonderful to hear them answer, "Present," as each name was called. All were present; all were safe on land. So when the storms of life are past and we land at last on the heavenly shore, the Captain of our salvation will call the heavenly rolls, and not one of God's children will be missing.

We won't be on Malta's old bleak shore or by a bonfire kindled by pagans, either, but upon Canaan's happy shore and there by the Sea of glass mingled with fire we shall answer Him, "Present—safe at last."

Dear Lord, the little ship I am in doesn't appear to be making much headway sometimes. Help me to rest assured in the knowledge that You are present in the storm and that my soul is safe in You. Praise Your Holy Name, Sovereign God, and for the sake of Christ, Amen.

Scripture: Hebrews 11:23-29

Key verses: "By faith, Moses when he became of age, refused to be called the son of Pharaoh's daughter, choosing rather to suffer affliction with the people of God than to enjoy the passing pleasures of sin, esteeming the reproach of Christ greater than the treasures in Egypt; for he looked to the reward." Hebrews 11: 24-26

Moses is at the forks of the road. Have you been there? Some stand still, others try one side and then the other, but Moses refuses one and steadfastly sets himself to travel the other. He shows himself a man of decision. Can you decide?

There are two elements in Moses' decision as there are in all decisions, the negative choice and the positive choice. He said a resounding "No!" to one. There was no weakness about it. But Moses did more than say "no". He refused to take one road, but he did not stand still. He went the other way. He also said "yes".

So many people think the Christian life is a life of negatives. But it is not what we quit, it is what we are going to become. It's a life of dos. There is a wax figure, down on Main Street. He is immune to the bootlegging, betting and carousing going on around him. To every temptation he resisted. But when I asked him to go to prayer meeting he was as unresponsive as many church members are to the collection plate. He didn't see it. Why, that wax figure is not a Christian. He is as far from a saint as death is from life. "No" is useless, without "yes."

Now, Moses' decision was costly. There was much to be given up. He went from Egyptian Prince to Hebrew Slave, the highest to the lowest. He said "no" to the pleasures of Egypt and all its treasure. His decision brought great disappointment to one who loved him, the Princess who adopted him. It was to her he owed his life, yet in the end he turned from her and all she offered.

But the cost of this decision is not to be measured by what he gave up alone. What he chose in place of it was also costly. What did he say

"Yes" to after all this "No"? He chose suffering. Amazing that with his eyes wide open he chose the road of suffering, agony, disappointment, battle, conflict, and tears. Why? Why did he do it?

He did it because he had a clear eye for distinguishing right from wrong, not what he wanted to do, but what he ought to do. He knew the pleasures and gains of this world are only temporary. How we need Moses' clear-headed perception. He had an eye for the things of real value. So clearly did he see that he chose and esteemed the things of God greater riches than the treasures of Egypt. He looked away from all but the coming reward.

Now what was the outcome of this decision? He received the reward of a Godly character. See him coming down from Mount Sinai, face like the sun. How? By looking not on gold, but on the Lord.

Through this decision he was able to render a great service to his own family and to the world. He gave the world a "Book" that kept his people safe from sin and disease. Based on the story of the transfiguration there were two men with Christ. One was Moses who esteemed the Lord more than the treasures of Egypt. What a great deciding day that was for Moses. Will you decide today to say "no" to the temporary things so that you might say "yes" to God's plan for your life?

Dear Father in Heaven. So often I am tempted and ask for Your help to say "No." I didn't realize You help me say "no" so that I can say "yes" to what You are asking of me. I know, deep in my heart what that is. Yes, Lord, I will. Amen

July 20   The Chemistry of Tears

Scripture Reading: Revelation 21: 1-7

Key Verse: "And God will wipe away every tear from their eyes . . . ." Revelation 21:4

The record of every life is written in letters of tears. Speak of them and immediately we recall some experiences of our past.

The first time the Bible mentions tears is in II Kings 20:5. It is the record of a king weeping. The last mention of tears in the Bible is a more pleasant picture. It is found in the words of our Scripture, "And God will wipe away every tear from their eyes . . . ." There is not a living person who does not need the comfort of having their tears dried at some time in life.

The chemist claims that a tear is sodium chloride in an aqueous solution. The physiologist will tell you that it is the lubricating fluid of the eye. But in its fullest meaning a tear is a distillation of the soul. It is the deepest longing of the human heart in a chemical solution. It is the concentrated extract, the final precipitate of the deepest feelings of the heart. True tears are not camouflage, but the picture of the soul on the canvas of emotion. They are portraits of our deepest feelings.

What is the purpose of these hot tears of humanity? Can a child by weeping repair the broken toy? Can a mother by crying bring back her lifeless child? No, tears cannot restore that which is lost; it can only express the grief of it. And yet I say to you that tears are an indispensable part of our being.

First of all, they make us willing to leave this old valley of tears when the time shall come some day. Because we are born to sorrow and tears like the sparks fly upward, we get to that place where we can say, "I am ready and I am willing to go now to that place where God shall wipe away all tears from my eyes."

Tears make us feel our dependence on God. When all seems lost God is there for us with comfort and love.

Our tears also birth the grace of sympathy for others. To be best fitted for the office of comfort and sympathy we must first be immersed in the baptism of tears. Sympathy is born of travail and if you have never felt the sorrow of loss, you have no sympathy to offer.

Then, there are the tears of a sinner. Peter denied his Lord then went out and wept bitterly. But those tears were sweet to him for there is joy in the presence of the angels over one sinner who repents. It is the shedding of the old and bitter and the filling with the newness and sweetness of forgiveness. These tears are the avenue of escape, restoration, joy, and peace.

Let us think of Jesus' tears at the grave of Lazarus, the tears He shed over Jerusalem, and the tears that fell in Gethsemane for us. He wept that your eyes might be dried.

One of the handkerchiefs that God will use to dry those tears away will be the revelation to us of the fruit of the tears we brought to Him. He will show us all of them recorded and each remembered. We shall then see what we often quote but don't truly understand, that "all things work together for good to those who love God, to those who are the called according to His purpose." Yes, "Those who sow in tears shall reap in joy."

There is a key behind the gates of heaven that unlocks every mystery. God's plans unfold like lilies, slowly and beautifully. We do not always see the movement, but it is there. Take your tears to God, beloved. He understands.

Dear Lord, You know my heart and what is breaking it in two right now. I bring it to You and I lay this burden down, along with all my heartache and tears, at the foot of Your throne of mercy and grace. I trust You, Lord. Amen.

July 21   Purpose is a Universal Tonic

Scripture Reading: Philippians Chapter 1

Key Verse: "For to me, to live is Christ and to die is gain."
Philippians 1:21

A great life's purpose will give inspiration, it will give a spirit of sacrifice, and it illustrates the correct concept of Christianity. Lives fail without the vision of Christ. The true purpose of Christianity is not something to carry on our backs; it is a dynamic that carries us.

Look at Paul. It is very interesting to hear him as he speaks of himself in the letter to the Philippians. He said, "For to me to live is Christ." This statement gathers force when we remember the exact position which he was in when he wrote this. He was a prisoner of the Praetorian Guard, awaiting the word of the Emperor, which would mean life or death. He looks at both roads ahead of him as he says, "To live is Christ" and "to die is gain."

If he shall live it will be to carry on the Word of Christ in the regions he has not traveled yet. If he is to die, it will be gain. Life and death have lost their old significance to Paul because there is one vision that fills the horizon. There is no darkness, no light, but everywhere he sees the Master as the crown of life. He is not only the author and finisher of life. He not only began, but He will also end the good work whether Paul is there or not. And when life ends what is it? It is Christ. What will be your chief joy in glory? Christ. That is why this man, Paul, stands and looks at Nero's little axe and says, "To die is gain." Do you see that executioner Paul? "No, I do not see him!" What do you see Paul? "Christ."

From the moment he was blinded on the Damascus Road and heard the voice of Christ saying "Why do you persecute me?" Saul was a new creature. He cried, "Who are You Lord?" and "What will you have me to do?" When we experience the new birth as Saul did, our lives begin there. The old life drops away, and we desire to know Him completely, and do His will.

Paul lived this new life under a new covenant. Not the law written on stone, but on his heart, the seat of affection. So when he wanted to know what God would have him do he did not have to go to some code of rules. He need only turn himself to silence and quietness and say, "O Christ, direct, control, suggest this day all I design to do or say." Christ was indeed the Lord of his life.

Now let me ask you to finish this theme for yourself. On a clean piece of paper write the story of your life honestly and faithfully and truly in a brief sentence as Paul wrote his story. Write!

For me to live is - - - money? Now be honest in God's name. If you have played the hypocrite before, do not do it now. Write it down not for man's eyes, but for God's. "For me to live is money." If that is true put it down.

For me to live is - - - pleasure? I want the enjoyment of pleasure of sin for a season, a good time with the world and worldly associations. Then write it down.

For me to live is - - - fame, or fill it in for yourself. Now finish it. And to die is - - -. No! I cannot write that for I know that to die is to perish, to be forgotten. What is fame when I am gone? I cannot write it.

No, my friends, you cannot write Paul's estimate of death after anything except Paul's estimate of life. If by God's grace you can write "For me to live is Christ." You can write, "To die is gain." It can only be gain to die when you have found Christ to live.

Dearest Lord, I can see that I've had actual idols in my life. I do not want them there. I want You to be first and foremost in my life. I want to be able to say with Paul, "For me to live is Christ and to die is gain." Amen.

July 22   The Meaning of Faith

Scripture Reading: Hebrews 10:32-11: 3

Key Verse: "Now faith is the substance of things hoped for, the evidence of things not seen." Hebrews 11:1

It stands to reason that if faith is the thing whereby a Christian lives, if it is the basis of his whole Christian life, then it is imperative that he know all he can about it. Where shall we go to find all this information and knowledge? Well, God has left us in His book, a heritage of rich experiences of faith as revealed in His Book by men and women who walked with Him.

Faith is such a big word that in one place God gives over a whole chapter of His Word to exemplify it in the lives of those who practiced it. Many have defined faith, but it is nothing until you put it into practice. L.P. Jacks once remarked, "Faith is reason in a courageous mood." All of us have seen a long jumper. Picture a man running down a cinder path to make a broad jump. He does not go hesitatingly up to the line to make the leap. He runs with all his might. He has made the decision to go forward at the beginning of the track, not at the end of it. Decision is the cinder track, faith is the leap.

That is what the author of Hebrews had in mind in our text. Moffet's translation reads: "We are confident of what we hope for, convinced of what we do not see." Faith begins with believing and ends with trusting.

Let us apply faith in the realm of our own soul. Someone has said, "There is a hero in every man." You and I need to see that hero, and make it our life task to allow God to shape you into that type of man or woman faith tells you that you can be. You may never be famous or wealthy, but you can be trustworthy. You can be dependable; you can be industrious and noble. You have a great many tasks to perform, but the greatest one is through faith, to allow God to make you what you can be, out and out for God and His kingdom.

Faith gives you the power of endurance to stay with the task. George

Washington Goethals, the great engineer, was sent to complete a task where men before him had failed repeatedly. Because he was a man who had a dream of things as they could be and not as they were, and because he dedicated himself to the task and would not surrender, we have today the Panama Canal.

The other day I saw a tourist, who had stopped by the side of the road, lifted up the hood of his car and was gazing in upon the motor looking for the cause of his trouble. When he came to a standstill he did not look at the outside, he knew the trouble was on the inside. Just so, in order to improve the functional life of humanity it is necessary to enrich the inner-faith life from which words and deeds emerge. Dealing with externals will accomplish little.

Real faith functions in practical matters. Man has a past, a present and a future. Vital faith takes care of man's past, his present, and his future. Faith accepts God's forgiveness of the past. Faith believes in the power of the blood for the present. And faith provides inspiration and hope which enables one to face the future with a smile. There can be no great Christians without a great God in the soul. This great God cannot be a great power in man without being appropriated by man, and faith is the only means that man has for appropriating God. Do you use your gift of faith?

Holy Father God, thank You for providing everything I need for a fulfilling, fruitful, and abundant life. I need only receive it by faith from Your loving hand and use it to Your glory. In the name of Jesus Christ, Amen.

July 23   Letting Our Enemies Get the Best of Us

Scripture: Esther Chapter 7

Key Verse: "So they hanged Haman on the gallows that he had prepared for Mordecai . . . ." Esther 7:10

The Bible shows by example two ways of dealing with our enemies. Let's look first at the wrong way, or how **not** to get the best of our enemies.

As the Viceroy of Xerxes, everyone bowed and saluted when Haman passed by, all but one, Mordecai the Jew. When Haman saw that Mordecai did not bow before him, he was filled with rage.

Never did a man plan such a terrible revenge. It was not only the destruction of Mordecai that Haman planned and plotted, but also the destruction of the whole race of Jews. This terrible revenge of Haman would have been accomplished, for he had persuaded the King to sign the death edict against the Jews of the empire, but for God, who intervened as He frequently has for His people.

The intervention was through two agencies. First, the restless nights of the Persian Despot, who, unable to sleep, had his secretaries read to him the records of the realm wherein he learned that Mordecai had saved his life on one occasion from assassination.

The next morning he asked Haman what should be done to a man the king delighted to honor. Confident that the man was himself, Haman suggested that a crown be put on his head, that he be arrayed in royal garments, mounted on a royal charger and be led throughout the streets of the city by one of the most noble princes of the realm with a proclamation shouted by criers, "Thus shall it be done to the man whom the King delights to honor." The humiliated and crestfallen Haman was compelled to lead his enemy in triumph through the streets and avenues of the city. But worse was yet to come, for Haman was seized, hurried to the gallows and hanged fifty cubits high.

Thus Haman is an illustration of the folly of permitting one thing to cloud our life. He had the respect and adulation of everyone in Persia except one man, Mordecai. Everything he might wish was his. There was not a tree, palace, treasure, or town that Haman could not have had for the asking. But when he saw one humble Jew refusing to do him honor, that spoiled it all. He centered his mind on the one thing he could not have.

That has been human nature from the beginning. Look at Adam and Eve. They had all trees for their enjoyment, but one. And it was that tree that blasted the happiness of the garden for them.

We must center our thoughts on the blessings we have, not on what we do not have. Haman allowed the disrespect of Mordecai to fill his heart with an all-consuming hatred. And hatred opened the door to transgression and sin. When a man has had his revenge, he discovers that the one who is most injured is himself.

We must dig a grave deep within our own heart where we shall bury far out of sight the injuries and enmities of life. We must not foster them, nurse them, magnify them, or brood over them. Satan is behind all that.

Jesus says, "Love your enemies." Paul says, "Forgetting those things which are behind." The better way is God's way, and tomorrow we will study it.

Dear God, Forgive me for nursing grudges for things that are behind me. The heat of anger burns me inside and causes deep scars. Please heal me and fill me with your love to overflowing so that even my enemies may partake of you. Amen.

July 24   Getting the Best of Your Enemies

Scripture: Genesis Chapter 50

Key Verse: ". . . And he comforted them and spoke kindly unto them." Genesis 50:21

Today, let us look to Joseph who took the right way, God's way, to treat the brothers who sold him into slavery. If Haman is the ugliest character in the Bible, Joseph is the most beautiful, the most Christ-like. There he is, the boy of many dreams with the coat of many colors.

Hated by his jealous brothers, he is sold into slavery and carried off into Egypt. There in the home of Potiphar a worse fate befalls him. He is accused of a terrible crime, committed to prison where he spent long and weary years. But at length the Daystar of Hope rises over his dungeon and he is delivered from the dungeon to interpret the dreams of Pharaoh, and the tide turns for Joseph. Everything goes in his favor. He is exalted to the second highest place in the Empire and wears Pharaoh's golden chain around his neck.

One day, Hebrews come down to buy corn, and when ten of them are ushered into his presence he knows them immediately as his brothers who had mistreated him. For a time Joseph deals severely with them to awaken remorse within the hearts of those cruel brothers. This he accomplishes in a most unusual way until they say one to another, "We are truly guilty concerning our brother . . . therefore this distress has come upon us." Having stirred their conscience, Joseph was no longer able to disguise his heart and in the privacy of his own chamber, reveals himself to his brothers.

What a marvelous scene, a beautiful triumph of forgiveness. Joseph had a great Christian spirit before Christ came. A Christian spirit is a forgiving spirit. His was a triumph, not only of love and affection, but of faith in the providence of God. His brothers had hated him, envied him, and sold him as a slave. Potiphar's wife had tempted him, falsely accused him and put him into prison. The Chief Butler had forgotten him. But God was in it all and through Joseph's life and faithfulness he saved the lives of his father and their people from starvation.

Joseph said "God meant it for good." That is a real triumph of faith, if through even the most painful experiences of life you can see that God's hand was upon you and leading you.

Here then are the two ways of dealing with your enemies. The way of Haman, to hate him, wish him ill, and seek to do him ill. The end of that way is misery and unhappiness. So there is a slogan which says "If you wish to punish yourself, hate someone else in life."

The other way is the way of forgiveness and reconciliation, the way of Joseph, and the way of Christ. Paul says "If your enemy is hungry, feed him. If he is thirsty, give him a drink; for in so doing you will heap coals of fire on his head."

When Washington's Army was at Philadelphia, a wicked and disloyal soldier in the army was court-martialed and sentenced to be hanged. On the day of the execution there appeared at Washington's headquarters a godly Quaker who had walked many miles to plead for the life of the condemned man.

Washington heard his plea but said he could do nothing to stay the execution of sentence. Then, as he turned to leave Washington said to the Quaker, "Are you a relative of the man?"

"No," said the Quaker, "He was my deadly enemy."

Almighty God who forgives me when I least deserve it, thank You for Your loving mercy. May I remember to freely give the forgiveness that You have freely given me. Amen.

July 25 Lost

Scripture Reading: Luke Chapter 19

Key Verse: "For the Son of Man has come to seek and to save that which was lost." Luke 19:10

One morning, I saw a man of 72 years stand on the curbstone looking over the ruins of a block on which the day before had stood a magnificent department store. It had gone up in smoke.

As I stood there, he said, "Preacher that represents the accumulation of a lifetime. I have lost my fortune." What a tragedy. But, while it is a tragedy to lose a fortune, or our health, those tragedies do not compare with the tragic prospect of a lost soul. There is no healing for the loss of the soul except in the blood of Jesus Christ.

Today, we will think about this one little word. Considered in the light of eternity, it is the most distressing word in all the languages of men. Now, this word is descriptive of the spiritual condition of every man and woman who has not trusted Jesus Christ as their Savior.

It is that little word, "lost." It is the darkest word in the history of the human race, indicating separation from God and eternal dwelling in the land of punishment.

Down in a West Texas town made up of cowmen and their families, there came word late one afternoon that a five-year-old child had wandered away from home. With no fences, and no real roads, only a wide-open country, you can understand the anxiety of the populace.

Every man and boy spent the night searching the country for that poor, dirty, little child. Now, they did not look for that child because it was good. No, fact was that child had run away in a rage at its mama. Nor did they search for that child because its family was rich. In fact, they were as poor as Job's turkey.

I will tell you why they looked all night for that child, not stopping until it was found. It was because it was lost. It was lost. And that's exactly why Jesus came from heaven, gave up His throne and power, became man and suffered and died and rose from the grave. It was to save men. It was not because they were good. Nor again was it because they were rich. It was because they—we—were lost.

Psalm 51:5 tells us, "Behold I was brought forth in iniquity, and in sin my mother conceived me." Yet again we are told, in Psalm 58:3, "The wicked are estranged from the womb; they go astray as soon as they are born, speaking lies."

The doctrine, so popular today, that men are born innocent and can be trained and raised up into Christianity, has no sanction in the Word of God. Romans 3:23 says, ". . . for all have sinned and fall short of the glory of God." Ephesians 2:3 declares, ". . . and were by nature children of wrath, just as the others." Sin was born in your soul. But, there is another side to the picture.

"The Son of Man came to seek and to save that which was lost," our text reads. Thank God for a seeking Savior! Thank God that through a dear Christian mother, or that godly wife, through a preacher or a faithful friend; you heard the message that Jesus was seeking you.

On the two arms of the cross of Calvary, there is held out the only hope for this world's redemption. Thank God we are no longer lost. Thank God for the redemptive power of the cross.

Father, Thank You for the love that led You to make such a sacrifice. Thank You for the limitless patience You show with this rebellious world. Lord, I am thinking today of those I know who are lost. Please draw them to You. Bring them to knowledge of Your love for them. Bring them to complete surrender and salvation of their souls. I pray in Jesus' name, Amen.

July 26   The Palm Tree Christian

Scripture Verse: Psalm 92

Key Verse: "The righteous shall flourish like a palm tree . . . ."
Psalm 92:12

Let us see what the palm tree can teach our waiting hearts today. First we notice that the palm tree indicates the presence of water. In Exodus 15:27 we read, "Then they came to Elim, where there were twelve wells of water and seventy palm trees; so they camped there by the waters." What a delightful sight to a traveler, exhausted and despairing, with a dry water-bag, with intolerable heat, his strength spent, to look up and see a great row of palm trees on the horizon.

Those distant palms speak to him of shade, blessed rest, comfort, companionship, and of life-giving water. The palms mean an oasis, a lovely spacious garden in the very midst of a blazing, pitiless desert.

Now, water is linked to every Christian life. Jesus says "If anyone thirsts, let him come to Me and drink. He who believes in Me . . . out of his heart shall flow rivers of living water." So, the child of God stands up in the desert wastes of this old world indicating the presence of the water of life. Perhaps we should catechize ourselves a little here. Does my life point the weary traveler to the water of life, the shelter of the oasis, Jesus? Does my life establish the fact that the living, exhaustless waters of salvation are at hand?

Next, we notice that the palm tree inclines upward. In Jeremiah we read "They are upright, like a palm tree." It stands straight up, a slender column aiming directly at the heavens, leaping up a living shaft reaching for the throne of God. So too, every Christian life stands upright like a pillar before God. Not because of anything they do, it is all God's work.

The palm tree represents internal development. Most trees grow up by adding to their outward girth, but the palm tree is different. It grows from within, from the center out. Christian experience is the same. It is not a putting on of moral habits. It is not an outward loyalty to Christ.

51

It is not concerned with forms and ceremonies. The Lord Jesus lays hold of the heart. Why? Because, out of the heart proceed the issues of life. Look what Christ did when He got the heart of Peter, Zacheus, and Paul. The Christian life is a heart-centered life.

The palm tree has infinite ministry. It is good for hundreds of uses. It is one of the most productive of all trees. It furnishes man with masts, posts, rafters, mats, roofs, milk, dates, nuts, oil, and endless other imperative needs. Christian lives are to be fruit-bearing lives, as well. Jesus said, "By this My Father is glorified, that you bear much fruit; so You will be My disciples."

The palm tree presents to us an indestructible symbol of beauty. God wants us to flourish, like the palm. To flourish means to thrive. And unlike other trees which lose their leaves and stand naked to the arctic blasts, the palm is perennial. It is always green and evergreens speak of eternal life. Theirs is continuous ministry. We read in Psalm 1 of the happy man. "Whose leaf shall not wither; and whatever he does shall prosper." There is no thought of decay, decline, defeat, or death.

The palm tree lives in the desert with its heat and dry wind and yet despite it all, the palm tree goes on. Why? Because its source of strength is out of sight. It has a root that has gone down until it has found the life-giving stream. Despite storms and the environment in which we live, we too can flourish like the palm tree.

Dearest Father, thank You for the picture of the palm tree. It is a reminder of how You intend our life to be lived. May I yield myself more and more to You each day and flourish like this lovely creation. Amen.

Scripture Reading: Matthew 5

Key Verse: "Blessed are the pure in heart, for they shall see God." Matthew 5:8

We are perplexed by the seeming impossibility both in the requirement and the promise. "How?" we ask.

The pure in heart are those who have exercised and received the previous qualifications and bestowments from God. They have the poverty of spirit which recognizes its true condition. There is the mourning which rightly feels the gravity and awfulness of that condition. The desire for the righteousness of God, and the spirit of meekness coupled with the true spirit of mercy, these will purge the heart of its self-regard until its eyes shall open to behold the light of God.

Dr. Moffett once said in class that this beatitude should be translated, "Blessed are they who are not "double-minded" for they shall be admitted into the intimate presence of God." The epistle of James indicates a similar meaning when it says "purify your hearts you double-minded." Double mindedness indicates instability, unsettledness, even deceitfulness and lack of integrity. We cannot be quite sure of a double-minded man, because he is not sure of himself.

The pure in heart are those who are not double-minded and unstable, deceiving themselves and others. They are single-minded and wholehearted. So, the first step toward such purity of heart is to have a will single to the good and to God.

The second step is to have an eye single to the good and the true. Jesus said, "When your eye is good, they whole body also is full of light." Cross-eyed Christians who have one eye out for good and one eye out for evil darken their minds and are double-minded. Single-mindedness is not narrow-mindedness or simple-mindedness, but a genuineness, a soundness at the core, an indifference to externals.

When we set our will to do God's will, our eye to see God's purposes and our mind to think on whatsoever things are true, honest, just, pure, lovely and of good report, light then begins to stream into our minds, dispelling the shadows of doubt. Our hearts and our thoughts are then cleansed by God's Holy Spirit, and thus we approach the state of being pure in heart.

We can turn our mental camera in almost any direction and get assuring pictures of God's presence. We can look at the earth and feel with Carlyle that nature is the very garment of God. We can look at saintly souls in their goodness, at scientists in their search for truth, at poets with their flashes of beauty, and all these seem to reveal God speaking through them.

Look at the stories of Jacob, Job, Paul, and so many others in the Scriptures whose lives and outlooks were transformed by a touch from God. Whether you call it a vision of God, or a communion with God, it amounts to the consciousness of His presence. It is the blessed assurance of loving relations with Him and communion in mind and heart, will and conduct. For these, purity of heart is central.

The blessing of "seeing God" is the one thing that will calm our distraction, which will supply our needs, and lift our lives to a level of serene power and blessedness unattainable any other way. And everything will be different when earth is crammed with Heaven and every common bush afire with God.

Holy and Almighty God, I surrender my double-mindedness and set my heart to do Your will, my eyes to see Your purposes, and my mind to think on whatever is true and lovely and of good report. I desire genuineness of heart so that I may see You. Amen.

July 28   The Power Of The Blood Of Christ

Scripture: 1 Peter 1: 13-21

Key Verse: ". . . knowing that you were not redeemed with corruptible things, like silver or gold . . . but with the precious blood of Christ, as of a lamb without blemish and without spot." 1 Peter 1:18-19

Let us sum up the wonder-working power of the blood of Christ in four great truths. The blood of Christ justifies, redeems, reconciles, and cleanses.

First, "justified" means the making just of one who has been unjust. Here the thought is that sin is the breaking of the law and a broken law demands a penalty. A holy and just God could not disregard the offense of sin. He solved this problem by permitting His only son to die for us on the cross so that man is not merely pardoned and set free from a penalty, but in the power and wisdom of God he is made a righteous man.

Over the portals of a church in Germany there is cut in stone, a beautiful lamb. A man at work on the steeple of the church lost his footing and plunged to the ground below. A flock of sheep chanced to be grazing in the churchyard and the fall of the man was broken on a little lamb. The lamb was killed, but the man's life was saved. In his gratitude he cut into the stone over the doors of the church, a replica of the lamb that saved his life. So we are forgiven and pardoned and saved from the penalty of sin and death by Christ, who is the Lamb of God.

The blood of Christ redeems. The word "redeem" speaks of bondage and slavery. In Peter's day, when a slave was in bondage, his family or some kind-hearted friend of means would redeem the man from slavery with gold or precious stones paid as ransom. Well, bless God, Christ paid the price of our redemption and oh how great that price was, nothing less than His own precious blood.

The blood of Christ reconciles. Man's condition is that of alienation and separation from God. Sin always separates man from God. Cain sinned and "went out from the presence of the Lord." Judas sinned and "went out immediately." How can men and God be reconciled? By the precious blood of Christ, it brings the unsurpassed peace of reconciliation.

The Blood of Christ cleanses. At first it seems like a strange paradox. How could blood cleanse? Blood makes a stain which is deep and distinct and which every evildoer dreads to leave behind him. Blood has always been the stain and evidence of guilt. But here is a great paradox; the blood of Christ, instead of staining, washes out the stain of sin. Instead of defiling, it washes white the soul of the believer. The awakened conscience feels the stain of sin and the shame of sin. But as for the blood of Christ as presented in the New Testament, the sinner can look upon it and be made clean.

How great the wonder-working power of the precious blood of Christ upon the souls of those who in faith receive Him and trust Him. If you have not received Christ, I plead with you to receive the ransom that was paid for you with the royal blood of the Son of God.

If you have received Him, won't you share with and pray for those you know who haven't? God longs for His magnificent gift to be received. Christ's part was to pay our debt. Our part is to accept His payment and share the good news of it with others so they may partake.

Dearest Holy Father, thank You for paying for the debt of my sin. I am so grateful. Today, I lift up to You the names of ----- --------, and, -----------. Please justify, redeem, reconcile, and cleanse them as well. Amen

July 29   The Wilderness or the Promised Land

Scripture Reading: Hebrews Chapters 3 & 4

Key Verse: "Beware brethren, lest there be in any of you an evil heart of unbelief in departing from the living God." Hebrews 3:12

Here is a great passage of warning and exhortation for the children of Israel so long ago and also for us today. Paul goes back to the story of the Israelites in their journey through the wilderness and he sums up their trouble. They had the leader, Moses. They had the message, because God spoke. But they disobeyed through unbelief in the Word of God. That was the reason so many never stepped into the Promised Land, and it is sadly the same today.

Notice the contrast between chapters three and four. Chapter three is like a drear November day when all the landscape is drenched by rain. Chapter four is like a still-clear day in summer when nature revels in bliss. Each chapter, however, represents an experience of the inner Christian life.

I think of Israel's wilderness experiences. Never was there a more victorious and proud nation than Israel that day on the shores of the Red Sea. Behind was Egypt, left forever; above, the fleecy cloud, the chariot of God, the tabernacle of His presence. Before them, a land of milk and honey about a two or three months journey away. But out of 600,000 men, flush with victory and hope, only two entered into the Promised Land. Forty years slowly passed away in which that wilderness became a cemetery. One by one the bodies were placed in that wasteland, the desert sands their winding sheet, the solitude their mausoleum. Forty years for 600,000 to die.

The wilderness experience is emblematic amongst other things of unrest, aimlessness, and unsatisfied longings. Tents were constantly being struck, only to be erected again. How few Christians have learned the secret of inner rest. How many are the victims of murmuring and discontent, bitten by serpents of jealousy, passion, hatred, ill will, broken vows, blighted hopes, purposeless wanderings, and the monotony of failure. They are always striking and pitching the camp, always seeing the same horizon. Life passes away amid fret and chafing disappointment, till we say with Solomon, "Vanities of vanities, all is vanity."

Think of the scourges of the desert, sandstorms with hot winds and powdery dust finding its way into the lungs, mouth and eyes, stinging the skin, making life nearly unbearable. Then there is also the mirage. Oh, deceived hopes, his thirst mocked, emblem of disappointment as found in seeking from the world that which does not satisfy instead of seeking in Christ who is our Promised Land and who will give us rest.

The cause of the wilderness experience? "They could not enter in because of their unbelief." Unbelief raises barriers which shut us out of blessing.

They murmured. They complained about the food, they complained about the water, they complained that they wished they had died in Egypt. They didn't listen to the voice of God and thought they could do better for themselves. The darkness of unbelief cannot live in the sunlight of fellowship with God. They failed to learn the lessons of the past.

What may we learn today? Guard against a heart hardening. Guard against a fickle heart, and guard against an evil heart. Renounce the wilderness and enter into Canaan by faith. The Almighty God wants to lead you into the abundant life; do not allow unbelief to deprive you of your blessing.

Lord, I don't want to spend my life running in useless circles. I want to learn from the past and follow You directly into the abundant life. Amen

July 30   The Perils of Discipleship

Scripture Reading: Luke Chapter 9

Key Verse: "Now it happened that as they journeyed on the road, that someone said to Him, 'Lord, I will follow You, wherever You go.' And Jesus said unto him, 'Foxes have holes, and birds of the air have nests, but the Son of Man has nowhere to lay His head.'" Luke 9:57-58

In the last six verses of the ninth chapter of Luke three incidents are related very briefly. Three men suddenly appear and then, just as suddenly, they are gone. We never hear of them again and the tantalizing brevity of it all leaves us wondering what became of them.

But while their visits are short, they are long enough to illustrate three perils of Christian discipleship. First, we see the peril of the uncounted cost. Next, we are introduced to the peril of the unburied corpse, and lastly, we hear of the peril of the unforsaken circle. Now, we need to remember that here we are dealing with discipleship, not salvation. The natural man cannot follow Christ, and they that are in the flesh cannot please God. We must first be born again by the Holy Spirit through faith in the Lord Jesus Christ as our Savior. Then we are challenged to deny self, take up the Cross, and follow our Lord. It is, therefore, to the twice-born who have set out to follow in His steps, that scripture presents three perils of discipleship.

Consider first the man in our text above. In Matthew's account of this encounter, we are told the man is a scribe. Now, up to this time, Jesus' choice of disciples had been fishermen and humble folk of lowly occupation. If He had an eye to earthly advantage, He would have lost no time listing a scribe among His followers. What prestige to have had a theologian among His group! But, with his usual perception, our Lord saw the tragic weakness in this man and answered him accordingly. It was really only another way of saying, "You only think you want to follow me. Have you counted the cost?" Yes, there are those who have plenty of sentiment, but make no sacrifice.

The second man reveals the peril of the unburied corpse. The first man was at least eager, this man is not eager enough! The Lord Himself calls this man, and adds a command to go and preach the gospel, but this man wanted to bury his father. Why does he then receive such a stern reply? The trouble lies deep. This was the sort of fellow who was ready to follow after all the "ifs" and reservations and provisos had been attended to. See the word in his request, "Suffer me <u>first</u> to go . . ." He had put something else ahead of Jesus, something more important than the kingdom. In such cases, there is always some corpse somewhere. Maybe it is a friendship, a fellowship with this world that needs to be forsaken. Dead issues, dead pleasures, dead interests, they keep so many of God's people from walking faithfully with God. Whatever it may be, leave it behind. God will not tolerate divided allegiance.

And, consider finally, the peril of the unforsaken circle. This last man went a step beyond the previous one. He said, "I will follow You . . . but. . . ." "But" is one of the most tragic words in the Bible. At first thought, one would say there can be little enough harm in saying goodbye to his friends and family. One must ask, however, then why were they sitting at home? Our Lord abruptly heads off the trouble. His kingdom is no place for a man with his head turned one way and his feet turned another. You must forget the things that are behind, and pay the price of consecration and dedication to the Kingdom of God.

Lord, open my eyes that I might discern which duties are simply distractions to be left behind. Amen.

July 31   The Supreme Offering to Christ

Scripture Reading: II Chronicles Chapter 17

Key Verse: ". . . Amasiah, the son of Zichri, who willingly offered himself to the Lord." II Chronicles 17:16

Who was Amasiah? He was a general in Jehosophat's army, commander of 200,000 men. Yet, this big, important man willingly offered himself to the Lord. Amasiah put God's cause first in his life. Everyone puts God's cause somewhere in their life, everyone must. But, the real question is where do we place God's call in our priorities in life? Amasiah put it first.

Jesus preached the same idea years later when he said, "Seek first the Kingdom of God . . ." "Seek first," he said, not seek second, or seek third, not incidentally, not partially, not optionally either. Seek it, and put it first in your life, then God will do the rest. Paul also illustrated the same truth when He said, "For me to live is Christ."

Now, this man Amasiah also points out something else for us. Not only did he live for the Lord, but he did it in the army, a difficult place to be foremost for God. There is no distinction, you see, between the secular and the sacred calling. We are to be just as much called to the Christian life on Tuesday as on Sunday. Out in the shops, and the factories, the stores and your social circle, wherever your elbows touch with the world, oh, beloved; let us make sure we are living the Christian life there.

One of the great pork-packing factories in the west was owned by a modest Christian man. He was once introduced, and the man questioned him, "I apologize, but I didn't quite catch, what is your business, exactly?" The owner of the factory replied, "I am a Christian, sir." "Oh, you did not understand, what do you do for a living?" Came the answer, "My business, sir, is to be a Christian. I pack pork to pay the expenses." O, beloved, our business in this world is to live for Christ.

But Amasiah has another lesson for us as well. Note that he offered himself. There was no conscription, no coercion. This was not a draftee, but a volunteer. He offered himself willingly. What a glorious thing for men and women to rise up and surrender to God!

Would you have your life count for the highest and the best? Then your life must be yielded to the guidance and mastership of the Lord Jesus Christ. The Bible says that the disciples were called Christians first at Antioch. Why? Because they believed in Christ and they practiced his teachings. They were endeavoring by their whole life to be like Christ. A Christian, then, was one who was actually Christ-like, putting Jesus first, foremost, and always at the center of their life.

So, what was the walk of Christ like? Well, Jesus walked with an eye single to the glory of God. He delighted to please God. Christ walked in utter disregard of self. He walked with a consuming passion for souls, and in complete surrender to God's will. This is what it means to be Christ-like.

And what about Paul? What difference did becoming a Christian make in the life of Paul? Every difference. Remember Paul as the persecuting Saul? After his encounter with Jesus, Paul laid claim to being a Christian on the ground that "Christ lives in me." He was indwelt by a living, reigning, conquering Christ, and so are you and I! The harvest of Paul's Christian life goes on today, dear friends, all because he put Christ first. With that Christ-like disregard for self, he surrendered to God's will, and lived with consummate concern for the salvation of others. What about you?

Dear Lord, like Amasiah, I want to live for You firstly, willingly, and in whatever situation I find myself. Today, Lord, as I go about my earthly business, use me in Your heavenly business. What an honor! Thank You, Lord, Amen.

August 1   Is Christianity Worth What It Costs?

Scripture: I Timothy Chapter 4

Key Verse: ". . . Godliness is profitable . . ." I Timothy 4:8

While it is free to acquire, Christianity requires much to maintain. It is not cheap in any way. You cannot play with it or play at it and succeed. You cannot put it on and off like a coat. It asks for sacrifice and consecration, full and completely. The fact is, this is where the shoe is pinching for some Christians, and they do not thank me for saying so.

But, beloved, I ask you to face it. You cannot drink the cup of the Lord and the cup of the world at the same time. Often the things we sacrifice are not inherently wrong, they are simply weights that hold us back. And, because Christ calls us to a higher place, some people are not willing to leave the worldly toys and distractions for the spiritual banquet He offers.

Christianity is not an organization, a superstition, an emotional journey, or an exclusive social club. Rather, the life of Christ and the Christlike life give us a true picture and an adequate definition. Our purpose is to become like Him.

There is a mighty force in our lives when genuine Christianity gets a chance with us. That is why the author of our text says "Godliness is profitable." Christianity bestows power for the taking to every Christian. It is the supernatural leap between the world and the provision of heaven. The same power that propelled the resurrection of Christ from the dead gives us dynamite in our lives. It is an explosion of power, deep and abiding joy, sight beyond the horizon, and a rock-solid foundation for every event of life. It is the electricity in the wire, the fuel in the plane, and the spark of life that brings a dead seed to a mighty and vigorous plant.

Dr. James Vance once told of spending an interesting day at the Grand Canyon. While he was looking at some Indian curios a gentleman came over to him and said, "You are Dr. Vance. You used to preach at Newark, New Jersey." He shook hands with him then went on to say that as a son of a poor minister he was in that city attending a night school trying to become a lawyer. "Often I was tempted to give up, but the biggest boost I got was on Sunday nights when I went to your church. It was what I got there that kept me going and put me through." The stranger introduced himself and presented his card as the attorney for the Erie Railroad.

That man found in Christianity a force for everyday living. Christianity makes the meek mighty. It strengthens us, puts heart in us. We find ourselves transformed, lifted up, and empowered for the moments we face. New birth has changed us to the extent we have surrendered to it, not only now, but eternally. We become eternal beings with eternal goals and issues. The sacrifices we thought we made for God now appear trite and trivial. Is Christianity worth what it costs? Yes, it is worth all that it demands, because it only demands the relinquishment of the things of this world, while bestowing the riches of heaven.

When Louis Agassiz, the great scientist, was at Harvard some years ago, the seniors would say to the freshmen, "Keep close to him and he'll show you something wonderful every moment." So too, I say, "Keep close to Christ. He will show you His glory. He will interpret life in a way that gives it meaning and significance." Christianity means harmony with His will, and dedication of our lives. That is a real cost, but it is not too high to pay.

Dear God, the price I pay to stay in Your will is nothing compared to the price You paid for me on Calvary. Thank You with all my heart. Amen

August 2 Behold

Scripture Reading: Psalm 51

Key Verse: "Behold, I was brought forth in iniquity, and in sin did my mother conceive me." Psalm 51:5

On a trip through the country, I always like to look at the signs along the road, the big, colored billboards and the old-fashioned Burma-Shave style signs. Well, someone has said that the Bible is God's true and faithful signboard for saint and sinner as they pass through this journey of life. And, truly, there is one word in the Bible that seems designed to capture our attention. It runs through the whole Bible, and God uses it again and again. It is the word "Behold."

The word means "note well," and indicates that there is a reason for your deep and lasting attention. Let us take a look at a few of the important "Behold" signs God has set out along our way.

The first "Behold" is that of our text. Yes, the first thing man has to learn in coming to God is that man is fallen, a sinner in the sight of God. Like Isaiah, who upon seeing the holiness of God, recognized his own sin. Isaiah's cry of "woe is me" reveals he had finally seen his life in perspective to God's holiness. Until a man realizes he is unclean, he talks of his own goodness. But when he gets sight of God, his mouth is stopped, as was Isaiah's.

The next "Behold" is good news; in fact it is The Good News! "Behold, I bring you good tidings of great joy, for unto you is born this day in the city of David a Savior which is Christ the Lord." This is the good news of the gospel; it doesn't simply tell you that you are lost, but it shows you how to be saved. It is a gospel of peace, peace with God. These good tidings are truly to all men, the good news of reconciliation.

So many people have the wrong idea of the gospel today. I heard of a poor woman in Glasgow once. She was in great need and poverty, and a kind, wealthy Christian man went to help her in her distress. But, as he knocked and knocked, he received no answer; she thought it was the landlord coming to put her out and so would not answer. That's the way with many people today. They say there is too much to give up to accept the gospel. How ridiculous! It is a blessing to give up rags in exchange for a new suit of clothes. It is a blessing to give up being a child of sin to become the child of God. And it is a blessing to give up nothing in exchange for everything. Jesus did not come to make life miserable; He came to give us abundant life!

Another "Behold" in found in John 1:29, "Behold the Lamb of God who takes away the sin of the world." Think of it, every sin you have ever committed has already been paid for. Jesus, the Lamb of God, came to save you. Bring Him your sin, and He will blot them out forever, exchanging them for eternal life. "Him that comes unto me I will in no wise cast out."

The last "Behold" I want to look at today is in Acts 9:11, ". . . for behold, he is praying." Saul has seen the Lord on the road to Damascus, and waits, blinded, upon the Lord. God is speaking to Annanias, sending him to lead Saul to the light. Beloved, is there one today, waiting perhaps for you, seeking the truth? Does God have a divine appointment for you today? One who needs the good news and thirsts for the eternal, abundant, life that only Jesus can give? Be ready to introduce them to the Lord today, saying, "Behold, the Lamb of God, who takes away the sin of the world."

Father, help me to be able to lay aside my own problems and tasks long enough to consider the position of others. If there is one to whom You would have me to speak of Jesus, please give me the words, the opportunity, and the boldness to do so to Your glory. In Jesus' name, Amen.

August 3   A Time to be Serious

Scripture Reading: I Corinthians Chapter 7

Key Verses: "But this I say, brethren, the time is short, so that from now on even those who have wives should be as though they had none, those who weep as though they did not weep, those who rejoice as though they did not rejoice, those who buy as though they did not possess, and those who use this world as not misusing it, for the form of this world is passing away." I Corinthians 7:29-31

In this solemn statement of the great Apostle Paul, we have our pattern of conduct in the last days. It begins and ends with a reminder of how short and changing are these fleeting times. Of course, there is a sense in which the time has always been short. It was short in Paul's day, for compared with eternity, the whole stretch of history is but a drop of water compared to the oceans.

Nothing is clearer in the Word of God than the fact that in these last days, Christians are called to unusual seriousness and special urgency. Especially does the Word exhort believers to be sober. If ever the church ought to live with her lamps burning, praying and living with the light of another world in her eyes, it is today.

It was for just such a time as this that Paul wrote the words of our text, expressing the urgency of the situation, and our proper behavior in it. "Those who have wives should be as though they had none," Paul declares. It means that believers should not be completely overtaken by domestic cares. We are not even to make home and family our number one priority. God comes first.

Paul also states, "Those who weep as though they did not weep." We also must not be too much taken up with our sorrow. We are not to nurse old heartaches, mistakes, and bereavements. There is just too much to be accomplished for the Kingdom of God to be occupied with our own troubles. Likewise, however, the Scriptures remind us that "Those who rejoice" should behave "as though they did not rejoice."

We are not to be too much taken up with our joys. No enjoyments, no pastimes or recreations are to occupy the pre-eminence in our mind.

Do you see it, beloved? What Paul is saying here is that these days are not ordinary days, therefore ordinary conduct is unbecoming. During great crisis people forego ordinary comforts, revise all their habits, and do things they never would do in ordinary times. Do we really believe that the age may soon come to a close, that Jesus is coming, and that we are Christ's witnesses in the end of the age?

"And those who buy as though they did not possess," the Scriptures go on to say. What we possess must not possess us. Oh, beloved, have you learned that even better than possessing many things is to be independent of them?

"Those who use this world as not misusing it," is the final admonition of our text. This world is our passage, not our portion, dear ones. Yet some of us are driving our tent pegs down as though we meant to stay. Oh, beloved, hear me. Life is too short, and eternity too long; souls are too precious and the gospel too wonderful for us to take it easy. Living in these perilous times, in a crumbling civilization, with men's hearts failing them for fear, if ever God's people ought to live as peculiar people whose citizenship is in heaven, it is now. Let us be sober, for the time is short and the fashion and form of this world passes away.

Beloved Father, Please teach me to live with a sense of urgency and seriousness as Your ambassador. In Christ's name, amen.

August 4   Our Royal Commander

Scripture Reading: 1Timothy 6:11-16

Key Verse: "Fight the good fight of faith . . ." 1 Timothy 6:12

The French soldiers reckoned the presence of Napoleon with his army as equal to ten thousand bayonets. Well, Jesus Christ is our Commander. The prophet Isaiah 55:4 says ". . . I have given Him as a leader and commander for the people." In the New Testament He is called the captain of our salvation. As such, His orders are paramount and to be obeyed to the letter.

Against the grim Welsh Coast a November storm was raging. Signals of distress broke out from a ship drifting helplessly toward the cruel reefs. Quickly the lifeboat coast guard assembled. An old sailor spoke up, "Captain, it's no use in this wind. We can launch the boat and perhaps reach the ship but we will never get back." Said the Captain, "Boys, we don't have to come back." This is the spirit of loyalty that must possess us as we seek to follow our incomparable leader.

In Korea, in the early days of the war, our troops were tragically handicapped because of lack of adequate equipment or supplies, and poor intelligence information. They had to retreat in the face of greater numbers, leaving the wounded behind to face certain death while they had to face the shame of bitter defeat.

But in God's army that will never happen for our leader, the Son of God is omniscient and almighty. We are on the winning side. It is impossible for us to lose the war. John sees Him coming to wage and make war. He was clothed with a vesture dipped in blood, and He sees the armies of the devil and his antichrist vanquished and destroyed.

Yes, the engagement is bitter and desperate. Our enemies are not flesh and blood but principalities, powers, and world rulers of darkness in this age. The war will come to an end some day. We hope it will be soon. But mark it well; our Lord is a Captain who has never lost a battle. Who wouldn't want to belong to the army of the Lord Jesus Christ?

Who would like to enlist today? God's recruiting station is wherever you are right now.

For your encouragement, look at the glorious traditions behind us. Our regimental flags have the names of historic battles won in Jesus' name. Oh, think of the immortal achievements of the Army of the Lord.

Look at some of those immortal men like Wycliffe, Huss, Ridley, Latimer, Knox, Wesley, Spurgeon, Moody, and a host of other heroes in God's Army. These inspire us to do or die as we march with our incomparable Lord.

When the soldiers near the end of the war, they can sense it, they can see it by the signs around them. They begin to look forward to the glory approaching. I believe the Lord Jesus Christ is coming very shortly for His own. It cannot be long. We shall be caught up together with the resurrected dead to meet Him in the air. A little later, we shall return with Him to the earth to share in His glorious reign of 1000 years.

> Hark the waking up of nations
> Gog and Magog to the fray.
> Creation's groaning, groaning
> For the coming latter day.
> Will you dilly? Will you dally?
> With your music and your wine?
> Up! It is Jehovah's Rally,
> God's own arm hath need of thine.
> (Arthur C. Cox, 1840)

Then will come the New Heaven and New Earth, as we continue in the fellowship and service of God throughout eternity. Onward, Christian Soldier, Onward!

Almighty Lord, I will follow You. I look for You. I trust You. I love You. Amen

Scripture: Genesis 18:16-33

Key Verse: "... Let not the Lord be angry, and I will speak but once more: Suppose ten should be found there?" And He said, "I will not destroy it for the sake of ten." Genesis 18:32

The earnestness of Abraham's plea as he intercedes for Sodom is palpable. God had tolerated the growing evil of this city until its wickedness had darkened the earth and pierced the skies, until the moment when He came down to visit judgment upon this wicked place.

After He appraised Abraham of His plan, this wonderful man of God and man of faith took it upon himself to ask Jehovah God to please not destroy the good in that city along with the evil.

Six times Abraham interceded, six times he made his request, and six times Jehovah answered him in mercy and agreed to spare the city. Now why did not Abraham ask yet again?

Perhaps he thought there were not only ten righteous men in Sodom, but more, so he left off his praying and interceding. Yet God found but Lot and his family who were worthy to be saved. According to the record, we have only three souls who escaped Sodom. The lessons of Sodom are many and great.

Without God's people, the great cities are lost, as nations are lost. Neither cities nor nations nor families nor individuals come to God of themselves; rather they go the other way, the way of ruin and death.

Apart from the intercession of God's people and God's answering mercy, all cities, all nations, and all individuals will surely plunge downward to death and hell.

God nowhere promises to save, or purposes to save, the lost cities and lost people except through His people. Only so far as God can find and use men and women like Abraham to live and intercede will a nation be saved.

It is a great truth that even a few of God's people can turn a whole nation toward righteousness and toward God, and they can change a community in the same way.

In order to begin in our own communities, what must be done? We must stand for righteousness, as Daniel did. We must faithfully bear witness for Christ in the home and everywhere. We must proclaim God's gospel to the lost. We must confess and reconsecrate our own lives through prayer, like Jonah did. And we must engage in real intercession for the lost.

How many Christians does it take to intercede for a community, or a nation? How many does it take to gather in Christ's name to pray thus? Just two or three.

Well, they would be a burdened two or three. They must certainly be a dedicated two or three. And, they must be a praying two or three. But, to these He promises His presence. In Matthew 18:19-20, He states, "Again I say to you that if two of you agree on earth concerning anything that they ask, it will be done for them by My Father in heaven. For where two or three have gathered together in My name, I am there in the midst of them."

He proposes to honor the agreement made between them in prayer. And, He proposes to grant the prayer of this gathering of two or three who are asking in Jesus' name. What are we waiting for?

Dear Father, I pray for my neighborhood and my community just now. In Jesus name, I ask for revival among those who already love You and a softening of the hearts of those who need to meet You. Help me speak of Your truth and love when You provide the divine opportunity to do so. Amen.

August 6   The Chemistry Of Light

Scripture Reading: I John 1: 5-7

*Key Verse: ". . . God is light and in Him is no darkness at all."
I John 1: 5*

There are three ways by which God reveals Himself to man: in nature, in the Scriptures, and in the Person of Christ.

From creation, man is able to learn a great deal about God. David tells us in the Psalms that "The Heavens declare the glory of God and the firmament shows us His handiwork."

The person of Christ is the highest revelation of God. In Colossians we read, "For in Him dwells all the fullness of the God-head bodily. Jesus Himself said, "He that has seen me has seen the Father." God is invisible as a spirit. He cannot be seen with our eyes. Only in Christ do we see God.

In the Bible we have a progressive revelation of God. We learn to know Him as a God of love, grace, mercy, justice and truth. The Scriptures teach us that God is life, God is love, and God is light. Today let us think about God as light.

Light is invisible; no one has ever seen the whole spectrum of pure light. We can see the objects which the light reveals, and the effects it has. Just so, God is invisible and we can only see Him as He is reflected in the person of Jesus Christ.

Light rays, from a source such as the sun, can be seen but never felt. Heat rays, conversely, are felt but never seen.

The Son, who is the light of the world, corresponds to the light rays. He is the one whom we can see but not feel.

The Holy Spirit corresponds to the heat rays, for He is felt in the lives of the believers but is never seen. Like the wind, we see His power at work and feel His presence in our lives, but cannot discern a physical form.

Remember that Moses made a very bold and peculiar request of God, saying, "Please show me Your glory." And God said, "You cannot see My face, for no man shall see Me, and live." And the Lord said, "Here is a place by Me and You shall stand on the rock. So shall it be, while My glory passes by, that I will put you in the cleft of the rock and will cover you with My hand while I pass by. Then I will take away My hand, and you shall see My back; but My face shall not be seen."

We know from I Corinthians 10 that this rock is Christ. Moses could not see God, but hidden in the Rock of Ages, which is Christ, he saw God and the Rock filtered out the wrath of God and allowed only mercy and love to pass through.

We today cannot stand before God without a mediator for "God is light and in Him is no darkness." We need a shield between God and us. So the Psalmist said "The Lord God is a sun and shield." Of course God could not be our sun unless He was also our shield, as He is in the person of the Lord Jesus Christ.

Are you hidden in the Rock? The abiding presence of God is both our sun and our shield. Take time to realize that you can never even stand in the presence of God without the Shield, the Rock, the Lord Jesus Christ.

Almighty God, thank You for providing all I need to stand in Your presence. I have accepted the Rock, the Shield, the Lord Jesus, but I am concerned that _____ and _____ have not as yet accepted You. Please touch their hearts and help them to see Your wonderful love for us and help them accept the salvation that You offer to all who will receive you. Amen.

August 7   Jesus Christ, the Same

Suggested Reading: Hebrews Chapter 13

Key Verse: "Jesus Christ is the same yesterday, today and forever." Hebrews 13:8

Have you ever thought what a boundless satisfaction there is for us in those first five words, "Jesus Christ is the same"? Some of us who once enjoyed good eyesight, good hearing, nerves tingling with the wine of health, now know that age has taken its toll. Your health does not stay the same. You have pains and aches that were never yours in the yesterdays, but plague you today.

Or maybe a few years ago you were in good circumstances, meeting your financial obligations and making money, but now adversity is a regular boarder at your house. You know that circumstances do not stay the same.

Then, there is the fickleness of human nature, your own, or those you count as friends. One day they eat you up, the next they act as though you've given them a belly-ache. You have trusted and been disappointed. Perhaps you must live or work with one that is as changeable as a chameleon in spirit and disposition. Oh, we cannot live long in this world without the realization that earthly relationships cannot and do not remain the same.

Since all that is true, what a relief to turn from these changing scenes to Jesus Christ the Same. Here is one who never fails the one who leans on Him for repose. Health may fail us, but His strength is made perfect in our weakness. Adversity may crash upon us, but He draws nearer that a brother and whispers "In the world you will have tribulation; but be of good cheer, I have overcome the world." When friends desert us, like Paul we might say "No one stood with me." But we can also say with Paul in the next verse, "But the Lord stood with me."

We may have to say with Jeremiah, "The crown has fallen from our head, woe to us." But the Lord says, "I will forgive their iniquity and their sin I will remember no more."

Even when death draws near He assures us, "I am the resurrection and the life."

Men may ask "Is the day of miracles past?" There is no day of miracles. Miracles are simply the supernatural operation of God and He is timeless. There is no day with Him. His supernatural power is always the same and wherever He regenerates and directs a human heart, there you have miracles.

There is abundant evidence all over the world to a wonderworking God and to a Christ who is the same today. There are thousands of lives that can be accounted for in no other way. The blind are seeing, the lame are walking, the lepers are cleansed, the deaf hear, the dead are raised up; the poor have the gospel preached to them.

Eyes blinded by the god of this world are still being opened, sin's cripples walk in newness of life, the dead in trespasses and sin are quickened to eternal life. He still does mighty works and when we pray more, we will see His hand moving more.

The Word declares that is "Jesus Christ is the same, yesterday, today and forever." Foundationally, behind the Bible, the Church, creeds, and church activities, stands the Eternal Christ. We must in our thinking, living, and witnessing, give Him the pre-eminence. Our need is to know Him. Anything less will be defeat and sorrow and loss for time and eternity. Anything else will not satisfy. He is the one unchangeable element in life.

Dear Lord, You are my great tower. I can lean on You and You will hold me. Amen.

Scripture Reading: Psalm 33

Key Verse: "Sing to Him a new song; play skillfully with a shout of joy." Psalm 33:3

Someday we will sing a new song with the ransomed hosts in glory, but even before that we may know something of that joy here on earth. David, in Psalm 40:3 says, "He has put a new song in my mouth." And the anonymous psalmist of Psalm 33 exhorts the righteous to praise Him. Indeed, it is only those who have experienced His great grace that can truly bless His name. David knew this.

In Psalm 40, we see that innumerable evils had compassed David about. His iniquities had taken hold upon him. Enemies had sought to destroy him and sin, like a fiery serpent, had coiled about him.

But instead of a cry of despair, David now has the song of victory. Instead of the throes of death, David now sings the thrills of life.

Yes, Christians too can sing this song of deliverance. When one is born again, he becomes a new creature. He is heir to a new covenant. He has a new home and travels a new way. And while on his way he is given a new song. The old song of doubt and hate and discontent fades out and the new song with its exultant notes of faith and hope and love fill the soul.

Yes, the psalmist had something to sing about, but so do we! On yonder cross of Calvary, Jesus reached His arms down to the lowest sinner to rescue him from the deep mire where there is no standing. So the redeemed soul has something precious to sing about. What deliverance! It would be abnormal if we did not sing!

We should note too that this new song is not dependent upon temporal things. Madam Guyon, in her French prison, could sing, "Content a prisoner to be, since, my God, it pleaseth Thee." For her, the freedom her soul had found in Christ was sufficient, though she was imprisoned for her faith. This song is not dependent upon the fame or fortune of this world. Indeed, many who have fame and fortune are destitute of song.

The new song is not something one works up within oneself. This song is born not of natural man; it is the song of a new heart. Before one can sing it, he must have a new heart with which to sing it. It is, primarily, a song of gratitude.

Our pleasure-mad, on-rushing age has about exhausted its thrills. The music of life has become jarring. Instead of the new song, the world sings the old discord of sin. Tired and weary, it asks, "What next?" only to find the same disappointment. The world has no new song. What promises to be a song, only becomes a yawn.

Contrast this with the bountiful, exuberant strains of Psalm 33, "Praise the Lord with the harp; make melody to Him with an instrument of ten strings. Sing to Him a new song; play skillfully with a shout of joy." What joy and hope are ours, because of Him.

Yes, the Christian life is not like the drab days of lowering clouds, but shines like the glad burst of a spring morning. We have exchanged certain death for certain life. We have exchanged the strength of a mere man for the strength of the almighty Creator, by whose word, "the heavens were made." We have exchanged fear for rejoicing, "Because we have trusted in His holy name." Oh, praise the Lord today, beloved, and let the redeemed of the Lord say so.

Mighty Father, my soul trusts only in You. Not only are You the Great Architect of the world, but You are the artist of my soul. Not only do You tend the great garden of the planet earth, but You number the hairs on my head. Praise Your name, most merciful and loving Lord! Amen.

Scripture Reading: Matthew 5: 1-12

Key Verse: "Blessed are those who mourn for they shall be comforted." Matthew 5:4

There is a vital progress and connection in the Beatitudes. The jewels are not flung down in a heap, they are wreathed in a chain that the wearer may have an ornament of grace about his neck. They are an outgrowth from a common root, stages in the evolution of Christian character. The true purpose of the gift of life is that we might become imitators of God as dear children. And there are few instruments more powerful for the creating of that type of character we are to make our own, than this sacred sorrow.

Not all sorrow is a blessing, even in disguise. Paul recognizes that there are grades of sorrow when he declares, "For godly sorrow produces repentance leading to salvation . . . but the sorrow of the world produces death." Hence, when we seek the sources of comfort we must first consider the causes of our sorrow.

What are we mourning for? Is ours a grief or a grievance? Is our sorrow rooted in self-centeredness or does it stem from the suffering of others? Are we painfully penitent for our sins, or merely bemoaning their penalties? Some sorrow may be only effervescing self-pity, foaming with the poison of bitter resentment. Before seeking the divinely given prescription for comfort we should analyze our tears and diagnose our sorrows.

Significantly, the second Beatitude with its promise of comfort follows the first Beatitude with its blessing on the poor in spirit. Mourning is the emotion which follows upon that poverty. The one is the recognition of the true estimate of our own character and failings. The other is the feeling which follows upon that recognition. And the quality of our mourning is to be tested by the humility of our minds. Sorrow due to injured pride, threatened prestige, or thwarted possessiveness does not receive the promise of divine comfort. But the "poor in spirit" who mourn for their sins, who feel the sufferings of others, who weep over love's losses, they shall be comforted. Godly sorrow will receive God's consolation.

The eye that never knows tears would lack essential tenderness. The mind that never mourns would not possess the mellowness needed for friendship and love. The heart that never felt a break would not be quite whole. There is a saying that "all sunshine makes a desert." If our lives were only sun-filled, our streams of sympathy would dry up, our eyes would become spiritually blind and our natures would be horribly selfish.

Man has feelings to get hurt, a conscience to gnaw at him, and anxieties to fret him. Every increase in capacity to enjoy higher values carries with it growing capacity to suffer. The ear that is most alive to harmony is most hurt by discord. The conscience which is most responsive is also most shocked by the evils around it. Suffering and sorrow faithfully borne, beget a clarity of vision and a depth of understanding which are an abiding comfort.

Sorrow is also the spur to discovery. Many people will not bother to learn the truth until driven to it by some dark experience. It is against dark velvet that diamonds are displayed to show their luster. When disaster overtakes, men do not always find consolation from their club-mates and fellow golfers. More likely they seek out someone so spiritually close that they may sit down with them in a silence too deep for words. Our most precious relationships are those in which deep calls to deep.

Holy Father, may I see each time of suffering and mourning as a time for learning and growing. May I relinquish my heart's pain to You and let You turn it into something beautiful for the Kingdom of God. Amen.

August 10   The Suffering Servant Comes

Suggested Scripture: Isaiah 52:13-53:3

Key Verse: "Behold, My Servant shall deal prudently; He shall be exalted and extolled and be very high. Just as many were astonished at you, so His visage was marred more than any man and His form more than the sons of men." Isaiah 52:13-14

There is nothing in the Old or New Testament more arresting than this portrayal of the Servant of the Lord in which we are conscious of appalling gloom and ineffable glory. We know too little about this Servant. We know too little and judge too lightly the ministry of suffering on our behalf that was accomplished by our dear Lord Jesus Christ. Let the truths of this chapter grip your heart and you will cast aside all your flippancy. Face these facts of suffering and sacrifice, sorrow and tears, and they will sober you, humble you, and cause you to be more appreciative of the blessings you now enjoy.

This marvelous vision of the Lord Jesus in His vicarious suffering was given 600 years before it came to pass, yet in every detail is correct. It begins with two questions, "Who has believed our report? And to whom has the arm of the Lord been revealed?" Not many people believed God when He was revealed by the lowly Nazarene, who was the power of God unto salvation. Verse one is a lamentation of God, because of the unbelief of the world, then and now.

In verses two and three, we have the description of the suffering Servant. "He shall grow up" brings His humanity immediately to mind. "A tender plant" means "a shoot from the root", and while Jesus was of royal descent, it was descent from a royal house fallen on evil days; a humiliated, humbled, house of David. Jesus the Son of God was certainly found in humble fashion as a man, born in a stable, growing up in a tiny village hidden in the hills of Galilee as a carpenter's son. But there is another point to notice here, and it is in the words "before Him." This means that the unnoticed growth of this one by the world was noticed by Jehovah. Though not cared for by others, He is tended and guarded by Jehovah Himself.

Naturally a shoot from a dry ground would show but little beauty, foliage or flower. It would be starved and colorless compared to well-watered flowers and plants. In effect, there was nothing about Him that we should desire Him. And we see the confirmation in Jesus' earthly years, that there was complete absence of any outward show, or that which pleases the spoiled tastes of sinful man. It is evident in the poor judgment of mankind, choosing the tinsel rather than pure gold, choosing the vulgar over the meek and stainless purity of Christ, crying out, "Not this man, but Barabbas." And that cry, which is in substance a cry for less perfection, less holiness, is still the cry of the world today.

Lowliness of condition and lack of qualities appealing to men's false ideals will certainly lead to being "despised and rejected." Thus we read of Christ, "He was despised and forsaken of men." His claims were ridiculed, His words of wisdom rejected. His love was repulsed. He drank the bitter cup of contempt and all His earthly life He walked in the solitude of uncomprehended aims. In the hour of extreme need, He appealed in vain for solace and companionship, and was deserted by those whom He trusted most. And, He brought it all on Himself because He would be God's Servant, and Man's Savior.

Dear Lord, how quickly I forget the scope of the love of Jesus. How often I fail to appreciate the greatest gift ever given. I am humbled by the thought of Your great love for me. Amen.

August 11 The Suffering Servant's Sacrifice

Suggested Scripture: Isaiah 53:4-12

Key Verse: "All we like sheep have gone astray; we have turned, every one, to his own way; and the Lord has laid on Him the iniquity of us all." Isaiah 53:6

As we continue to look at this chapter of Isaiah, we press on to verses four through six, where we find the vivid description of the crucifixion of Christ. He was smitten, afflicted, pierced through. He was crushed. He was scourged. He was chastened. Yes, here we have the accumulated sorrows—our sorrows, our transgressions and our iniquities—as the cause of His multiform afflictions. He bore, He carried, He was wounded and afflicted, He was bruised. The stripes of our iniquities were laid on Him. Why? All for our salvation. Yes, this suffering was caused by our transgressions, and yet, how little we think about it.

The physical violence that was heaped upon our Lord, our blessed Lord, can you picture it? Dare you? The glory of it all is that all was for the end that we should be saved. His bruises, that we might be healed. His chastisement, that we might have peace. His stripes, that we might be spared those stripes. He is not simply a teacher, or an example, or a benefactor! His work is to bear our grief and be bruised for our healing.

Verses seven to nine give a graphic description of the unresisting endurance of the Servant, and the misunderstood end of the Servant's life. May God lay on your heart the sad facts of the days of His passion. Picture the suffering before Pilate, and before Herod who had no right to question Him. In the face of the spitting, buffeting, smiting, He stood silent. His lips were opened only in witness, but not in complaint or remonstrance. Why? Because He was willing to embrace that cross for us. Because He loved the Father and would do His will. Because He loved the world, and would be its Savior. These verses refer to the unfair trial and mockery, for His death was a judicial murder. He died alone on that cross that none of us must ever face death alone.

And now, just a moment to look at verses ten through twelve. These verses state clearly that His sufferings were divinely inflicted in the light of the fact that in the determinate counsel and foreknowledge of God, He delivered Him up. His soul was made an offering for sin. It was a trespass offering, representing sin or guilt as a debt and the sacrifice as making compensation. Did not Jesus state in John 10:15 that He would lay down His life as a ransom for many? His death was the communication of life. Having died, the Servant now lives. Having died, the Servant carries into effect the divine purposes.

In verse eleven we read a fitting crown upon the Servant's head and heart. The note of coronation is that the Servant will be content. He will be content to have borne all the grief and sorrow, content with the results, when He gazes upon the Church purchased by His own blood. Hallelujah!

The closing scene is that of a conqueror. Here is picture of the victory Christ has accomplished. Jehovah's Servant shall reign, and of His throne sacrifice and intercession are to be the foundations! Look at His life, His death, His suffering. Look at that grave and resurrection, that coming glory, that inexhaustible intercession and undying love. Look into your own heart, and measure the depth of your gratitude, and then, make it right with Him.

Praise You Father God, for your great gift. Praise You for Your unchanging nature. How great, how deep, how inspiring Your love is to me. Thank You. Amen.

Scripture Reading: Deuteronomy 30: 11-20

Key Verse: "I call heaven and earth as witnesses today against you, that I have set before you life and death, blessing and cursing; therefore choose life, that both you and your descendants may live." Deuteronomy 30: 19

Jesus looked upon all men as entitled to share in the joys of life. Contrast this with the Greek stoics, who said that life truly worth living is possible only for a few rare souls. Or Buddha, whose basic aim was to suppress not only selfishness, but also all human desire. His search was for an escape from life rather than for the enjoyment of it. Jesus saw and shared men's longings for happiness. And He made much of the points that He knew would bring happiness and fulfillment to the lives of men.

The first requisite for being happy is to settle the seat of sovereignty in one's life. There must be a place of final authority. To Jesus, God was the center of reference in all things, at all times, in all places.

The great knowledge of the ages has been gifted by God to man. Tested by the ages, universal in its truth, we can trust the counsel of God in regard to all matters of life. There need be no confusion, no relativity, and no changing opinions, only unchanging, dependable, trustworthy truth.

To some, the Sovereign is not God, but self. The thought process is, "I pray for world peace but my deeper prayer is that I may be secure and undisturbed." Hence when Christ confronts us with His gospel of blessedness, it is His Kingdom of God against our Kingdom of self. Self says, "Be aggressive, climb over others, get to the top, scratch and claw for your part of the pie." Jesus says, "Blessed are the meek for they shall inherit the earth."

Which is the real world, the one Jesus saw, or the one we see? Is it not logical to say that the most truly real world is the world as it looks to God who created it? How small and petty we would be to choose "our way" because it is what we can see and hold and contain in our human brains. How much more far-reaching is our view when we trust the One who can see beyond the horizon.

Jesus saw the world more clearly than any other one who ever trod this earth and he laid down the rules for living as He knew them to be. We reveal ourselves as ignorant when we ridicule these principles as impractical because they do not seem to fit our little man-viewed world. It was said of the Apostles that they turned the world upside down. In reality, Jesus' teachings turned the world right-side up. So, the first secret of happiness is to change the seat of sovereignty from self to God.

Have you noticed the central objective in new-fad teaching of religion? It is simply how to use God for the satisfaction of our own self and interests, how to make Him an ally in our campaigns for personal popularity and business prosperity. All this is very pleasing to modern congregations who call it good, practical, down to earth preaching. That is its defect. It is down to earth rather than up to God.

The core of what Christ teaches us about happiness is that by forgetting self we find ourselves, and by giving we receive. When we move our minds and hearts out of the kingdom of self into the kingdom of God, the secrets and sources of the higher happiness are revealed.

Father God, You are the authority of my life. No guessing, no confusion about what to do, Your will is what I seek, knowing that it will bless me as fully and richly as You intended all along, Amen.

August 13   A Reasonable Religion

Suggested Scripture: Micah Chapter 6

Key Verse: "He has shown you, O man, what is good; and what does the Lord require of you but to do justly, to love mercy, and to walk humbly with your God?" Micah 6:8

Micah's message was so constructive and so inspired that he defines for us the will of God both for the individual and for the world. Some writers feel that no man has given in such beautiful simplicity and truth a more improved definition of real religion. What does the Lord require of you? Or, in other words, what is necessary to please God? In his answer, he passes by ritual; he passes by sacrifice, to give the simple and profound answer in our text. How beautifully simple, that a child can understand it. How vastly profound, that the wisest of men cannot run past it.

But, what is it to "do justly"? Justice is fair-mindedness in action. Just conduct is the outward expression of inward honesty and sincerity. This doing justly, playing the game fairly, is to cover the whole circumference of life. It is to govern our play, and our business relationships. It was just such lack of justice between man and man that filled Micah with indignation. As he looked about him, he saw priests prattering oracles for pay. He saw so-called prophets who would pronounce a blessing if they were paid, but would pronounce a curse if they were not. He saw judges accepting bribes and the powerful rich taking such advantage of the poor that Micah accused them of stripping the hide off their flesh.

And so, Micah's word is a needed word in every age. There is a pressing need for justice between capital and labor. We are concerned that the employer pays a just wage, but if we are just we are also concerned that the employee does a just day's work. We should handle the tools of our trade as honestly and religiously as we handle the communion cup on Sunday morning. And, we have a race problem in this country. We proudly pledge allegiance to the flag and promise, "Justice and liberty for all," yet again and again racial prejudice crushes the minority races and holds in subjection those of other color. Justice is needed in the home, between parents and children, in the community, and in the church.

Why does God ask us to be just? Because justice is a badge of character. God is eager that we be just, because He wants us to be like Himself. He is eager for us to be just because injustice is a time bomb which sooner or later will explode and blow the building we have built on a foundation of injustice to bits.

But, God asks not only that we be just but also that we be merciful. Mercy is the child of love. The world today is dying for this everyday kindness. The closer our relationships, the more it is needed. In the home, in the church, in business and in the community, mercy makes living easier. It enriches both the giver and the receiver.

And, finally, God requires that we walk humbly with Him. To walk with God, there must be fellowship and communion. There must be love and imitation. God is so eager for our companionship that He emptied heaven to secure it. God longs for our fellowship not because He cannot be satisfied without us, but because He knows that we can never be satisfied without Him. Finally, God longs for our fellowship because He knows that it is only as we walk with Him that we shall really be just, or merciful.

Please Lord; help me to please You by doing justly and loving mercy. Let my light so shine before men that it glorifies only You. Amen.

August 14   Walk in the Light

Scripture Reading: Ephesians Chapter 5

Key Verse: "For you were once darkness, but now you are light in the Lord. Walk as children of light." Ephesians 5:8

Here is a revelation of the difference between the kingdom of this world and the kingdom of heaven. This world's kingdom is the manifestation of midnight darkness. God's kingdom, however, shines with the light of mid-day.

Our Lord told us that before His second coming, human society would sink to the very lowest levels such as prevailed in the days of Noah. Verses three and four are a litany of sin and unrepentant behavior. Praise God that the topic doesn't end there. "But now you are light in the Lord," verse eight reminds us. But now, the past is gone forever. But now, a new present is begun in vivid contrast to the past, marking the boundary line between darkness and of light.

"You are light," Paul reminds us. We are so identified with light, yes the Light so indwells us, that we have become light itself. We have been translated into the kingdom of light; we have been made a child of Him who is light; and we have become partakers of the life that is light. In Him we become what He is, light.

"Walk as children of light," because character determines conduct. Everything in the walk of the Christian should be different from that of the sinner. Notice that our conduct and our conversation betray us. They reveal our citizenship.

The vile sins that are the lifestyle of the kingdom of darkness, are not even to be mentioned among the citizens of light. To even discuss them is to pollute ourselves. Nothing is purer than this light. The works of darkness are degrading and destructive, but light is fruitful and edifying.

What then are the characteristics of those who are the light in the Lord? Paul mentions three. He first says the fruit of the light is "goodness." That means beneficence in action towards all persons.

Goodness holds back the Christian from doing anything that would be detrimental to another.

He will guard his influence and gladly give up even a lawful thing if there is in it the possibility of leading another away from Christ. Goodness is the most practical virtue, banning every form of selfishness and compelling the Christian not to seek his own but the other's good.

The next fruit of the light that Paul mentions is "righteousness." Now this righteousness is wiping the slate of every form of impurity and dishonesty and fleeing from even the appearance of evil. This righteousness gives the Christian a conscience void of offence toward God and toward men.

Finally, we are told that "truth" is the final fruit of light. There is no sham or pretence, no compromise, no secret evil alliance in the life of a citizen of the Light. Rather, there is a life of reality, open-hearted sincerity, and purity. Rather, there is a life gladly welcoming of every scrutiny from above.

Now beloved, to walk as children of light in these days is most difficult. We are to live our lives for God.

Filled with the Holy Spirit, we are to let our light shine before men that people may see our good works and "glorify your Father in Heaven."

Dear Lord it is only through you that I have the righteousness of Your Son to clothe me and protect me from the darkness of this world. Please fill me with Your Spirit, that I may live life in Your Light, as a testimony and a witness to your grace and love. Amen.

August 15   Deposed

Beauty, the wise man said, is vain. But, here we have the story of how God used the beauty of two women to save a nation from destruction and carry forward His eternal purpose.

The story of Esther is a drama that opens with a banquet, which for wickedness and beauty, splendor and length has perhaps never been surpassed. Ahasuerus sits in royal state at the center of the table in the great banqueting hall, and about him are arranged over 127 princes from his far-flung Empire. For one hundred eighty days the king has been engaged in showing these guests the riches of his glorious kingdom, and the honor of his excellent majesty.

For the last seven days, a great banquet has been in operation, and the king has been flanked with princes, attendants, army officers and other guests gorgeously arrayed with their robes and jewels flashing in the light of myriads of candles and candelabras. The floor of the banquet hall is of marble, mother-of-pearl, and precious stones. The couches upon which the revelers recline are in keeping with the splendor of all else that night. Every cup at the banquet is of purest gold. Slaves and eunuchs pass to and fro with liquors and food, sensuous music floats down from the galleries, and fountains throw their silver spray up as the sweet incense of Persia fills the air.

Ahasuerus is thinking to himself, "What more can I do to entertain and impress my guests?" Then, to his alcohol-inflamed brain, comes a new idea. "The Queen, the beauty of all the earth," he thought, "I will bring in Vashti and display her beauty to all." So, through his trusted eunuchs, Ahasuerus summons the queen, Vashti.

Startled by so wicked and unprecedented a proposal, the drunken lords no doubt sit up in eagerness to await the coming of the far-famed queen. But they were doomed to disappointment. She refused to expose herself to the lascivious gaze of the drunken mob. Vashti said, "No," and it is surely one of the great God-inspired "no's" of all history.

Let all women, and all girls remember her "no." This queen was known in her time as an unparalleled beauty, but to history she is remembered because she had character. She loved her soul and her principles more than life and riches. That single word, "no," made Vashti immortal, and it made Esther immortal too.

Had it not been for that "no" of Vashti's, Esther would never have been heard of. The refusal of Vashti lost her crown and began the chain of events that would place Esther in position to aid in the deliverance of her people from destruction. God was working behind the scenes.

Faith in God's providence gives us confidence that the affairs of this troubled world are in His hands. He never lets go of the helm. If He is in the lives of nations, He is also in the lives of individuals. God has a plan for every life. God has a plan for your life, and for mine.

Dear Lord, whatever Your plan for me, whatever the divine appointments You have set for me, I ask You to help me meet them with grace, with boldness, and with integrity. If like Vashti I am to face testing and persecution, then let me face it with dignity, firm in my confidence. If, like Esther, I am to require the courage to act, let me act with boldness and speak from faith. For Your glory, amen.

August 16   What the World Wants Most

Scripture Reading: Matthew Chapter 5

Key Verse: "Blessed are the peacemakers, for they shall be called sons of God." Matthew 5:9

Christian people are not merely to bear injuries and to recompense them with pity and with love, but they are actively to try to bring about a more wholesome, pure state of humanity and to breathe the peace of God which passes understanding over all the jangling and struggles of this world. If we give the due depth of significance to that name, "Peacemaker" we shall find that this grace worthily completes the whole, linked, series of Beatitudes and is the very jewel which clasps the whole chain of Christian and Christ-like characteristics together.

Some thirty months after the guns ceased firing in World War II, a radio questionnaire was submitted as to what the world wanted most from America. The answer proved that the dominant desire was for peace. But when we say that we desire peace what do we have in mind? In the tense world situation today, most of us think of peace between nations. When the air is filled with threats and warnings and national budgets are pyramiding skyward by the fear of future war, all thoughtful people pray fervently for international peace.

But, if we should prove able to resolve the international tensions and organize the family of nations under world law, would we then enjoy peace? What we suffered in Korea was in spite of, and in the face of, the Security Council's efforts and power and that of fifty-nine nations. Several lands also have recently been reddened with blood, although they were not at war with any other country. Peace between nations does not guarantee peace within nations. And peace within nations does not guarantee peace within our social and domestic circles. In fact, many persons are so taken up with frictions in their near-at-hand situations, that they give little thought to large social and world problems. Consider the example of the soldier who wrote his wife begging her to stop arguing with him so that he could fight the war in peace.

Where does peacemaking begin? It is said that the longest journey begins with the first step. For the peacemaker, that first step is with himself. The man whose own life is not orderly is like a ship whose ballast has become loose. That ship rolls unmanageably, a menace to itself and to other craft. He who feels frustrated easily becomes the tool of the agitator and warmonger.

If a house be divided against itself, that house cannot stand. Jesus saw the lack of inner peace, and so He taught us to cut ourselves loose from the past. Said He, "Let the dead bury their own dead." That was the Master's short, surgical way of saying that we are simply to turn our backs on some things and go on. But He does more. He turns us from remorse, which is futile regret for a past that cannot be changed, to repentance, which is a redemptive turning toward the future. In owning our faults, we disown them. In confessing our sins, they cease to be ours. Christ breaks the power of cancelled sin to continue to assault us, and sets the prisoner free.

Tomorrow let us continue to explore this first step of being a peacemaker as well as the steps that lead to waging peace in the world around us.

Father God, please shine the light of Your truth into my heart and reveal any sin that is causing a backward pull in my life. I forsake this sin of _____ and ask Your forgiveness for it. Thank You for the inner peace that You bring to my heart in preparation for sharing this peace with the world around me. Amen.

August 17   What the World Wants Most II

Scripture Reading: Matthew Chapter 5

Key Verse: "Blessed are the peacemakers, for they shall be called sons of God." Matthew 5:9

Yesterday we learned that the first characteristic of this peace we are talking about is the peace of reconciliation with God. The cause of all other fighting in the world is that men's relationship to the Father in Heaven is disturbed by their antagonism, indifference, forgetfulness, and opposition to His will.

The first thing to be done to bring men to peace with one another and with themselves is to rectify their relation to God and bring peace there.

It is not accidental that the beatitude of the peacemaker follows directly the blessing on the pure in heart. The wisdom that is from above is first pure, then peaceable.

When God is given charge of an individual's life, He sets it in order as a mother straightens a child's nursery where toys are littered on the floor. When a person has achieved such a peaceful ordering of his own life under the primacy of love, he is fit to be a peacemaker among others.

But, we must not mistake peacemaking for peacekeeping. We may keep the peace because we are too indifferent to care what goes on around us or too good-natured to feel any righteous indignation at wrongdoing or too selfish or lazy to risk any unpleasantness for the sake of setting things right.

Jesus could have kept this peace by remaining in Galilean villages, basking in His popularity, healing the sick, and preaching comfort. But no, He set His face toward Jerusalem where critics and a cross awaited Him.

He was a minister of active reconciliation. The peacemaker is called not to a sheltered passive role, but to an active aggressive program.

He speaks convictions when a moral issue is at stake. He enters into controversies to correct falsehood, but he speaks the truth in love.

The peacemaker keeps above personalities in these controversies, counteracting prejudice, suspicion and hatred by the sanity of his mind and the sympathy of his heart. By deeds as well as thoughts and word, the peacemaker is a minister of reconciliation.

He does not merely discuss the problems of brotherhood between racial and religious groups; he enters into the experiences and fellowship with individuals of other groups.

He does not try to do by agitation what he fails to do by demonstration. He prepares for world citizenship by practicing the principles of brotherhood in his own community.

He knows if he cannot get along with his neighbor it is futile to talk about a family of nations. And if he does not keep his word man to man, he is not consistent in asking governments to stand by their treaties.

The peacemaker takes seriously the command of the Lord, "Love your enemies, bless those who curse you, do good to those who hate you, and pray for those who spitefully use you and persecute you, that you may be sons of your Father in heaven."

The paradox of peace is that we can have peace only by fighting for it. We must wage peace with more zeal and energy that men have used in making war and thus hear our Lord call us sons of God. Man will not, but it matters little what men call us and it matters everything what God calls us.

Holy Father, may I be a tool in Your hands for bringing peace wherever I go, for I bring You and You are the Prince of Peace. Amen.

August 18   The Seed Plot of the Bible

Scripture: Genesis Chapter Chapter 3

Key Verse: "And they heard the sound of the Lord God walking in the garden in the cool of the day, and Adam and his wife hid themselves from the presence of the Lord God among the trees of the garden." Genesis 3:8

Some believe Genesis Chapter 3 is the seed plot of the Bible, because so many of the truths of our faith spring from this place. Here we find the foundations upon which rest many of the cardinal doctrines of our faith.

But Genesis 3 holds even more. In its verses we behold the utter powerlessness of man to walk in the path of righteousness when divine grace is withheld from him and we discover the spiritual effects of sin as we see Adam seeking to flee from God. We see our merciful, gracious God seeking after the guilty sinner and learn of the provision that He made to meet our greatest need. We mark the universal tendency of human nature to cover our own moral shame by a device of our own making, and the utter failure of that attempt.

The devil is introduced in this chapter, without any word of explanation concerning his previous history, but we are shown the sphere of his activities, the method of his approach and the form of his temptations. We watch as he throws doubt on the Word of God, and substitutes his own words for those of our dear Lord. Praise God, we learn of the certainty of his ultimate overthrow and destruction in this chapter as well.

In Genesis 3, we see God confront Adam face to face with his sin, and we see Adam excusing himself. Mankind today still refuses to confess sin in brokenhearted shame. We are still passing the blame with excuses. And God is still calling with the call of yearning love, "Where are you?" It is the call of divine justice which cannot overlook sin. And it is the call of divine love which offers redemption from sin. To each and every one the call of Genesis 3 is reiterated, "Where are you?"

Everything recorded in this chapter has much more than a historical significance. We see clearly defined the wages of sin and death, and then we see it carried out when Adam is expelled from the garden. And, most blessed of all, here we have the promise of a redeemer, "He shall bruise your head, and you shall bruise His heel." We are told He shall be born of the seed of woman, but not of man. 4,000 years later a virgin was with child in fulfillment of this word. Oh, how much of our hope and future springs from this early seed plot God planted in Genesis.

Thank God for His revelation of the reality of sin. Our iniquity is really an assault against the nature of God. Like leprosy, sin contaminates and spreads, issuing in death. But, in Him we find forgiveness of sin and renewed relationship with our Creator through His provision of a Redeemer. Like Adam, we have a tendency to blame others, to hide our sin. Like Adam, our paltry excuses and our hiding will never make our relationship with God right. Only Christ's sacrifice at the cross can do that, only our acceptance of His provision, only our willingness to own up to our sin, and receive His forgiveness.

And thank God for this little passage at the beginning of the Old Testament that can bring encouragement and joy as it testifies to the Sovereignty of our Lord. Sin does not take Him by surprise. His plan is right on schedule, and the fulfillment of it is sure.

Dear Father, It gives me such peace to know that nothing has surprised You; nothing is too big an obstacle for Your plan. Make my life be evident testimony to those around me. Amen.

August 19   What God Tells Us in Prophecy

Scripture Reading: Isaiah 21: 8-12

Key Verses: ". . . 'Watchman, what of the night? Watchman, what of the night?' The Watchman said 'The morning comes, and also the night. If you will inquire. Return! Come back!'"
Isaiah 21:11-12

This is a dramatic prophetic utterance that reveals a picture of night, gray and foreboding. The moon is thickly veiled behind the clouds. The wild wind whips the mountain trees and whistles through the rocky teeth of ledges and buttresses piled high against the sky. Yonder is a fortress wall dimly seen in the ghostly light. A lone watchman paces from turret to turret with his swinging lanterns casting shadows over the rude stones.

I see a shadow move beneath the wall and a voice cries hoarsely above the wind's shrill whine, "Watchman! What of the night?" In long drawn syllables that ride in the wind, the sentry shouts, "The morning comes, and also the night."

Such is the picture of the prophecy. In this chapter, Isaiah himself is the watchman. He speaks not his own words, but the inspired word of his Lord. He speaks not for the temporal, but for the everlasting. Not for time alone, but for eternity.

Men are beginning to recognize our age is one of night. They will soon learn after the peace-table that there is no power in self-seeking nations to bring righteousness to pass upon the earth. The night of human suffering will deepen into the blackness of despair because no morning comes at the hands of men. God alone gives the answer and tells of the coming morning.

God tells us that it has been night in the world ever since sin entered. He sent the Light but the world knew Him not. Then the lovers of darkness put out the world's Light and held carnival around the cross. And there was darkness over the land. Yet, the church today has a message for the world, a message of hope and courage. It is a cry from the Prophet Isaiah and from the heart of one greater than Isaiah, the Lord Jesus Christ. That cry is "The morning comes!" Oh the beauty of a sunrise after the darkness of night.

There will be a glorious morning for the nation of Israel, "Cry out to her that her warfare is ended, that her iniquity is pardoned." The nations are working their way to Armageddon, the Antichrist, and judgment. There will be the morning of universal peace after the awful night of prolonged war. What blessings. Yes, there is a glorious morning coming. As these times come upon us, let us remember the words that angels speak whenever they touch us in our world, "Fear not." Though the tumults rage around us, let us face the horizon and watch for the promise.

The story is told of a lovely seventeen-year-old girl, one of a crowd of vacationers who had sat about an open fire in the Western mountains and listened to the thrilling stories of an old Ranger. Late at night the company retired. Finally toward dawn, she fell into a fitful sleep but soon awoke and with a wild scream cried, "Fire, fire, fire!" "Where?" shouted the old Ranger as he sprang to her side. "Out there! Don't you see?" she cried. Sure enough the whole sky was ablaze with light darting up from behind the wooded horizon and the great peaks far above. Gently, the old Ranger placed his hands upon the terrified girl's arm and said, "Why dear child, that's not fire. That's the dawn of a new day." Watch, beloved, a new day will come soon.

Lord God, thank You for reminding me in these dangerous days of war and violence that this has been foretold since the beginning of time. It is all seen and known by You and I need not be afraid. I trust You dear Father. Amen.

August 20   The Bible and You

Scripture Reading: II Timothy 3:10-17

Key Verse: "All Scripture is given by inspiration of God, and is profitable for doctrine, for reproof, for correction, for instruction in righteousness, that the man of God may be complete, thoroughly equipped for every good work." II Timothy 3:16-17

The entire trend of the day in human affairs is to emphasize the place and value of society to the exclusion of the rights and importance of the individual. But when you come to the Bible you will find it a personal book. It talks about individual sin and a personal God who has sent His own Son to save men from sin. The gospels stress the importance of the individual. In its chapters you find Christ and individuals. The church is a personal thing; individual believers lead others to Christ, not usually whole societies at a time. Because the Bible deals with us as individuals, both our blessing and our responsibility are personal ones.

We can truly thank God that the Bible is the property of the average man. It is not God's purpose to gratify the mental demands of a few, but the heart-hunger of the many.

The Bible calls itself food. The value of food is not in the discussion it arouses but in the nourishment it gives. Good food must be taken in and digested to produce healthy bodies. The Bible calls itself water. Water must be drunk to be of value. The Bible calls itself a sword. Battles are not won by just debating the value of swords, but by using them. Our task under God is to read and release it to others. The book offers itself to every man as a staff upon which to lean, a lamp to show the way, and a light to keep the feet from stumbling. The man who reads and hides the Scripture in his heart finds himself truly equipped for life's trying experiences.

Here is an old man tottering toward the grave. The thought of tomorrow is as a nightmare. He is without God and without hope in the world. Here is another man growing more feeble with each rushing day, but trusting in Christ as revealed in the Bible. He quietly nestles in the assurance, "The Lord is my shepherd; I shall not want . . . . Yea, though I walk through the valley of the shadow of death, I will fear no evil, for You are with me." And so the believing heart is comforted.

Here is a young man facing life's most overwhelming temptation and at last he resigns himself to a life of lowered ideals. But here is another young man, taught to trust the word of God. He knows that Christ was also tempted in all things, yet was without sin, and is able to give strength and comfort to all those who are tempted. The young man finds the path to victory.

In this book the lost find a Savior and the poor find encouragement. For the rich there are reminders of their obligation to help the poor, for the weak, the Lord will be their burden-bearer, and the strong are reminded to help the weak. Pride and selfishness are condemned, and humility and kindness are commended.

Because the Bible is the property of the average man there are some duties he has in relation to it if he and others are to benefit. He must take time to study and meditate upon it. Then, we must make it available to others. Every father and mother needs it. The sailor and the soldier need it. The policeman, the prisoner, the teacher, the clerk, the salesman, the laborer and the farmer all need this book. We must give it to them. Pass it on. Pass it on!

Dearest Father, thank You that You did not leave us without comfort or direction. Please help me to be faithful to follow the leading of the Holy Spirit and to take in Your word, the Bible, hungrily. Then show me ways to share Your word with others. Amen.

August 21   Why Pray?

Scripture: James Chapter 4

Key Verse: ". . . You do not have because you do not ask."
James 4:2

Jesus tells us of a restless young man who grew tired of the restraints of his father's house. Therefore he asked his father to give him his inheritance, and with it he started out for a far country. He was out to live his own life. He was out to do as he pleased. He captured the prize he set his heart upon but by so doing he did not find what he wanted. Listen to his confession—"I perish with hunger." And that experience is not unique. To fight God's law is to fight God Himself. To break God's law is to break ourselves.

God is infinitely eager and infinitely able to meet our needs. Prayer is a power that makes it possible for God to do for us and through us what He does not otherwise do. Whatever else life has brought to us; it has not brought the best unless we have learned how to pray.

What kind of praying receives results? James says "The effective, fervent prayer of a righteous man avails much." First then, prayer must be earnest to be effective. The reason God cannot bless many of us is that He cannot get our attention. Even God cannot give what we are not interested enough to take. And so, you'll be without God in your life just so long as you are content to be without Him.

But, when you get to the end of yourself, when the mighty hands of desperate need put their weighty load upon your shoulders and press you in utter weakness to your knees, then are you prepared to pray effectively. When you cry with Knox "Give me Scotland or I die," when you vow with desperate Jacob "I will not let You go unless You bless me," then you'll make it possible for God to answer. I tell you, prayer is earnest business.

It is not only the earnest prayer, but the righteous one that is a mighty power. James does not mean that in order to pray we must be perfect. What he does mean is that prayer, to be effective, must be offered by one whom, if not right, is at least willing to be right. For God to answer the prayer of one who is in rebellion against Him would be to create anarchy in His own kingdom. For God to answer the prayer of the Prodigal in the far country would not be a blessing but a curse to the Prodigal.

We try to pray when there is a quarrel between God and us, or a surrender we are unwilling to make, a task we are unwilling to perform, a wound that we are unwilling to heal. That is what Jesus meant when He said "If you bring your gift to the altar and there remember that your brother has something against you, leave your gift there before the altar and go your way. First be reconciled to your brother, and then come and offer your prayer."

Finally, prayer to be effective must be offered in faith. "Let him ask in faith with no doubting." Faith laughs at impossibilities and cries, "It shall be done." When we pray we cease to carry on alone. Our strength becomes the strength of the Infinite God. It is the means of receiving God Himself. And it is the means of releasing the power of God in our lives and the lives of others.

How prayer changes things. Let us remember to ask the One who yearns to bless us. It is a royal service, a royal duty, and a royal privilege.

Dear Father God, thank You that You have made it possible for me to communicate with You, the Lord of the Universe. What an honor and an opportunity. Let me not waste it through lack of use. Amen.

Scripture Reading: Song of Solomon Chapter 6

Key Verse: "Who is she that looks forth as the morning, fair as the moon, clear as the sun, awesome as an army with banners?" Song of Solomon 6:10

The picture of the church presented here is the picture of a conflict, "awesome as an army with banners." It is no doubt true that the church is fairest in the eyes of God when it is foulest in the eyes of men. Christ incurred the world's hatred because He fought sin so effectively. The Bride of Christ is the salt of the earth because it is a company of unified, if separate, believers following in His footsteps.

The church is God-given, and as such must magnify God's Word in the world today. It is only God's Word that reveals all human need and offers a remedy for them. It has a message for every human heart. It radiates light, and offers life. It meets every condition and need of man.

The church is militant, because it centers in Christ. He is the one life-giver, the one sin-forgiver, the one hope for the lost human race. Christ regenerates lives and transforms nations, Under his power, Saul became Paul, Cephas became Peter, weaklings became giants and vagabonds became kings. Christ was not only willing to come into our world to live, but He was willing to come to die. Oh, beloved, the message of the church is the heartbeat and the life-throb of the Son of God.

The church of Jesus Christ has stood the test of time because the gospel message is a message unlike any other. For the work of salvation, liberation from the bondage of sin was the church established. It is true of the individual and of the church that "He that wins souls is wise." The militant church is ever seeking to lift men and women from despair to new life. This type of church runs counter to entrenched evil and human nature on all sides. It is naturally opposed by public opinion, by learning, by prejudice, and by war.

A military conflict has raged in the world from the day that Satan entered the Garden of Eden until this hour. Against the church, the rage of earth and hell has been unleashed. No institution, which condemns the evil desires of men, attacks their cherished lusts, and insists on the practice of self-denial and sacrifice can hope to escape ridicule, attacks and onslaughts. But, in spite of the fiery darts of the evil one, the church has marched with militant stride down the highway of the centuries. The church cannot straddle the fence. Where principle is involved, it does not only believe in right, but champions it.

And, finally, the church that is live, virile and aggressive undertakes the impossible. It was true of Apostolic Christianity. The followers of Christ then were undaunted. They gave themselves to Christ with such abandon that they dared to risk their lives for His cause. Today, if we possess that same faith in that same Lord, it will bring the church in our day to grips with the impossible and a passion will be born in our souls that will change the temperature of the world.

The church is the symbol of inaugurated, organized opposition to hell. Its banners have been lifted high and unfolded above every embattled field and scene of combat between good and evil. Go out to meet the world in the knowledge and understanding of your calling as a part of the church militant, the Bride of Christ.

Father God, revive in my heart today the zeal for Your house, for Your service, that brings glory and honor to Your name and victory to the cause of Christ. In His name and for His sake I ask it, amen.

August 23   Body Essentials

Scripture Reading: Ephesians Chapter 1

Key Verses: "And He put all things under His feet, and gave Him to be head over all things to the church, which is His body, the fullness of Him who fills all in all." Ephesians 1:22-23

In this wonderful chapter of the letter to the Ephesian Christians, Paul reveals the purpose of God concerning the Church as the instrument through which the work of His only begotten Son should be carried forward.

That church consists of all who believe on the Son and have received eternal life through the acceptance of Jesus Christ. We are therefore His witnesses and representatives in our different localities and His partners in His continuous work of redeeming the world and in the ministry of the gospel. In Christ we are all members of His body. We love one another because we all love Christ.

Can you imagine this ludicrous story? One day there arose a schism in the human body. The foot said, "My position is far too low to suit my taste. Why should I wade through mire and mud to please the body? See how high the hand is? He does not carry the load, I am made to carry it, so if they make me a hand I'll stay in the body, if not, I'll secede." Then the ear began to make complaint, "Why should I be put on the side of the head? The eye is in front and has every prominence. Were I the eye, I would remain in the body, but being but an ear, I will withdraw myself from this fellowship." How absurd. How childish to talk like this, says Paul. No, each member helps each other by being true to his own particular calling and gift.

Is your church in a spiritual drought? We can put an end to this drought just as Elijah of old did when he went up to the top of Mount Carmel and cast himself upon the ground and put his face between his knees and prayed to God, and the refreshing rains came.

How are we to put an end to spiritual drought? Like Elijah we must go to the top of the mountain with God. Our power as churches is in our separateness from the folly and frenzy of the world and not in our affiliation with them. Then we must surrender ourselves to God. Proceeding still further we must seek the blessing with an exclusiveness of purpose. As Elijah put his face between his knees, so we too must concentrate on this great business of prayer for the lost and of the outpouring of God's presence upon His church.

We might list many components of the growing, thriving, spiritual body of the church, such as love for one another, solid teaching and training, opportunities for exercise of our spiritual gifts, deep worship, and adoration of God. It is true that all of these are necessary for a healthy church. But they also naturally flow from a church rightly connected to the Father. He supplies the love for one another, the inspiration for life-changing teaching, the fruition of our spiritual gifts, and the desire and fulfillment of worship and adoration through the Holy Spirit.

If the Holy Spirit is filling the believers of a church that church will function as it was made to function. Love, outreach, increase of wisdom and salvation of the lost will simply happen. These things are naturally occurring where the Spirit is leading. Beloved, do not quench the Spirit, for it is **the** essential for the body.

Dear Lord, let me not be one who interferes with the work of the Holy Spirit in my church family. Help me remember to not be a complainer or trouble-maker. Sometimes I want to just straighten them out, but that is Your job. Help me pray to You instead, so that You will either send correction in Your own way or change my heart. Amen.

August 24   The Great Chemist

Scripture Reading: Psalm 113

Key Verse: "The Lord is high above all nations, His glory above the heavens. Who is like the Lord our God, who dwells on high, who humbles Himself to behold the things that are in the heavens and in the earth?" Psalm 113:4-6

Indeed, as we think of this wonderful creation of our God, we have to wonder at those who declare from their hearts, "There is no God." Where do they live that they cannot see His glory amidst the miracles of creation? Where have they gone to school that the unfolding mysteries of science and the great parade of history has not revealed to them the guiding hand of a great and mighty God?

"When I consider Your heavens, the work of Your fingers, the moon and the stars which You have ordained, what is man that You are mindful of him?" the psalmist cries. On such a clear night, with the stars proclaiming the gospel through their various constellations, men can feel the grandeur of God. He has pictured the salvation story, from the constellation Virgo, portraying the virgin birth, through the Lion of the Tribe of Judah come conquering. He has hung these pictures for the viewing of earth's inhabitants alone. Who is He to consider us? But He does.

And what of the composition of this earth? For instance, the water that makes up so much of our own planet. The chemist calls it H_2O, that is, two parts hydrogen to one part oxygen. Combined in this way, God provides for our needs. It is the stream the Good Shepherd provides for the physical thirst of His sheep. It is the cascading waterfall and the crystalline lake. Yet each of these separate elements is among the most flammable known to man.

Is it not just like our Lord, the Great Chemist, to continually put before us these seeming contradictions that point over and over to Him. Oxygen and Hydrogen are flammable and potentially dangerous on their own. Yet, we use water to put out fires that are caused by either one of its elements. Yes, this is my Father's world.

Yet, the Great Chemist is also the Great Physicist, and the Great Biologist. The balance of nature shouts the presence of God. Earth is perfectly positioned; just the tiniest bit one way or the other wouldn't work. The atmosphere is just right for us to thrive, a bit more of this and we couldn't breathe, a bit less of that and we would be baked by the sun's rays.

"The heavens declare the glory of God, and the firmament shows His handiwork. Day unto day utters speech and night unto night reveals knowledge." Yes, it is so. The more intimate your acquaintance with creation, the more time you spend out of the company of man and in the company of the great outdoor cathedral built by His own hands, the more you will find this to be true. On a clear night when there are no man-sounds to be heard, the stars seem to throb with their joyful song, and the pulse of the Creator is nearly palpable in His creation.

"Those who wait on the Lord shall renew their strength; they shall mount up with wings as eagles, they shall run and not be weary, they shall walk and not faint." Take time to get to know His creation, beloved, and recognize the testimony it speaks. Watch the sky for the jewels He has strung in pictures. In Him are strength, rest, and wonder.

Oh Holy Creator God, truly, You are worthy of praise and adoration. Thank You for the privilege of living in the midst of Your creation, and for the even greater privilege of looking forward to eternity in Your heavenly creation. Amen.

August 25 — A Cold Pancake

Scripture Reading: Acts Chapter 2

Key Verse: "And suddenly there came a sound from heaven, as of a rushing mighty wind, and it filled the whole house where they were sitting. Then there appeared to them divided tongues, as of fire, and one sat upon each of them. And they were all filled with the Holy Spirit." Acts 2: 2-4

What's worse than for the world to come against a cold Christian? It's worse than a cold pancake and who would want to eat one of those? But oh, those lovely hot-hearted ones with butter and honey. They make the world hungry to know Jesus, with their joy and satisfaction in His presence. Oh the joy of the fire in these hot, yielded hearts.

Beloved, we need the Pentecostal fire today, in our hearts and filling our churches. When I was a boy I heard the comment "You can't have a successful Church unless you have a spiritual membership." I have never forgotten that remark and I wish to insist on the truth of it.

"Spiritual and membership" are two vital words. How can you define the word spiritual? You really don't need to. It is hard to define but easy to recognize. Here's an example. Two men rise at prayer meeting. The first talks very knowledgeably about the laws of the spiritual life. There is no response or comment. He takes his seat. The second, neither learned or eloquent, tells of a recent trial, the Savior's presence with him through that trial, and how His Holy presence was so real and comforting. He then takes a seat. The people weep for they have been lifted to the realms of blessedness.

So you know what was the difference in those two men? It was the presence in one and the absence in the other of that quality that marked the lives of Peter, John, Paul, Stephen and others who were filled with the Holy Spirit. They were filled with that love-fire that turned their lives and their world upside-down for Christ: the Spirit that carries men to God through the Lord Jesus. If we are filled with the Holy Spirit, it is to serve, and give, and pray, and testify to the wonderful Savior we love.

Now, concerning membership, do you know that the center of the church's strength is not in the pulpit, but in the pew? Even one man filled with the Holy Spirit can accomplish much for God.

John Livingston in the Kirk at Shotts, Scotland preached and five hundred were saved after one sermon. What was the secret of that power? This, the church had been fearful lest the day pass without any mark of Holy Spirit's power and on Saturday night they gathered and prayed. They spent the whole night in prayer.

Jonathan Edwards preached his famous sermon at Enfield in July, "Sinners in the Hand of an Angry God." People were so mightily moved that they grabbed the arms of pews to keep their feet from slipping into perdition. But, beloved, he read his sermon. His face was buried in his manuscript. No, the power was not him. The people were so consumed with a desire to see a great outpouring of God's blessing, they assembled the previous evening and wrestled with God till the morning dawned.

Oh dear one, there is no doubt a pew in touch with God lends power to the pulpit. A church filled with the Holy Spirit will do great things even if the pulpit is commonplace. In Acts, the church was praying when the blessing came. Are you praying? Are you?

Father God Almighty, please fill me with Your blessed Holy Spirit and let me go out in power to serve You. In Jesus' name, amen.

August 26   The Price of Souls

Scripture Reading: Psalm 126

Key Verse: "Those who sow in tears shall reap in joy. He who continually goes forth weeping, bearing seed for sowing, shall doubtless come again with rejoicing, bringing his sheaves with him." Psalm 126:5-6

There is nothing as priceless as the human soul. Jesus had this fact in mind when He said, "For what will it profit a man if he gains the whole world and loses his own soul?" Other things are fleeting, but the soul is eternal. Every person born into the world will outlive the stars. The soul will live to see the stars fall and go out like scattered sparks driven by an autumn wind. When this world is no more, when the never-ending columns of the ages go marching by, the soul will live on somewhere forever, either in celestial joy beyond the power of the pen to portray, or in horror.

It is our privilege, a privilege coveted by angels, to seek to win precious eternal souls to the Savior and to the heavenly home. Rich will be the reward of those who are found faithful. Great will be the disappointment of those who go in empty-handed. The price of souls is tremendous. It calls for intense zeal and complete dedication on the part of those who labor for the Lord.

How great a value Jesus places on souls. He, who had been rich in the possession of the entire universe, became the pauper son of peasant parents and yet His condescension was only the initial payment on the great sin debt. He came to this cruel, sinful world to tread the winepress of sin's wrath alone. From Bethlehem all the way to the blood-sweat of Gethsemane and the cruel cross of Calvary, where He died in agony, He was paying the price of souls.

When they mocked Him, and spat upon His face, He was paying the price. When they plucked His beard and thrust the crown of thorns upon His head, He bore it all for sinners. It was for sinners' souls that He was tied and scourged. It was the priceless value of souls that were lost, that drove the nails through his quivering flesh that raised the cross, and left it hanging between earth and sky.

It was the value of each one of us to Him that made Him stay there while His friends wept and the soldiers gambled and the multitude mocked. It was His love for souls that made Him endure until the Father turned His back upon Him and the darkness hid His near-nude body from the insulting gaze of the passerby. I tell you, my friends, souls are priceless to God. Are they priceless to you?

For the value of a diamond, men dig into the heart of the earth in search of the precious stones. For the yellow metal we call gold, men have risked and lost their lives. And there are souls of pure gold, diamonds in the rough, buried in the mar of sin. We are the miners, the explorers. It will cost us something, too, to go in search of them in the name of our Lord. It calls for intense separation from the world, a life of prayer and consecration, and complete selflessness. Oh, beloved, He thought the price of souls was not too steep. Let us thereby seek to unearth these hidden jewels, that they may adorn heaven forever.

Dearest Lord and Savior, I am always in awe when I remember the terrible price of my salvation. I know that You want all to come to knowledge of You, and I ask Your help in more thoroughly devoting myself to being Your witness at home and away. Please plant in me today that desire to seek after those who need You, and to share the wonderful good news of Your love and provision for them. Amen.

August 27   A Remarkable Man

Suggested Scripture: Isaiah Chapter 38

Key Verse: "Go and tell Hezekiah, 'Thus says the Lord, the God of David, your father: I have heard your prayer, I have seen your tears; surely, I will add to your days fifteen years.'" Isaiah 38:5

Good King Hezekiah was a remarkable man. Soldier, statesman, architect, poet—he was all these. But there is a sense also in which he was the most remarkable man who ever lived. He was the only man who ever knew for certain just when he would not die, and just how long he had to live. His is a unique and royal biography. But, there is more to it than that. This is the one and only mortal who foreknew the year of his death. He preaches irrefutable truths to us across the ages.

How did Hezekiah use those added fifteen years? Well, in view of all the available data, Hezekiah used those added years so profitably that we are still reaping the benefits today. Hezekiah would have been the last man on earth to waste those years of special grace. He understood how precious they were.

Remember, II Chronicles tells us that Hezekiah was the man responsible for cleansing and reopening the temple and restoring temple sacrifices. A bit later, we find that he instituted the great National Passover, of which it is said, "since the days of Solomon, the Son of David, there was not the like in Jerusalem," and later yet destroyed the idols and false gods and altars throughout the land of Judah.

In fact, every time we read the Old Testament, we are in debt to this good king and his men, for Hezekiah formed a guild of men specially set apart for such devout literary work as the arrangement and transmission of the Old Testament Scriptures. Hezekiah, you see, did not just begin well. He finished well.

His epitaph in Scripture is an epitaph we would all be glad to have applied to us, I am sure. "He did what was good and right and true before the Lord his God. And in every work that he began in the service of the house of God, in the law and in the commandment, to seek his God, he did it with all his heart. So, he prospered."

And what about us? We do well to reflect on the fact that just as truly as those extra fifteen years were a special gift of God to Hezekiah, so are the days and years which we may ourselves yet live on earth.

It is God who portions out the lives of all human beings. Although no prophet comes to us to inform us how long we are yet to remain in the body, God nonetheless allots the number of years to each of us. What then shall I do with God's lease of years to me? Well, I must follow Hezekiah's example. I must use every year that God gives me for purposes of practical godliness.

I must count my life in terms of opportunity for serving God. I must redeem the time because the days are evil. The only worthy purpose in life is doing the will of God, so if we ourselves are truly living in and for the will of God, our life will be preserved until God's purpose through us is fully achieved. George Whitefield said, in the very thick of persecution, "I am immortal 'till my work is done."

Dear Father, I know my years, days and hours are in Your hands and I desire that, like Hezekiah, I would be of use to You in every minute of it. Help me to learn the practical godliness that Hezekiah exuded in every area of his life. Help me to redeem each moment You give me in order to further Your kingdom. In Jesus' name and for His sake I pray, amen.

August 28   He Went A Little Farther

Scripture Reading: Matthew 26: 36-56
Key Verse: "He went a little farther." Matthew 26:39

Our Lord's experience in the Garden of Gethsemane on that never-to-be forgotten night is an experience as black as midnight. The agony He suffered is expressed in His own words; "My soul is exceedingly sorrowful, even to death." Judas, one of the trusted, was out in the city betraying Him for thirty pieces of silver. Eight of the twelve were at the entrance to the garden, asleep. The other three, Peter, James, and John were but a stone's throw from Him, but they too were asleep. With the coming of Judas and the soldiers, all would leave Him and flee. A little later on in the night He would sit alone in the judgment hall, with Peter outside denying Him with oaths as the cock crowed. Blood stood on His brow in great beads of sweat. Was there ever a midnight any darker?

Yet, in the very depth of this darkness, He could pray. It is out of this deep, dense darkness that a most brilliant light and heartening encouragement comes. Out of such darkness, light shines the more brilliantly. For it was on this night that Jesus went a little farther. His act reveals the white radiance of eternity.

The blaze of noon is seen in His demeanor, in His acts, in His purpose, in His steadfastness on that awful night. He went a little farther. Jesus sets the example, paces the march, reveals the spirit, and charts the course for us all. "The little farther" that He went was not far when measured by the tapeline, but what a distance when measured by the actual line of Christian experience.

The disciples were sleeping, and He was agonizing. They were dreaming of thrones and kingdoms, Jesus was thinking of the plan of salvation and how it was to be made possible by His death on the cross. This "little farther" marks the difference between the average, the ordinary, and the out- and-out Christian. In this willingness to lay down His life, to be a living sacrifice, to go the last and most difficult step, here is our example.

Think back upon that night and how He went a little farther in prayer. He first prayed that if it be possible remove this from Him. Then He prayed, "Not as I will, but as You will." He went a little farther you see. How much farther? To the place of full surrender, "Not as I will, but as You will."

How rambling, weak, heartless, and indirect we can be in our prayer life. We need to go a little farther in our prayer life this year.

We need to follow Jesus into Gethsemane. There was no formality there. His prayer was burning with earnestness, blazing with desire, and baptized with blood. And, if we will go farther with prayer, we will go farther in submission, in advancement, in consecration and in our spiritual lives.

In the longest journey, it is the last step that delivers us to the goal. Let us persevere, let us be steadfast when we think we can't hold on another moment.

Do we grow weary of doing good in the face of no appreciation? Do we finally tire of praying for the salvation of those we love? Do we trek twenty miles and stop when our goal is only one mile around the bend?

No, beloved, we go a little farther, and a little farther more through the agony of the garden, and the cross and into the resurrection and the life. This is the pattern Jesus gives us.

Dear Father, help me to go a little farther with You this year. Please help me to walk more closely, obey more fully, surrender more completely and love more selflessly. Amen

Scripture Reading: Exodus Chapter 20

Key Verse: "You shall have no other gods before Me." Exodus 20:3

The Ten Commandments could easily be called the "ten rules for living." By this, I do not mean they speak the final word on human conduct. I am not forgetting that Jesus summed up these ten words in the one law of love, "You shall love the Lord Your God with all your heart and with all your soul and with all your mind and with all your strength and your neighbor as yourself."

But in these days when so many are confused, when so many seem to have flung away their old convictions, and when so many have let go their moorings, I believe these rules might serve as guideposts to finer and fuller living. These are not mere arbitrary rules like the law that compels us to drive on the right side of the street rather than on the left. No, these ten partake of the nature of great principles. To violate them brings disaster to the individual and society as a whole. To observe them is to plant our feet on the road to a fuller individual and social life.

Very appropriately, the Ten Commandments begin with God. That is always the best place to begin. The first commandment has a brief preface, "I am the Lord your God, you shall have no other gods before me." This begins with a great assumption. It assumes the reality of God. It begins by asserting that "God is," and that He is available.

I may say with Thomas, "My Lord and my God." I may shout with the victorious Paul, "My God shall supply every need of yours according to His riches in glory by Christ Jesus." Every man who asserts this ancient law may have God for his very own. Whatever else we might miss in life, beloved, no man need miss God. How clearly and insistently Jesus declares this truth.

But, how may we come to posses God? We find the conditions in germ here in this ancient law, which is made clearer in the New Testament. "You shall have no other gods before Me," the Scriptures say. In other words, we find God when we are willing to give up all else in order to find Him. The Scriptures also say, "You will seek the Lord your God and you will find Him if you seek Him with all your heart and with all your soul."

Israel in that day could have God only as they were willing to let the gods of the surrounding nations go. We today do not believe in these lesser gods, but in spite of that fact, we are as truly polytheistic as they.

We no longer think of the mythical war-god Mars as a person, but we worship the things for which he stood with the same loyalty and devotion of those long ago. We no longer believe or bow at the shrine of Venus, the goddess of love, but that for which Venus stood still lays its enslaving and defiling hands on millions. We would never dream of worshipping Bacchus, the god of drink and revelry, as a person. But perhaps he has never been given greater homage and respect, nor had more willing worshippers than in the world today.

Yes, the other gods are still with us. While we may chuckle at the notion of the Israelites bowing before a golden calf, we worship with the same fervor at the altar of our own sacred cows, do we not? And yet, here stands the ancient law, saying that if we will give up these lesser gods, we will find the real God. And in the birth of Christ, this commandment became not merely a forbidding law, but a radiant gospel.

Dearest Father, reveal to me any idols that may exist in my life, and help me to bar them from my heart and mind. The throne of my heart belongs to You alone. In Jesus' name, amen.

August 30   Stooping to Conquer

Scripture Reading: Mark Chapter 9

Key Verse: ". . . This kind can come out by nothing but prayer and fasting." Mark 9:29

The quest of the ages is the quest for power. By it, man has traveled from cave to mansion, dog sled to airplane, gibberish to eloquence and barbarism to culture. When Jesus was present on the earth, He radiated power and He promised power. He said, "You shall receive power after the Holy Spirit has come . . . ." In fact, nowhere was the overwhelming power of the glory of the Lord revealed more eloquently than on the Mount of Transfiguration. Jesus was on the mount not for a baptism of new glory, but for the revealing of the veiled glory that was in Him. The Father spoke, and the disciples were silenced by awe.

Now every form of power has its own specific medium of transmission. Electric power is transmitted by wire, water power by pipe and conduit, steam power by tubes, and spiritual power by prayer. The one thing we have failed to grasp, it seems, is that there is no substitute for prayer. The manufacturers of the world have learned about the specialization of power long ago. Each form of power has its own specific and absolute medium. Nothing else will do. And so it is with spiritual power as well, it is transmitted from the source by nothing else but prayer.

We can see in our text that if we want to wield the kind of spiritual power for the Lord that can change ravaged lives, we must take prayer seriously in our own lives first. "This kind can come out by nothing but prayer and fasting." The Lord Jesus made prayer a pattern in His life, and so should we who go out in His name. But how should we pray?

Well, as you prepare to minister in the Lord's name, pray for yourself. In genuineness of heart, pray the prayer of the publican, "God be merciful to me a sinner." Pray the prayer of David, "Create in me a clean heart, O God, and renew a right spirit within me." We must develop a consciousness of sin and disarm pride in our own lives, so that through repentance we can become fit vessels to transmit God's love to others.

Next, pray for an awakened church. Pray that as at Pentecost, each member of the Body of Christ would be charged with the power of Almighty God for the spreading of the gospel.

Finally, pray specifically for those to whom you are going to minister. Praying for those who need the Lord is a life-saving process. Now, have you ever seen a lifeguard coming in with fifty victims in his arms? No, he concentrates on one at a time. It is so with our praying for the souls of nonbelievers. Pick out specific persons whose names you can take to God, rather than just praying in general over a group. Put names on a card and pray for them as a lifeguard goes after a drowning soul. Don't stop, but like the guard who jumps in, put your best stroke into prayer that you may reach that drowning one for Jesus.

In our text, a father has brought his needy son to the disciples to be delivered from Satan's power. What could they do? Nothing. They found themselves helpless before this need. They lacked the vital power which would bring victory. For Jesus, however, there is no case too difficult, no situation too hard. Prayer is simply drawing on His resources. To conquer in this world, we must fight with the weapon of prayer.

Dear Lord, as I go out today to the place of ministry You have given me, I ask for guidance, direction and boldness to speak the truth in love as You give opportunity and leading. In Jesus' name, amen.

August 31   Where Are You Staying?

Scripture Reading: John 1: 35-42

Key Verse: ". . . Rabbi, where are you staying?" John 1:38

The disciples wanted to know more about Jesus. They wanted to know where He lived, where He was at home, where He was rooted and grounded. Thus, they asked where he lived. And you, my friend, where are you staying?

It's a natural and common question, yet if we simply name a city, what does it tell us? It is not simply a question of geography that I ask you today. You cannot tell where a man lives by looking at a map, city guide, or directory. You must examine the contents of the man. It is a question of his own dominant interests and so in this deeper sense, where are you staying?

The answer depends, not so much on what is outside, as what is inside. Let me illustrate. I take my dog with me to some beautiful art gallery. He sees all I see, physically speaking, yet after visiting every room I find that "The Sistine Madonna" or "The Lord's Supper" are not in his world. It is not an issue of eyesight, but insight. It is the mind and heart that sees, not the eyes. Things only become real to me as they enter into my experience.

In the blind man's world; the beauty of form and color is not. Rainbows and sunsets do not exist for him. There is the deaf man's world. Melody and harmony are not in his world. He cannot hear the prattle of the child or the warbling of the bird. In every case, the presence or absence of faculties determine the range and reality of the world for that man. So, to the spiritually dead man, spiritual forces, values and blessings do not exist.

Give me your full address and by it I will have a definition of the world you live in and I shall know the quality of your life. There is the shopkeeper who lives in a stream of commodities running to and fro, grinding out of the wheels of business the grist of profit. He eats it, sleeps it, dreams it, and works it. Talk to him about any other subject and he is dry as a pine stump.

Or another man, who lives in a world of books and ideas, he is interested in outlooks, insights, and discriminations. He feels that wisdom is the principal thing. He strives for understanding and that is his world.

Another may live in a world of distrust, hate, suspicion, insinuation. He seeks for the immediate and the debased. He lives in that kind of world.

There is also a man whose head is filled with visions and dreams of better things. He appraises everything through spiritual eyes and values. Christ is his experience and his life. He lives in a world where God is real and heaven is near. He lives with God.

I do not care whether you have two rooms in your house. But, where do you, as a child of the Eternal God, find yourself at home? Do you, as Jesus did, live with God? Not as much or as often as you'd wish? Then, how splendid, how encouraging this closing fact. It is always possible to move. It may not be so outwardly, but inwardly it is possible. Today, here, without noise or dust, with no need to send for the furniture van; you can do it yourself by your own choice and resolve. If you are tired of your old abode, move out; move up, up where you belong.

Move into God's world where you can stretch up and out and grow. Up where you can breathe, and the air is fresh and pure. Move into the glorious sunlight of His love. He bids you "Come and see."

Almighty God, I really want to examine where my life is right now. Around what do my thoughts and time revolve? Where am I staying in my emotions? Lord, there are places I want to evacuate and places I want to move to in order to realign my life with You. Thank You for the power and mercy You give. Amen.

September 1   Renovate or Regenerate?

Scripture: Romans Chapter 10

Key Verse: "For they being ignorant of God's righteousness, and seeking to establish their own righteousness, have not submitted to the righteousness of God." Romans 10:3

The Spirit of God and the Word of God works the will of God in human lives and that will is regeneration, a new life, a new walk, a new heart, a new birth, a new creature. To renovate is man's plan to change the human heart. To regenerate is God's plan to change the human heart. The first works on the surface and never reaches the trouble. The second goes to the source and changes the whole entity and everything it touches. Getting man converted closes doors of vice, but closing doors of vice never gets men converted. God's way is regeneration, then renovation. Man's way is regeneration by renovation - impossible.

So many well-meaning Christians are engaged in programs of goodness. But Christ left us one program and only one, "Go therefore and make disciples of all the nations, baptizing them in the name of the Father and of the Son and of the Holy Spirit, teaching them to observe all things that I have commanded you." This is the main work of the whole church in the whole world throughout the whole age.

But the church has set aside the divine program and accepted the substitute program. You can never change the nature of a hog or impart to him a new nature by closing up the place where he wallows, nor change the nature of a turkey buzzard by removing the carrion. No, the hog must be changed into a sheep and the buzzard into a dove and that is possible only by divine power. It matters very little whether a man goes to Hell a down-and-out drunkard or a cultured, educated, morally sober man.

We have the ministry of reconciliation, not renovation. What did Jesus do? He told Nicodemus "You must be born again." You may say, "But renovating and rebuilding men seeks noble ends," yes, but you are turning from God's commands. You say, "But who will rebuild men if Christians don't?" I say "Who will do the real work of introducing men to the One who regenerates if Christians turn aside to make men righteous on their own?"

Hear me! Jesus came into the world and found all sorts of evil. Yet He never organized a temperance movement or a personal purity society. He organized nothing. But He made provision for an organism, the Church.

You see, beloved, God's plan is to make man immune to the attacks of the bacteria of sin. Jesus never said a word about putting a clean man in office. But He did pray that His disciples be kept from evil. Man's whole idea of renovating the world is about better environments, better pleasures, better buildings, better education, better social life, better movies, better this and that. And still humanity is unsaved and goes on denying and rejecting the plan of God, the Word of God and the Warning of God, building a godless civilization.

What is the remedy? Intensify social services? Force cleaner movies? Have better legislation? No dear ones. We must listen to the Master who said "you must be born again." Let us live the gospel, preach the gospel, rebuild lives and men by the gospel, which starts on the inside by the magnificent power of God.

Almighty Father, Help me know that whatever I do, the first aim and the point of it all is to glorify God and see to the reconciliation of my brother. Amen

September 2   The Man Who Stumped the Devil

Scripture: Job 1:1-12

Key Verse: "You have heard of the perseverance of Job."
James 5:11

Man is born to trouble as sparks fly upward, and from the battle of life there is no discharge. But of all the sufferers, Job is the supreme example of the man who in spite of his troubles holds fast to God, and in the end sees the vindication of his faith. As deepest waters are clearest, so is the message here, both clear and simple.

Job was a good man and had prosperity of soul, health and worldly things. He had seven sons and three daughters, thousands of his sheep whitened the desert, five hundred yoke of oxen and five hundred donkeys ploughed his fields while three thousand camels transported his products to the markets of the world. He was the greatest of all men of the East, but in his prosperity, he never forgot God.

In heaven, we are introduced to a conversation. God says to Satan, "Have you considered my servant Job, that there is none like him in the earth, a blameless and upright man, one who fears God and shuns evil?" The devil sneers that Job only does it for what he gets out of his allegiance to God, and if these worldly things were removed Job would be faithful no more. God allows Job to be tested by permitting Satan to touch all that Job has, Satan is only forbidden to touch Job himself.

One by one messengers come to Job to relate one catastrophe after another that befall his sheep, then his oxen and donkeys, then his camels, and finally, a messenger informs Job that all his children have been killed. When Job hears this, the climax of his calamity, he rends his mantle and falls down in sorrow and distress on the ground. But, he does not renounce God, instead, in his intense grief, he simply states "Naked I came from my mother's womb, and naked shall I return there. The Lord gave, and the Lord has taken away, blessed be the name of the Lord. Even stripped of all his possessions, and all his children, he still believes in God.

But Satan is not yet convinced that Job is impregnable in his faith, so he asks God to let him take Job's health from him, leaving him in agony and pain. So, Job is smitten with boils. His own wife, perhaps out of an ungenerous heart, perhaps out of sympathy with his terrible distress, advises him to curse God and die. But Job still holds fast. "What?" he said to his wife, "shall we indeed accept blessing from God and shall we not accept adversity?"

Then come the three friends. Their fundamental proposition is that all suffering is the result of sin and since Job has suffered so much, he must be the worst kind of sinner. Though Job doesn't understand God's justice in his life he never curses God or renounces Him. Always Job is stretching out his hands to find Him. The creed of his life is "Though He slay me, yet will I trust Him." God restores Job to his former state. His material possessions are restored as well as seven sons and three daughters who were the delight of his life and Satan slinks away, defeated.

In your hour of trial remember Job and remember the tender mercies of God. He is shaping us, forming deep spiritual qualities. Sometimes it is excruciating to be tested, to have our possessions pulled from tightened fingers. But wait for Him. Wait on the Lord, trust Him and He will bring you from the furnace purified, better, stronger, with wider, deeper faith, prepared for wider, deeper service.

Dear Father, help me to learn from Job and surrender everything to you; knowing this life is only a place of testing, purifying, and growing, and will be gone in a breath. Amen

September 3 God's Favorite Word

Scripture Reading: Mark 10: 46–52

Key Verse: "So Jesus stood still and commanded him to be called." Mark 10: 49

What is God's favorite word? What was the word that God spoke to man before He destroyed the earth with a flood? What is the word that brought Peter to Jesus? What is the word He spoke to the little children and to the weak and heavy-laden?

The word is "come." With that one word, come, I can sing the whole story of redemption. "Come" is the great word of the gospel. "Go" is the word of the law. The law shows the gulf between God and the sinner. The gospel bridges that gulf. The law drives, the gospel leads. Christ ever and always goes before, as a shepherd before His flock saying, "Come, come."

In the days of Noah there was such wickedness in the world that God's orders went forth for the destruction of the world. Noah was called by God to build an ark to save his family and all others who would come in. When the ark was finished God said to Noah, "Come into the ark, you and all your household." Then floods prevailed over the earth. Only Noah and his household in the ark remained alive. To all others it meant death.

That ark is a type of salvation and God still calls to man saying, "Come into the ark, come, come." The last word is come; the first word is come. It is God's favorite word.

Blind Bartemeus finds a sunny spot against the wall and waits to see what the day will bring him. He hears in the distance the hum of voices and the shuffling of feet. He asks what the stir is all about. It's Jesus of Nazareth, the crowd replies. "Jesus of Nazareth! Son of David, have mercy on me!" he cries. The louder he cries for Jesus the more the bystanders rebuke him. You know it's a bad thing not to come to Christ ourselves, but a worse thing to stand in the way of others. If you will not come yourself be sure that you do not hinder others.

Hearing the cry, Jesus stood still. Many other shouts were going up but that was the one Jesus heard. Jesus said to tell him to come. And Jesus healed Bartemeus' blindness. Notice in the Scripture what the beggar did. He called. He ran, He believed, and He saw. Now notice what Jesus did. They are the same things He does today. He was passing by. He stood still, and He called for Bartemeus to come to Him.

Jesus was passing through Jericho for the last time that day. Had Bartemeus not gone to Jesus when he did, there would be no other chance. He may be passing through your town today for the last time. We don't know. He is still saying, "Come, come."

There's the "come" of the little children "Let the little children come to Me and do not forbid them." Or His words to those who labor and are heavy laden. "Come unto me and I will give you rest."

But all the "comes" of the Bible are summed up in this last gracious invitation of the Bible that sums up and unites all other invitations. "The Spirit and the bride say, 'Come!' And let him that hears say, 'Come!' And let him who thirsts come. Whosoever desires, let him take of the water of life freely." As the body must have water so the soul must have the water of life.

The Bible closes with the invitation to drink of that life-giving water. The invitation takes in every one who will come. God sums it up in this one word so beautiful, so full of tenderness, love, and compassion, "Come."

Dearest Father, I lift _____ up to you. Please soften their heart so they may be like Noah and the little children and Bartemeus, who came to You upon Your loving call. Amen.

September 4   Heavenly Vision

Scripture Reading: Acts Chapter 26

Key Verse: "Therefore, King Agrippa, I was not disobedient to the heavenly vision . . ." Acts 26:19

Paul is unquestionably the greatest embodiment of the argument for Christianity there ever has been, and perhaps there ever shall be. Paul became a believer because of the pressure within his heart, his soul, and his life through the vision he had of the Lord Jesus Christ. And those of us who believe would do well to learn from Paul the necessity of constantly keeping that vision before us.

That vision of Christ convicted Paul of his sinfulness. Paul realized in that blinding flash that none of his works could save him and that he needed the salvation of God. Christ's presence compelled Paul to throw himself upon the Lord, stripping him of every sense of personal merit and constraining him to relay on the mercy of God through the blood of Christ.

But, beloved, when Paul said to King Agrippa, "I was not disobedient to the heavenly vision," he meant not only was he not disobedient to the vision that saved him, but also that he was not disobedient to the heavenly vision that sent him out to serve God. Yes, he was called to salvation, but he was also commissioned to service, and so are you and I.

Today, we see a world lost in sin. Men, women, and children all about us are lost, without hope or understanding of all God has for them. If in your heart there is not a burning compassion for the souls of men, a yearning sympathy for those so enslaved in their own misery and sin, you must ask yourself if you have stayed true to your vision of Christ. Paul was true to the vision that sent him to Calvary for his own supply of life-giving blood. Then, the vision sent Paul with that blood to a world lost in the depths of sin. What about you, beloved?

But, there is more. Paul was not disobedient to the heavenly vision that saved him, he was not disobedient to the heavenly vision that sent him, but he was also not disobedient to the heavenly vision that sustained him. There never was a man of God in all the history of Christianity who had as much trouble as Paul. He suffered at the hand of authorities. He was maligned, ridiculed, and criticized.

When Paul could find help nowhere else, this heavenly vision sustained him in the constant joy of the assurance of his own salvation, and in the fruitfulness of his own life in service to the Lord, and with the satisfaction of being able to say, "I have fought the good fight." We dare not lose sight of our precious Savior. We must keep our eyes on Him.

Beloved, the vision that saves us is available to every one of us by faith in the Lord Jesus Christ. The vision that sustains us in the assurance of our own salvation and the salvation of others will constrain us to say today, "I do not care what others may do but as for me and my house, we will serve the Lord." Oh, that God would now give everyone of us a renewed vision of Christ Jesus our Lord. That vision will sustain us until that day we drop at the feet of our Redeemer and receive the crown of reward awaiting every one of us. God grant it through Jesus Christ our Lord, Amen.

Dear God, I need that vision of Jesus. Please help me to fix my eyes on Him through the portrait Your Word paints. May His loveliness, His perfection, His brilliant righteousness block out all the worldly distractions that vie for first place in my sight. I want to see only Jesus, today and every day, for the rest of my life. Amen.

September 5   Fellowships and Joy of the Christian Life

Suggested Reading: Psalm 89

Key Verses: Psalm 89:15-16 "Blessed are the people who know the joyful sound! They walk, O Lord, in the light of Your countenance. In Your name they rejoice all the day long."

The Christian life is a life of privilege, power and blessing. The first word of the Psalmist, blessed or happy, is in some ways the keynote of the whole book. It appears nearly fifty times and always occurs in our relation to God. Scarcely ever do circumstances enter into this blessedness.

So, it is not what we have or what we know, or what we can do, but what we are that constitutes blessedness. Look again at the Psalm. Here is a verse that expresses the joy and blessedness of the Christian life.

Now we are to know the things that are freely given us of God. So here we see what the Bible means by the Christian life, that life which we are to meditate upon, to understand and, by the mercy of God, to experience.

First then, is that it is a life of perpetual fellowship. "They walk, O Lord, in the light of Your Countenance," (or face). The countenance of God is a symbol of Divine Presence. It also means Divine Favor. The benediction we like to offer and which was offered upon Israel is "The Lord lift up His countenance upon you and give you peace." We have the favor and presence of God.

Walking also implies progress. Walking in the light of the Divine Countenance means guidance as we take our journey and make progress through life. Now we ought to ask ourselves, what do we know about this walking in the light of His Countenance? Is this the experience of our life?

The Scriptures say that Noah walked with God. He was a practical preacher of righteousness. He had no convert, but he had a life of perpetual fellowship with God. This is the life intended for us.

The Christian life is a life of unchanging joy. "In Your name they rejoice all day long." Now, there is a vast difference between joy and happiness. Happiness depends upon circumstances of life. Joy is independent of circumstances and is dependent upon our relationship to God. Happiness is like the surface of the sea. Joy is like the bed of the ocean.

There is joy of retrospect as we look back at the past. There is joy of aspect as we look around on the present, and there is joy of prospect as we look forward to the future. There is the joy of memory, the joy of love, the joy of a peaceful conscience, the joy of the grateful heart, the joy of the teachable mind, the joy of the trustful soul, the joy of the obedient life, the joy of the glowing hope.

"In Your name they rejoice." Joy is not dependent upon ourselves, but upon Him. "In Your name," that is, not according to circumstances, but under all circumstances. This is what Paul meant when he said "Rejoice in the Lord always." He did not say "Be happy in the Lord always." No, we can't be happy always. We may be sorrowful, yet rejoicing. Our joy is independent of our happiness because it is associated with God. Oh how we need this in our Christian life, this unchanging joy. If we do not know what this means in our daily life, we are lacking in one of the essential features of Biblical Christianity.

Almighty God, help me to walk in the light of your Divine Countenance and partake more fully of the ocean of unchanging joy you give to me. Amen.

September 6   Song at the Supper

Scripture Reading: Psalm 116, 117, 118

Key Verse: "And when they had sung a hymn, they went out to the Mount of Olives." Matthew 26:30

Jesus was in the upper room with the eleven after He instituted the memorial supper to commemorate his death. They sang triumphantly of His death which He should accomplish the next day at Jerusalem. Not until we have seen Him singing with His disciples at the supper have we seen, in its completeness, the divine portrait of our Lord.

We've seen Him as the pleasant Christ, with children thronging around Him, fellowshipping with friends at the wedding at Cana, working, laughing, visiting and living with His community of family and friends. We've seen Him as the sympathetic Christ, not ashamed to weep at the grave of His friend Lazarus. We've seen Him as the sorrowing Christ when in the garden He said, "My soul is exceeding sorrowful unto death." We have seen Him as the kneeling Christ, praying through every crisis and every victory. We have seen Him as the suffering Christ and we have heard the cry on the cross, "My God, My God, why did You forsake me?"

But here He is, the singing Christ, singing with His disciples after He had delivered the message that should comfort their hearts and all disciples for all time as He is about to face Gethsemane.

I have wondered what song they sang. I wished it might have been preserved that we might sing it too. If you will turn to Psalm 118 you will find the hymn that is possibly the very song they sang. Psalms 116, 117 and 118 were sung at the close of the feast of the Passover and the 118th Psalm was the Passover Doxology.

This song was the prophetic confirmation of that glorious day when the spotless Lamb of God would make His own blood an offering for the sins of the world. You will notice, if you read it that is a song of faith. "The Lord is on my side," they sang.

It is a song of boldness. "I will not fear. What can man do to me?"

Pilate marveled at His boldness. It is also a song of gladness. "This is the day the Lord has made; we will rejoice and be glad in it." It is a song of praise and adoration, "You are my God and I will praise You; You are my God and I will exalt You." So did Jesus sing a song of praise in death, as He became the light of the world. It was a song of sacrifice. Think of it, Jesus singing as He faced Calvary.

It is a song of victory. "I shall not die but live, and declare the works of the Lord." Yes, He saw death, but it was death slain. He saw the grave, but it was the grave plundered. He saw judgment, but it was judgment silenced. He saw hell, but it was hell vanquished.

Moody said, as he closed the Northfield conference, "One of these days you will pick up a paper and it will say 'D.L. Moody of Northfield, Massachusetts is dead.' Don't you believe it. At that moment I will be more alive than I have ever been in my life."

Beloved, can you sing bold hymns of praise, triumph, and victory as you face what is before you today? Yes, you can, for Christ will either take you out of it or through it. But go with your head high and your eyes steadfastly on Him, with a song in your heart and on your lips.

Dear Father, I never knew that Jesus went singing to Gethsemane. I am awed by the remarkable trust He set as our example. I want to remember to praise You in the midst of all my circumstances, both joyful and sorrowful. Amen.

September 7   The Gospel of Labor

Scripture: II Corinthians Chapter 6

Key Verse: "We then, as workers together with Him . . . ." II Corinthians 6:1

In this Labor Day season, let us consider our Master. One of the glorious things about Him was that He was a worker. Whereas most founders of religion lived lives of contemplative ease, Jesus worked with His hands. By this He dignified the labor of man and taught us several lessons concerning work.

Jesus said, "Man shall not live by bread alone." A full dinner pail is no assurance of a full life. We must see beyond our work to its true meaning; then we find even the plainest jobs not only bearable but a source of satisfaction, pride, and joy.

Said a great architect to some men working on the building of a great cathedral, "What are you doing?" The man replied that he was mixing mortar. To the next man the architect asked, "What are you doing?" The man replied, "I'm building a great home for God and the soul." Which man do you believe went home bursting with energy and joy?

There is a story told about a man who lived with two wives. He was middle-aged while one wife was young and the other was old. The man was getting gray-haired. The young wife did not like that so while he slept she pulled out his gray hairs. The older wife wanted him to appear older and nearer her own age so she pulled out his black hairs. Soon the poor man was bald. The economy of our nation, our family and our own pocketbook is going to be in just such shape if every group takes only that which serves its own interest. Manager, consumer, boss and worker all must recognize that the interest of each is bound up with the interest of all.

The work of man is related to the work of God. Perhaps we have all felt that a large part of Christian life was spent in doing things apart from the rest of our life. We need to see that any useful work done

137

honestly and with a vision of its end purpose may be a token of our partnership with God.

We are apt to think that the only way we can serve God is to go to church, teach a class, or sing in the choir. And God needs all that for His work. But God needs the daily secular work of man if His will is to be accomplished on the earth. After all, there is little separation between the secular and the sacred, for in Christian service we do all to the glory of God.

God can use us all in His great work-shop. There He has an opening for every one of us. It is when men learn to do their work in partnership with God and honor Him in their tasks that the spirit of man will soar with purpose and dignity. Jesus teaches us that if we do something as simple as give a cup of cold water in His name we will be blessed.

Christianity makes common things holy and in daily service we find the greatest expressions of life's devotion. Let us as Christians rededicate the labor of our hands and the tasks of our lives to the service of God.

Lord, let me remember my employees, honoring them with fair wages and respect. Let me see in their faces the face of my Lord and treat them as Christ would want to be treated. For, once He labored with His hands for others also. Amen.

Dear God, help me to be a faithful and trusted employee. Let my attitude be one of service, gratitude and diligence to Your glory. May I see my co-workers and my supervisor as people You have brought into my life to serve and uplift, and may I recognize and accept that they are sometimes Your instruments of training and refining. Amen

September 8   That I May Know Him

Suggested Reading: Philippians Chapter 3

Key Verse: Philippians 3:10 "That I may know Him and the power of His resurrection."

When a person becomes a Christian the natural process is this: first the living Christ enters into his soul and development begins, then quickening life seizes upon the soul, assimilates surrounding elements and begins to fashion it. According to the great law of conformity to type, this fashioning takes a specific form, the form of the artist who fashions it. And all through life that wonderful, mystical, glorious, yet perfectly definite process goes on until Christ is formed in you.

Paul has one great longing, one ambition that knows no compromise. No persecution can daunt it, no suffering hinder it. The very longing of his soul is to know the Lord better. A fire has sprung up that nothing could put out. The Lord has centered it in his heart. Paul is able to say "I count all things loss . . . that I may gain Christ . . . that I may know Him and the power of His resurrection and the fellowship of His sufferings." Oh, how he wanted to know Christ.

But, Paul should not be the exception. You and I must be captivated by the same desire. Paul's experience, love, yearning for righteousness should be ours as well. Of all knowledge, the most precious, the most desirable, the most necessary, is the knowledge of God in Christ Jesus.

My greatest desire for you is that you might draw closer to Him, increase in your heart a burning, a yearning, a constant hungering to know Him better that you may be grounded in the faith.

So then, how can we know Him better? First, we must have a right conception of Him. He is more than a good example, a mere pattern for existence. He is the Christ, the Son of the Living God. He is the Divine manifested in the flesh and seated in His glorified body at the right hand of God; a Christ who loves you more than anyone else possibly could.

Secondly, if we are to know Him better we must know more of His book. God says "My people are destroyed for lack of knowledge." If you want knowledge of eternal things, and earthly things as well, read your Bible.

Prayer cannot be divided from study of the Word. Jesus Himself took time from His needed sleep and "having risen a long while before daylight, He went out" to pray to His Father. To Him, as to us, it was daily bread, vital air, the gate of heaven. He tells us "When you pray go into your room, and when you have shut the door, pray." Do this and you will know victory. Make Christ your constant companion and pray to Him in secret. Heart to heart communication with Christ will change your life.

Moses, alone with God, saw the burning bush. Isaiah was alone with God when he had the Great Vision. Paul was alone with God when he was caught up to the third heaven. John was alone with God when at the Isle of Patmos he saw the Holy City. Have you ever been alone with God?

Keep the company of Christians. "He who walks with wise men will be wise." Go where God and Christianity are honored.

Lastly, engage more actively in His work. Get busy for God. Go into His vineyard today, and get busy, and stay busy. At the factory, in the store, do you speak a word? At the office, do you live Jesus? Be at peace with all men, study, pray, and most of all walk with God, so one day you will hear, "Well done, good and faithful servant."

Dearest Father, I yearn for more of You. Help me to give You more of me. Amen.

September 9 Triumph of Uncompromising Living

Scripture Reading: Exodus Chapter 10

Key Verse: "Then he said to them, "The Lord had better be with you when I let you and your little ones go!" Exodus 10:10

This mighty monarch Pharaoh set himself to resist the Sovereign will and course of the Most High God in reference to His people, their lives, testimony, and destiny. Pharaoh is doing his best to drive a shrewd bargain with the people of God. Four times he offers them a compromise, but the battle goes on until the people of God win everything because they refused to compromise themselves. And, so, four grand lessons come to us out of this incident.

The first offer of compromise we see when Pharaoh, in Chapter 8 of Exodus, called for Moses and Aaron and told them to go and sacrifice to their God. Here Pharaoh is endeavoring to hinder the thorough separation of God's people from Egypt. Satan's object is fully achieved when people accept a worldly religion and fail to come out and be separate. God's purpose in the deliverance of His people was that "My name might be declared in all the earth." What declaration could there be then, or now, with His people still in Egypt?"

Note well Moses' answer to Pharaoh, "We will go three-days' journey . . ." Nothing less than these three days could satisfy God. Three days is the power of Resurrection. Three days is beyond the land of death and darkness.

Pharaoh's second compromise offer was, "I will let you go that you may sacrifice to the Lord your God in the Wilderness, only you shall not go very far away." If he could not keep them in Egypt, he would at least keep them near, that they might be brought back. There is always much more serious damage done to the cause of Christ by persons seeming to have given up the world and returning to it again, than if they had remained entirely in it.

The third offer Pharaoh extended was even more tempting, "Go now, you who are men, and serve the Lord." Pharaoh here extends a deadly blow to the testimony of the name of God in Israel, a partial deliverance which is useless to Israel and dishonoring to God. God expects us to bring our children up in the nurture and admonition of the Lord. Sending the fathers off to worship, and leaving the children in Egypt is not acceptable. And, oh beloved, we today should not exclude little children from our worship either.

Finally, Pharaoh's last compromise was "Go, serve the Lord; only let your flocks and your herds be kept back. Let your little ones also go with you." Oh, with what perseverance did Satan dispute every inch of Israel's way out of Egypt! He first sought to keep them in the land, then near the land, then part of them in the land, and finally Pharaoh would send them out without sacrifices!

But, Moses said, "Thou must also give us sacrifices and burnt offerings that we may sacrifice to the Lord our God. Our livestock also shall go with us; not a hoof shall be left behind . . ." Egypt is no place for anything which pertains to God's redeemed. God is worthy of all we are and all we have, body, soul and spirit. God will have all, or none. As Christians today, we need to say, "I cannot leave my substance to be the world's, I cannot leave my children in Egypt, and I must go the full three-day journey through the Red Sea, all the way, with all I have."

Dear Lord, all I am, all I have, and all I can do is at Your disposal. Help me to recognize the seemingly little compromises that would steal the strength of my testimony, and help me to stand firm against them. Thank You, Lord, Amen.

September 10   Passage of Faith

Scripture Reading: Hebrews 11:23-29

Key Verse: "By faith they passed through the Red Sea as by dry land, whereas the Egyptians, attempting to do so, were drowned." Hebrews 11: 29

Today, let us work in the orchard. For, I've long believed that the only way we can improve the fruit is by improving the tree itself. If the way to cleanse the streams of a fountain is to cleanse the fountain, so the only way we can improve the functional life of the Christian in his thoughts, deeds and activities is to go back into his inner life, to the springs of his life, and see that he is rightly related to God. The fruitful Christian lives by faith and all his activities are governed by the relationship he sustains with God. Real faith produces results.

In terms of faith, we ordinarily look to individuals as our examples. Today, let us look to a nation. "By faith they passed through the Red Sea." We see them, by faith, extricating themselves from a dangerous place and conquering impossible handicaps. Ordinarily, people find safety in flight or fight, but the children of Israel could find safety in neither. To fight the Egyptians was absurd, and it was impossible to flee into the mountains. All they could do was to depend on God and that was the third way out. Of these the Word says, "By faith" they crossed over. How many times has faith been the liberating force in our lives?

It was a dissatisfying faith. Had the Children of Israel been satisfied to have stayed in Egypt and suffer affliction there they never would have left for the Promised Land. But faith made them see better possibilities for themselves and a better place to live. Thus their faith created a holy discontent. It was also a goal-determining faith. They had a promised land before them and by faith they crossed over because a goal-determining faith made them see the land flowing with milk and honey before they were able to partake of it.

The faith of the Children of Israel was a waiting faith. There are times when we need to rest, to get our breath, to pray, to meditate and

143

to get the right perspective of things. God called through Moses and said to Israel "Stand still." Motion is not always a sign of progress.

Their faith was a faith that ignored outward conditions as they appeared, and accepted a new set of conditions as God gave them vision. That is exactly what the Children of Israel did. Functioning faith takes hold on God and removes fear from the heart.

Theirs was a faith that accepted leadership. Whenever faith moves in a group, that group must move as one. The faith of passage united them with God and united them with one another.

Then, this faith that came into their lives produced results. They did not stand still for long, only long enough to see their dilemma and long enough to see God's salvation. And so we read that the Children of Israel marched forward and crossed the Red Sea on dry land. When they put feet to their faith God's resources came into play and turned the impossible into the possible.

Oh beloved, what a sense of satisfaction comes to our hearts when we realize that whenever we are doing God's will His resources are put at our command. It is when we march forward with God that He has promised divine power in the marching.

Almighty God, thank You for lifting my eyes higher, to Your faithful sufficiency in everything I face. Help me to take Your hand and march forward on the dry land of Your will. In Jesus' name, amen.

Scripture Reading: Deuteronomy Chapter 34

Key Verse: "Since then, there has not arisen in Israel a prophet like Moses, whom the Lord knew face to face." Deut. 34:10

What a tremendous assertion, yet it is the sober truth. Moses is the outstanding character of the Old Testament. Among the towering prophets who stand like lofty mountains against the sky, he is the tallest of them all. He is great in character and he is great in his achievements. He brought a new nation to its birth, and so taught that nation that he succeeded in bringing every living man into his debt.

He was born in Egypt of a foreign and subjected people. Many years before his birth, his ancestors, then a meager handful of nomads, had been chased into Egypt by the hounds of hunger. They had been permitted to settle in that fertile part of the country called "Goshen." There they had prospered and multiplied rapidly until their few score had grown into many thousands. Then the Egyptian leaders changed their attitude toward these foreigners. Instead of making them welcome as in other days, they began to persecute them until the Israelites were enslaved, and all male babies were ordered killed to diminish the population.

It was to parents living in bondage, in a hut on the banks of the Nile, that Moses was born. Not only was he born a slave, but he was born with the threat of death upon him. His parents, in spite of the order of the Pharaoh, were faithful, believing that God had a purpose in the life of their boy. They took a basket, lined it with pitch and with prayer, put their baby in it and hid him among the bulrushes of the Nile. He certainly did not have a promising outlook. Oh, what God can do through people that are seemingly crushed by heavy handicaps.

Some years ago, a man died in the South who had been born a slave. As a small boy, he was traded off for a broken-down race horse. But that boy, who was seemingly of such little worth, when grown to manhood ultimately contributed by his discoveries millions of dollars to the economy. But he contributed even more by his Christ-like character. His name was George Washington Carver. And even so, God took this Hebrew slave and used him for no less a task that the bringing about of the birth of the nation of Israel. Oh beloved, this great leader was no accident. God had a definite purpose in his life as He has in yours and mine.

In the case of Moses, this greatest of all prophets, back of all of his natural abilities and the endowments of education that came from the privileged position of the Pharaoh's palace, was God's plan.

Moses' life work was due not to these, but to the faith which knit his soul to God. The writer of Hebrews lays bare the secret of the marvels affected by the heroes of the Hebrew story in the three little words, "By faith, Moses . . . ."

God has a plan for your life, as well, beloved friend. Whatever the handicaps or hindrances in your life, knit your soul to God. "We know that all things work together for good to those who love God, to those who are the called according to His purpose," Romans 8:28 tells us. And just so, God can use your circumstances, and your faith, to be a channel of blessing to those around you.

Dear Lord, when I read of the heroes of the faith in Hebrews, I am really reading about Your deeds through ordinary people who had faith in You. I believe that You are working in my life, Lord, and I desire to be a blessing, and a testimony, by faith. Amen.

September 12   Taking Your Temperature

Scripture: Revelation 3: 14-22

Key Verse: ". . . You are lukewarm . . ." Revelation 3:16

A startling statement to this church, you say, but it does not apply to me. Some of you are filled with ardent love and a consuming passion for the Lord. Yet, history is full of illustrations of men and women who at one time in their life were wholehearted for God and then the flame burned low. Solomon started well but his heart was turned away. Demas was a fellow-laborer with Paul, yet there came a day when Paul had to say "Demas has forsaken me, having loved this present world."

Now, what constitutes luke-warmness? The answer is in verse fifteen. "You are neither hot nor cold." In other words tepid, insipid, the same temperature as the crowd of whom it would never be said that they burned for God, just luke-warm folks whose spiritual life was unmarked by enthusiasm or zeal. Is this true of you? Were you once hot but you have now cooled down? Do you remember how you burned with a passion for God just after your conversion?

This luke-warmness would not be tolerated anywhere else in the world. Can you imagine a city business manager being luke-warm? He would soon be paid off. Can you imagine anyone in the political world carrying through some social reform if he were lukewarm? Then why is it that in the spiritual realm where we deal with eternities, the most important of all, that men and women can be lukewarm? Lukewarm in the face of our Lord's burning, consuming zeal? In the face of His compassions for the souls of men? In the face of the passion of the early disciples and martyrs who died for the cause of Christ? Lukewarm? Are we not ashamed?

Oh that we might discover the cause and find the remedy. Did your fall come, like David's, through inactivity? He had been a warrior, but was now idle, doing nothing. A selfish, self-centered, idle Christian can never be blazing with a passion for God and His service.

Or has your lukewarmness come by lack of spiritual exercise? Are you still in fervent, daily prayer? Are you still partaking of the daily manna of God's Word, the Holy Scriptures? Shall we come closer home? Is it some sin? Sampson once burned for God, but along came Delilah and he lost his consecration. What is the remedy? What is the cure?

"Behold, I stand at the door and knock. If anyone hears My voice and opens the door, I will come in." That is the remedy. Imagine a church in a building with everything complete, a church that said to itself "I have need of nothing." Yet, is it possible? Yes! Had you gone outside you would have found Christ craving for admission. He, the head of the church, the one who died for it, lonely and knocking, and craving admission yet all the while shut outside.

It is at your heart's door, lukewarm Christian, and before your heart's door He knocks now for admission. You hear Him. You know His knock. He is waiting for you to open it. He will never force His way. He is longing for your company, your fellowship, your love. And He will never be satisfied until He stands in the very center of your being. The only remedy is for Christ to come in.

You can continue being lukewarm, joyless, powerless, going through the motions, or you can make up your mind in the quiet of this moment that you shall be the Lord's and He shall be yours and surrender to Him the keys to your life.

Dear Lord Jesus, I do surrender to You. Come into my life and fill me with Your power, joy, and purpose. I hold nothing back. Amen.

September 13   Epitaph For a Ruler

Scripture Reading: Mark 10:17-22

Key Verse: "But he was sad at this word, and went away sorrowful, for he had great possessions." Mark 10:22

If we were to visit a corner of the Bible Character Cemetery where lie those who rejected Jesus, we would find the headstone of a young man known as the "rich young ruler." The epitaph on his grave is one of the saddest of all in the Bible. All three apostles, Matthew, Mark and Luke are careful to record the fact that he went away sorrowful. It must have haunted the disciples, and it haunts us today.

What was this young man like to have made such an impression? Mark tells us that the young man ran to meet Jesus and kneeled before Him when he asked the great question about eternal life. So he was enthusiastic about his soul. He wanted to make the most of his life. When Jesus asked him about keeping the commandment he could say that according to his light and standard he had kept them from his youth up. He was rich, religious, clean, and loveable. But by coming to Jesus he was asking, "I have missed something. What is it?"

Jesus did not send him away saying "You have arrived." Instead He said to him. "You lack one thing." It was not decency, uprightness, or integrity. It was not earnestness and high courage. It was not reverence. He was still able to bend the knee. What, I ask, had he missed?

He had missed eternal life. He had missed the life that comes from knowing God through Christ. "This is eternal life; that they may know You, the only true God, and Jesus Christ whom You have sent."

As the young ruler knelt at the feet of Jesus, He told him how he might find what he missed. What did He tell him? His answer was drastic. Often times we preachers seek to perform a major operation but we fail to make an incision. Not so with Jesus. He fairly laid the patient open with this word, "Go your way, sell whatever you have and give to the poor . . . come, take up the cross, and follow me." Of course Christ does not demand that of every man. Why did he ask it of this man?

He saw that while eager for eternal life, he was yet more eager for things. He had great possessions but possessions also had him. But what is universal in this command? It is this: "Follow me." That's the one essential. The Rich Young Ruler might have complied with the first part and still lost out. What Jesus was after was not the selling and giving. He was after the young man himself. He was after obedience. That is Christianity, the whole of it. It is Christianity in its course and consummation.

When the young man went away sorrowing, Jesus said with aching heart, "How hard it is for those who have riches to enter the kingdom of God." The disciples, amazed at what they saw, turned to Jesus and said, "Who then can be saved?"

Who indeed? The answer is, anyone who is willing to follow and obey. Look at Matthew. He was also a lover of money. He loved it so much that he sold his good name for it. But when he encountered Jesus his sorry bargain began to break his heart. Then one day the Master said, "Follow me." Then what? Did Matthew give all his wealth away? I do not know. Did he sob or shout or sing? I do not know. But I do know this. He did the one essential thing. He did that which brought him newness of life. He followed Jesus.

Today, Lord, I have decided that following You is more important than anything I might cling to here on earth. I surrender all and choose to follow only You. Amen.

September 14 Summer Fruit

Scripture Reading: Amos Chapter 8

Key Verse: "Thus the Lord God showed me: Behold a basket of summer fruit." Amos 8:1

A basket of summer fruit is so lovely, is it not? It speaks to us of the rich provision made for us by Him. The summer season is such a purposeful season. The energies of earth and sky and man work together, with rain and sun, cool nights and brown soil. These and the labors of man all appear in the clusters of the vine, the laden branches of the orchard, and the blazing beauty of ten thousand gardens. And it is so with life.

Human life too means purposeful production. Paul expresses sound Christian thought when he expressed this thought, "This we commanded you, that if any would not work, neither should he eat." Drones cannot be tolerated, neither physical nor spiritual drones. Upon the higher and truer plane, life also means spiritual production.

Jesus places the truth of life before us in a language a child can understand. He says that life is like a garden, and God Himself tends it. Jesus and his friends are the vine and the branches of that vine. We are a living organism and the constant care and concern of the Almighty. We are to bear fruit, and Jesus emphasizes that any life not vitally in union with Him cannot produce fruit, "Apart from me, you can do nothing."

Summer is also a diversified season. Into it are woven light and shadow, storm and calm, sunlight and shower, day and night. At times the program seems a hopeless mass of contradictions and confusions. So it must have seemed to Moses. He was a child of slaves, raised a darling in the palace. He was the outlawed shepherd who became the emancipator of a nation and finally the disappointed veteran on Mt. Nebo who saw the Promised Land but could not enter. Joseph, too, might have thought the pattern of his life confusing. He was his father's favorite, hated of his brothers, a slave in Egypt, and finally the lord of all the land. There seems to be no key, no pattern that we can discern. Yet, out of the drenching storms there will emerge a chastened spirit, a rich and disciplined life that will be worthy in the eyes of the Divine Husbandman.

Summer, after all, is a short season. In the Canadian Northwest, spring is sometimes late; the plowing and seeding are rushed. Summer comes sweeping them off their feet, and the farmer is obliged to work from sunup to sunset, and that means 20 of 24 hours up there. Then, before he realizes it, the wind has teeth and the frost warns of winter's approach. Similarly, life is short for us all. We revel through the sunny days, starry nights, sunrises and sunsets. The delicious, delirious days are as a dream. But the crystal moments, golden glorious hours, gallop off into the shadows and summer is gone. And, it is exactly so with life.

At the end of this age, we all shall stand before Him to give an account of what we have done with Christ and how we have used our talents. Out on a farm somewhere today, men are working feverishly to reap the harvest of past months and store it safely away. No time is wasted. No indifference is present. Every muscle is extended, every person, vehicle and tool is in use. All work, plan and labor toward that important end, harvest. They are wise and prudent. And, how shall it be with us?

Dear Father, it is true. I revel in the days of my life, often remembering that they are numbered, and I should be about my Father's business. The summer basket of fruit is lovely, but lovelier still the spiritual fruit of a life lived for You. Help me to live vibrantly for You. Amen.

September 15   Having the Right Enemies

Scripture Reading: Matthew 5:1-12

Key Verse: "Blessed are those who are persecuted for righteousness' sake, for theirs is the kingdom of heaven. Matthew 5:10

To be picked on is a heartbreaking experience, whether it is a child on a playground or an adult at his job. We are designed to love and be loved, and it is painful to be reviled by others. To be persecuted is to live in an atmosphere of suffocating suspicion, to have one's security invaded by intrigue, to be pursued by persons in a malignant spirit, and to be sniped at by enemies lying in wait. It is to be hounded and harassed with unjust penalties for alleged offenses. Among all the ills that flesh and spirit are heir to, persecution can come about the nearest to making life a hell on earth. Hence, the beatitude seems to be about the most paradoxical of all. "Blessed are those who are persecuted . . . ." It seems completely implausible.

The mere fact of being persecuted is no proof of virtue and is worthy of no blessing in itself, for more people suffer for the wrong than for the right. When the raw recruit is out of step his first need is to listen to the cadence to see if he is not at fault. Before we conclude that we are being persecuted for righteousness' sake we should study ourselves in the light of the Word of God. Do we match up to the love, selflessness, and sacrifice for others we are called to? In more cases than not, we need improvement. But there are times when some are persecuted for righteousness' sake. Jesus Himself embodied love and selfless sacrifice to perfection, yet He was persecuted with unspeakable cruelty.

We must face the fact that Christ-like goodness did and does arouse cruel opposition. Antagonism is inevitable between a Christian and the world because the characteristics and principles of a Christian are in direct opposition to many of the opinions and views of the world.

Goodness stirs unbelief and dislike because it disturbs the inertia of those who are set in their ways of thought and life. There is a story about the time when Orville and Wilbur Wright made their first flight at Kittyhawk, North Carolina. One of their neighbors in Dayton, Ohio on hearing the news is reported to have said, "I don't believe it. Nobody's ever going to fly and if anybody did fly, it wouldn't be anyone from Dayton." This is the type of thinking which lies in wait for pioneers and prophets, especially in their own country.

Christ- like goodness is persecuted because it interferes with those who want to be bad. The righteous are a standing rebuke to wrongdoers without uttering a single word. They haunt the evil ones with goodness as the smile of Stephen haunted Saul of Tarsus. They exercise a silent veto and though the unrighteous may override it, the effect is not erased.

When Jesus was reviled He did not answer, but His silence did not mean surrender to the principles of those who persecuted Him. The Christian is called to be a good soldier for Jesus Christ. This means he must stand, and having done all, stand. Thus are the principles of Christ like goodness pushed up to the advancing frontiers of human experience.

Yes, beloved, when you set out to live Christ's kind of goodness you can expect to be persecuted for the sake of righteousness. Tomorrow let us study the blessings that come with persecution.

Holy Father God, may any persecution lead me to deeper self-examination before I conclude I am without blame. I want to change for the better if I am to blame. But if not, then may I be brave and keep my eyes on You as You walk with me through this trial. Amen.

September 16 Having the Right Enemies II

Scripture Reading: Matthew 5:1-12

Key Verse: "Blessed are those who are persecuted for righteousness' sake, for theirs is the kingdom of heaven."
Matthew 5:10

Dwight L. Moody used to say that when any considerable time passed without someone attacking him, he became concerned about the vitality of his message.

If you never stand up for anything which somebody wants to knock down, if you never say anything which somebody does not criticize, if your righteousness has never aroused any ridicule or reviling, if all men speak well of you, then beware because you do not bear the mark of God's true servants in the past. A man is known by the enemies he makes as truly as by the friends he keeps.

Yes, persecution reveals the real stuff that God's people are made of. One thinks of Paul and Silas singing as they lay chained in prison. We think of Neimholler of Germany and Bishop Bergrav of Oslo Norway interned by the Nazis.

It was real stuff that made Hugh Latimer cry out in confidence as he went to the stake, "Be of good cheer, Mr. Ridley, and play the man. We shall this day light such a candle by God's grace in England as shall never be put out."

When a follower of Christ tries to rise toward his Lord's high goodness, he finds in opposition what a flier finds in a headwind, namely, that which enables him to get off the ground.

We find ourselves assuming responsibilities which could have been evaded, loving our enemies, blessing those who curse us, doing good to those who hate us and praying for those who persecute us.

When you turn the other cheek and go the second mile; then says Jesus, "You show yourselves children of your Father which is in heaven."

Suppose no Francis of Assisi had risked ridicule and persecution to alleviate the sodden mass of medieval cruelty? Suppose no Wilberforce had been willing to suffer scorn in his effort to rid England of the African slave traffic? Suppose no John Howard had opposed those people of his day to cleanse the prison conditions?

Had it not been for those who went beyond the paved roads of conventional goodness and cut across hostile country to reach the higher righteousness, there would be no advance in decent society and our civilization would stagnate in a pool of malice.

Life is like a relay race. Others ran before us and we start from the point where their lives touch ours. How vital that we touch them and carry on the torch.

So with our lives on this earth. They do not begin with our birth nor end with our death. Society is a compact between the living, the dead, and the great unborn.

To keep faith with those who have gone before and those who are to come after is the duty of every Christian. The honor of our service calls for endurance through weariness and courage through persecution. Christ waits to give you all you need.

Dearest Lord, let me step up to the plate when You call me to extraordinary service. Let me never hesitate with thought for my own discomfort or trial. I trust You to walk with me every step of the way and accomplish Your will as You give me the grace to be obedient. Amen.

September 17   The Secret of a Great Church

Scripture: Acts Chapter 2

Key Verse: "And they continued steadfastly in the apostle's doctrine and fellowship, in breaking of bread, and in prayers." Acts 2:42

To those early apostles like Luke and Paul, the church was grandly thought of. The most heartbreaking thought to Paul was the memory that he once persecuted it. Afterward, he fairly taxed his great vocabulary to tell his converts and all others of the beauty and worth of the church. He sees the church as the body of Christ, that living organism through which our Lord still speaks.

Even a cursory study of the church of the first century would show that they possessed many things which are not the possession of most churches today. Not material things, of course, for the church of today far exceeds that of the first century in material things and possessions. No, the outstanding thing that the early church possessed was a one-ness of heart, a singleness of purpose, a unity. They felt responsibility to the organization for which Jesus Christ had given His life. And the secret to this great church is found in four simple facts.

First, the early church was a church-going group. Even Pentecost was possible because all the people were present. No church can be great unless the members actually attend. We must love the house of God, and enter it when the doors are opened. The Body of Christ must be a top priority in our lives.

Next, the early church was a studying group. They spent much of their time in study at the apostle's feet. No church can be really great that does not have members who are hungry to know the Word of God. They searched the Scriptures, and so should we. Their members were diligent to learn the truth, so they could put it into practice.

The early church was also a praying church. Who can estimate the power of prayer? We far too often underestimate it! The mighty church is one that goes down on its knees to God, who alone can give power. How we need praying fathers and mothers. How we need all the Body of Christ to take seriously this responsibility to pray. How precious the privilege of coming into the presence of God, dear ones. Make full use of this blessing.

And, finally, the early church was a witnessing body. This is the greatest secret. These early church members arose from their knees to go into houses. They did not cease to teach and preach Jesus Christ. They did not cease, and sometimes we have trouble starting. We must develop the passion for souls, the love for the lost that can only originate with God.

You see, they knew the secret. Victory was certain, and problems were few. It was truly a conquering church. We are each one either a problem or a solution to our local church body. Let us each, from this moment on, determine to be part of the solution.

The prescription of the early church, consistently followed, will change problems into solutions. Let's all take this prescription today, for the sake of the Body of Christ, and for the sake of those whom we are to reach!

Oh, Dear Father God, I desire to be a fully functioning part of Your Body. And so, Lord, I ask that You would ignite that passion in me to see others come to know You. Help me to be a blessing to my local body, and an encouragement to its leaders, for your sake. Amen.

September 18   Tabernacle of Faith

Scripture: Exodus Chapter 25

Key Verse: "There I will meet with you, and I will speak with you from above the mercy seat, from between the two cherubim which are on the ark of the Testimony, about everything which I will give you in commandment to the children of Israel."
Exodus 25:22

To the Israelites, the tabernacle was the sign of settling down, dwelling in the land. It was the dwelling place of the Lord, a final stop after much moving and a long pilgrimage. This tabernacle was given to a chosen people at a chosen time and a chosen place.

This was a people delivered by the direct intervention of omnipotent Jehovah. The tabernacle was given so that God might dwell among His people, that He might evidence His oneness with them. He met their needs, and He demanded holiness in their lives. The tabernacle taught Israel the holiness of God, revealing by contrast their sinfulness and need of Him.

Now, in II Timothy 3 we are told that all Scripture is profitable. It is profitable for teaching, for reproof, for correction and instruction. We also know from God's Word that what was written before was written for our learning. This passage is no exception. It is rich with meaning. The tabernacle has been described as a type of both Christ and also of the Church as a habitation of God. We learn the importance of attention to detail in the work God gives. We learn that all true giving springs from recognition of stewardship and a personal consecration to the Lord.

In the construction of the tabernacle, we find that God was the architect. He had His own plan for the building, which he made known to Moses on the mount. God was explicit, precise, definite, and complete in his instructions on how to build His dwelling place. We are told exactly how and of what the tabernacle was built. It was of simple design and construction, yet of costly material, artistic grace and unparalleled beauty. There was a sense of majesty about the tabernacle, as is fitting for the first religious structure in which God condescended to dwell.

It is worth noting that God worked through the will of men. This is true in all of our Christian experience. As Israel built the tabernacle, the spirit of the people was thoroughly liberal and self-sacrificing. They were enthusiastic in their support, and obedient to God's instructions. Like the people of Nehemiah's day, the children of Israel had a mind to work.

Exodus tells us that God gifted Bezalel specifically for this ministry. Likewise, God gives specifically gifted people to the church today. When the church works in cooperation, allowing those with specific gifts to function in their roles, the result is truly astounding. But, Bezalel was not to rear up the tabernacle. The boards and bars and pillars were put into place by Moses' hands only, we read in Exodus 40. So, too, it is only the Lord that can set the members into the church today, as it pleases Him. Man is but the surrendered channel through which God the Holy Spirit works to build His church.

Like Israel, we long for rest, yet our souls can find no rest except in the presence of the Lord. As Israel rejoiced in the building of the tabernacle so that God might come to dwell among them, so we need to continually live in the presence of the Lord. In His presence are protection, guidance, love, and rest.

Dear Father, as I read over the details of the building of the tabernacle I am all the more thankful for the fact that You were willing to tabernacle with us yet again, in a body of flesh, that Your presence might always be with us, that Your forgiveness might be freely available to all who would believe. Amen.

September 19   The Angel That Goes Before You

Scripture Reading: Exodus Chapter 23

Key Verse: "Behold, I send an angel before you to keep you in the way and to bring you into the place which I have prepared." Ex. 23:20

You and I are travelers. We are strangers, pilgrims, and sojourners looking for a better country, a Heavenly one. We have come from God and we are going back to God. Our lives are made up of "goings out" and "coming ins". And during all of this, we are under the watchful care of God, "You are the God who sees."

Reason and argue as you may, as the years go by we are conscious that our days are computed, our career is mapped, and our way is ordered. "My times are in His hands," says the Psalmist. This day is yours with God from the rising of the sun till the going down thereof. And all through the watches of the night, He cares for you.

You are on your way toward tomorrow. You have been traveling toward this day, this year, since the hour you were born. Tomorrow may change your life's course and affect your very destiny. God knows. Will the way be rough, or smooth? Will the fare be plentiful or scant? What is that to you? Follow Him! The way may not be to your liking, but He will go before you. No plague can come near your soul's dwelling. Is there a cup of affliction before you? Well, it is only a cupful. Jesus your Lord drank His cup of the world's woes. Don't be afraid of your cup. Follow Him.

The plumage of the young swan is black, ugly, and dingy in color, but as it grows older it grows whiter. So you shall put aside the dusty robe of the pilgrim for another, a robe of splendor, for "He that overcomes shall be clothed in pure white." One day, as your earthly life was ready to begin, God's hand reached out and touched the pendulum of your heart and it began the millions of its beats. Someday, His finger will reach out and touch your heart again, and its beatings will be over. When? I know not, but you need not care! "To live is Christ, to die is gain."

When the enemies tried to take Jesus, they could not until He said, "Now my hour is come." So then, why should you worry? All is well. Now is your time to live your life that God has given, and live it to its fullest for Him.

Why did I awaken to live in this country and this century? I do not know, God knows. Why is my skin the color it is? I do not know, God knows. Why was I born in North America, instead of deepest Africa? I do not know. But, listen, what is that to me? What is that to you? Follow Him!

But say, my friend, you precious child of God on your way from earth to heaven, let not your heart be troubled. There is not a mile of your life's track, not a sharp turn of providence, not a stopping place that He hasn't gone ahead to provide for you. In your every tomorrow, He has been before you.

Yes, even though you must pass through the gloomy valley, "I will fear no evil for God is with me." You will come out of the darkness into the fields of living green, don't fear. Wait for Him. "I have gone to prepare a place for you," Jesus said.

Do your life's plans seem to go wrong? You can afford to wait on Him. Are answers to your prayers delayed? You can afford to wait on Him; your petitions are in the hands of a God who loves you and who knows your tomorrows. You can afford to wait.

Oh, God, waiting is so difficult. My flesh wants to be in control, but my spirit knows I must lie still on the Potter's wheel, as You shape me like the Potter shapes the clay. Help me not to wriggle under Your hand, Lord, but to wait. Amen.

September 20   Door Number One?

Scripture Reading: Deuteronomy Chapter 30

Key verse: "That you may love the Lord your God, that you may obey His voice, and that you may cling to Him, for He is your life and the length of your days . . . ." Deuteronomy 30:20

Our lives are, to a great extent, the sum of our choices. Each day presents us with choices large and small, of little import or of immense, life-changing importance. The Scriptures give us clear guidelines for every choice we face, especially for the ones that affect our lives the most. God's desire is that we choose wisely so that we might have the abundant, full, life of blessing that He designed for us, now and for eternity.

We are affected by our environment; Jesus was also affected by His. He wept in sympathy with Mary and Martha and over Jerusalem. But it is one thing to be moved by events and it is another to be mastered by them. Even in the shadow of the cross our Lord said, "Be of good cheer, I have overcome the world." A peace, a joy so secure, can come only to those who are initiated into the secrets of the Kingdom of God.

When a person submits to God's sovereignty and seeks to minister, rather than be ministered unto, many of the anxieties about rewards or recognition disappear and many petty insults and criticisms lose their sting. The man or woman who walks with God, his mind on high thoughts, never worries about keeping up appearances, "He shall hide me in His pavilion; in the secret place of His tabernacle He shall hide me."

Furthermore, Christ-like contentment is above the reach of physical ailment. As a healer, Jesus knew of bodily pain. He did not ignore the body; he mastered it. His followers found the power whereby they could say, "discipline my body and bring it into subjection."

I made the acquaintance of a blind man and I could hardly have told he was blind by anything he said or by the expressions on his face. In fact I found myself thinking, "Is it true? Is he really blind?" He would say, "Yes, I see . . . now, I want to see the church yard, and then let's see your rabbits." And I took him around looking at these things. Well, I found out that he had made up his mind that his blindness should not affect his spirits. His whole attitude revealed a triumph over what others called a tragedy. He is one of a mighty host who have found through their faith, a peace and power that physical ills could not shatter.

Still further, this higher happiness has a security that withstands the ravages of time. Worldly achievement or fortune does not insure happiness. Cecil Rhodes was met by one of our American statesmen, who congratulated the empire-builder of South Africa on his success. "You ought to be happy," said the American. "Happy?" cried Cecil Rhodes, "Good Lord, no! I spent a life amassing a fortune only to find that now I have to spend it all, half on doctors to keep me out of the grave, and half on lawyers to keep me out of jail."

When we get right with God by submitting to His sovereignty, we begin to lay up treasures in His kingdom "where neither moth nor rust destroys." We have what time or circumstance cannot take away, the peace of God which passes all understanding. Surely here is the call of life. It is the call of a choice; the same choice offered thousands of years ago by God to Moses and the children of Israel. Will we choose life and God or death and evil? Let us choose life.

Almighty Lord, You are the unchanging One. We can rest secure in the knowledge of Your love and provision for us. Time and circumstance are not Your master; may they also not be mine. Amen.

September 21   Spiritual Breathing

Scripture: Jude 1:20-25

Key Verse: "But you, beloved, building yourselves up on your most holy faith, praying in the Holy Spirit." Jude 1:20

In addition to good, suitable and regular food, the body requires pure atmosphere in order to have a healthy and vigorous life. So in the spiritual life a Christian must have both the food of God's Word and also the pure atmosphere of prayer if it is to be thoroughly healthy, strong and true.

Let us consider some of the aspects of prayer as the Christian's vital breath and native air. Breathing is the function of a healthy natural life. It is a spontaneous, unconscious, incessant act and habit, and marks the person as in normal health and vigor. So also if the spiritual life is healthy, prayer will be the natural spontaneous and unceasing expression of it. This is continuance in prayer.

What does that mean? Continuance includes the idea of clinging closely to and remaining constant in. It implies continuous devotion, and expresses itself in steadfastness and earnestness. It is more than frequently recurring times of prayer because prayer is something vastly beyond the utterance of words. It is the relation and constant attitude of the soul to God. This attitude towards God consists of several elements including submission, desire, trust, and fellowship.

What does it do? Continuance in prayer makes God's presence real. This presence brings peace which calms the soul in the presence of danger. It brings joy which cheers the soul in the pathway of difficulty and duty. It brings glory which illuminates the ordinary task and soul with the light of Heaven. It makes God's power very manifest. The heart is guarded against sin. The soul is therefore armed against temptation. It makes God's will clear. We learn to understand the guidance and providence of God, to perceive what things we ought to do and have grace and power faithfully bestowed to fulfill those things. It makes God's service easy. We are strengthened with all might according to

His glorious power. His calls are readily met because we are prepared. His yoke is easy, His burden light.

What does continuance in prayer require? We must honor the Holy Spirit of God. The Spirit of God is the source, the atmosphere, the power of prayer. We must meditate on the Word, the food of the Scriptures. All true prayer must be based on, warranted by and saturated with the Word of God. We must include prayer for others, for intercession is a prominent part of every real prayer. The life is fed by staying in the presence of God in prayer. It is this continuing presence that is the reservoir, the surrounding pool of daily power and progress.

The supreme object of prayer is not the attainment of some desire, but rather it is to know God. Knowing God we know His purposes, and knowing His purposes we desire them above our own. And, desiring His purposes, it then becomes safe for God to entrust us with His power.

But God will not give us power for unworthy purposes. Suppose you walked into a room where Jesus was sitting, what would you do? Would you hand Him a list of the things you wanted, as children do to Santa? Would you ask Him the explanation of a dozen problems you have been unable to solve? No, you would fall on your knees. You would kiss the hem of His garment, and being with Him, all your desires would be satisfied. That is where we are when we are in fellowship with God through continuance in prayer.

Dear Father, I desire to remain in Your presence throughout my day through continual prayer. Amen.

September 22

Compromise and Consecration

Scripture: II Corinthians Chapter 6

Key Verse: "Do not be unequally yoked together with unbelievers." II Corinthians 6:14

When we speak of Egypt as the type of the world, we think of the world which challenges the admiration, dominates the thought, inspires the desires, entices the indulgence and corrupts the nature of its people. It is a place where ethics are substituted for spiritual life, where humanitarianism takes the place of spiritual religion and where, indeed, man is deified and God is humanized.

Israel is the Child of God in type. Now the Child of God is opposed by Egypt, held in bondage, oppressed, and expected to serve its interests. From such bondage, it can only be delivered by the hand of God.

And the illustration continues with Pharaoh as a type of the Devil. He claims the right to control man and to receive his homage. He undertakes to put his will into the hearts of men against God's will. God is calling, calling his people out of Egyptian bondage. Satan is opposing their deliverance. As it was then, so it is today.

This then is the demand of God: separation, holiness, fellowship. Our response is the presenting of our bodies as a living sacrifice, for we are bought with a price.

Satan has an immediate and equally imperative response, typified in the reply of Pharaoh to Moses. "Who is the Lord, that I should obey His voice and let Israel go?" Intimating: "You cannot go to serve God. I am the god of this world. You must serve me. I am the god of society. Without me you must suffer ostracism, no success, no progress, no friends." Oh how the Devil would hold you back. Satan will surrender ground, but he will never surrender souls.

Another device is for him to say "If you must serve God, do it tomorrow, think it over, wait." Let our voices say "I hear the voice of God and I obey, now!"

Then the Pharaoh says "Serve God yourself, but leave your children. Go by yourself. Leave your flocks and herds." But listen to Moses. "Not a hoof shall be left behind."

The world will not tolerate the presence of a man whose life is wholly surrendered to God. And so Pharaoh kicks Moses out and says to him as the world says to you and me, "Take your flocks and your herds . . . and be gone." Happy is that man, for God is with him.

Holiness is entire separation unto God. It is a matter of relationship to Him. Righteousness is a matter of conduct. Holiness has been defined as the attitude of the will in which Jesus Christ is supreme.

Thus Paul says to the Corinthians, "I have betrothed you to one husband." A perfect wife is one who abides in the perfection of the marriage relationship. She may neglect her duties, burn her bread, forget to patch the socks, but she is no less his wife. So the soul married to Christ must be absolute in that relationship. There can be no compromise.

God said, "I will take you as My people and I will be your God." Therefore, yield yourself to Him. Come out into the open. Serve Him. Forsake the old affiliations. Become a new creature with new allegiance, new law of life, new Lord, new home, and new inheritance. For our inheritance is reserved for us in heaven.

Separate yourselves from the world, from the clutches of Pharaoh, as individual believers, His witnesses to shine as lights in the world, holding forth the word of life.

Almighty Lord, help me cross the sea on dry land as I separate to you as the bride separates to her husband. Amen.

September 23   Beginning in Philippi

Scripture Reading: Acts Chapter 16

Key Verse: "Now a certain woman named Lydia heard us . . . The Lord opened her heart." Acts 16:14

Philippi was a Roman colony, eight miles in from Neapolis and a major commercial city in Macedonia. Paul was now near to the center of earthly government. Little did Rome realize that the army of its ultimate conqueror had taken possession of its frontal defenses.

The eventual conquest of Rome for Christ began with the story of a woman, Lydia of Thyatira. On the Sabbath Day in places where there was no temple, religious Jews customarily would meet in a place of prayer. On this Sabbath Day, Paul and those with him went to the place of prayer in Philippi, which was on the river. A little group of women who recognized their relation to God gathered there, just outside of this city of idolatry under Roman rule, and Lydia was among them.

The first convert in Europe was made here, a woman of Asia, a Jewish proselyte and a businesswoman. Lydia's heart is touched and opened to the Lord, constraining the apostles to accept her hospitality. Later, Paul mentions in Philippians that the Church at Philippi was most dear to him, his chief joy and crown of his ministry.

Looking at this little group, meeting on a riverbank, we see the small beginnings of great movements embodied. One woman's heart is opened and how wonderful the victories which followed. Don't ever despise the day of small things, friend. God was acting and working in the heart of this willing woman toward a victory that would sway an empire. One heart in Philippi was opened, and Rome was doomed to lower its flag that the banner of the Cross might be supreme.

Thus Paul's work in Europe began. And, now, look at Europe today. In spite of all its spiritual desolation, in spite of its post-modern philosophies and post-Christian society, we see the testimony of Christ. Think of her architecture. The soaring buttresses of a hundred cathedrals support the stained glass gospel displayed for all to see and believe. In the galleries of her greatest museums are displayed countless paintings inspired by Christ and the Scriptures. Examine her literature and see what has been made possible because of Paul's faithfulness in small things. The poems of Chaucer, Spencer, Donne, and Milton, the prose of Bunyan and so many others all stand as mute testimony to the presence of the gospel in this land.

But, it does not end there, my friend. From yet another small band of believers, facing incredible odds with only the conviction of their beliefs and the confidence of His guidance, England sent out the seed of the gospel to another. A daughter nation was born; a seedling, fledgling government sprung from the faith of her mother's heart. The United State of America owes its Christian beginnings to the same humble roots of Lydia's faith in Philippi.

Do you ever wonder at the sheer odds of it? Does the number of those following the narrow way seem to pale in the face of the hostility of those who command the broad way? Do not despair. Do the numbers grow thin? Do not falter. God is able. On a riverbank just outside of Philippi, He began a mighty work that spread throughout an empire, then a continent, and finally to shores across the sea. But he began with just one heart.

Dear Father God, what an encouragement Lydia is to my soul. I pray that You would find a welcome foothold in my heart, Lord, from which to reach out to the world today. In Jesus' name, and for His sake, amen.

September 24 The Hardest Word

Scripture Reading: Genesis Chapter 39
Key Verse: "But he refused . . . ." Genesis 39:8

What is the word which lays a foundation upon which to build character? What is the word that in the great crises of the life of Jesus Christ, He pronounced to conquer Satan?

That word, the hardest in the Bible or out of it, the hardest in English, French, Spanish, Arabic, or any other language, is the short but mighty word, "No."

The difficulty of saying "no" has made men slaves to others and still worse, slaves to their own passions and fears. For the lack of a "no" spoken to the tempter, man fell in the beginning and millions have fallen since.

Adam was a great man. He must have been a notable lexicographer, a master of vocabulary; for we are told that he was able to give names to all the birds of the air and beasts of the field. But Adam was not able to pronounce the most useful, most difficult word in human speech, "no."

Let us look at Joseph and his forceful "no." After the temptation of Christ Himself, Joseph's is the most celebrated story of temptation in the Bible. Joseph's temptation was unusually strong because of the person of the tempter.

He was young; she was a woman of rank, beauty and fashion. Physically, it was undoubtedly a strong temptation. But it was also a strong temptation because she tempted him day after day. Constantly, he was under this temptation, yet he repulsed it.

Also, Joseph was in a foreign land, where his values were not understood. It would have been very easy to excuse giving in to this lovely tempter. Yet Joseph met this temptation with a magnificent "no." He refused.

He suffered and lost everything the world counts precious, but he held onto his character and to God. And God, as the Scriptures tell us, kept hold of him. It was because of this integrity in Joseph that God was able to use him as an agent of deliverance from starvation for the embryonic House of Israel.

Joseph's is not the only wonderful "no" in the Bible. Remember Shadrach, Meshach and Abednego? Daniel's three friends refused to bow down in worship to the golden image that the king had set up. These Hebrew lads had been brought up on the Second Commandment, "You shall not make any graven image. You shall not bow down to them, nor serve them." Therefore, they refused to prostrate themselves. The king's wrath landed them in a furnace, but God rewarded their fidelity by a great deliverance. They stood up for their convictions. Do I?

And what of Christ? There were three memorable occasions when Jesus said, "no." The first was when the devil tempted Him in the wilderness and thrice tried to sway Him from His mission. The second "no" came in the Garden of Gethsemane, when Satan again tried to turn Him from Calvary. The third and last time was when the mob at Calvary mocked Him, calling out, "If You are the Christ, the Son of God, come down from the cross. Save Yourself and us." Jesus' answer was no, except He said, "It is finished." Satan was finished.

Christ told us that the great business of His followers is to say "no." We are to deny ourselves, take up the cross, and say "no" to the world as we follow Him.

Dearest Jesus, help me to turn my back on the alluring calls of the world, and set my sights firmly on You. Strengthen my resolve, dear Lord, to live a life that is pleasing to You in every aspect. Help me say "no" to the world, in order that I can say "yes" to You. In Jesus' name, amen.

September 25   The Heroic Highwayman

Suggested Reading: Luke Chapter 23

Key Verse: "Lord, remember me when you come into your kingdom." Luke 23:42

The man who prayed this prayer was a highway robber. Even then he was dying the death of a rebel and of a murderer, yet I believe you will agree with me that this highwayman was no ordinary man.

Look at the situation. It was a holiday in Jerusalem some nineteen centuries ago. Rome was going to execute three prisoners. She would let her subjects see what it is to rebel. The crowd was more eager to see this show because the three men who were to die were well known. Two of them were highwaymen. They were not unpopular men, even looked upon as heroes.

The other man who was to die came into prominence in an altogether different way. He preached in their synagogues, taught in their temples, touched lepers into purity. He opened the eyes of the blind, raised the dead to life and proved himself a leader and teacher of great power. For this reason, some loved Him with a love stronger than death, while others hated him with a hatred that would not endure His being on earth. His name is Jesus.

Then, upon a skull-shaped hill outside the city gates, the victims were stretched upon the cross. There was the spraying of blood, the tearing of flesh, the straining of tendons, then these trees, so lately planted, stood laden with their fruit of infinite pain.

The soldiers made themselves comfortable at the foot of the cross with their drink and their dice, for death by crucifixion is such a slow-footed monster that they must amuse themselves while their victims die. Can you hear the jeers and scorn of the crowd? To the amazement of two of these sufferers, the one to whom the reviling was directed did not reply at all, but cried out a protecting prayer. "Father forgive them, for they do not know what they do."

Now the scene that will soften one heart will often harden another.

Two men hearing the same sermon and one's heart is broken and the other is only made harder. This was the case of the two robbers. One seems maddened and railed on Jesus. The other turned to the hardened robber and said "We receive the due reward of our deeds, but this Man has done nothing wrong."

Look at the insight and daring of that statement. Rome declared Jesus guilty. The religious leaders, the mob, the graybeards of the church declared him guilty. But all these could not disguise from this discerning man the truth. It stole into his heart, an absolute conviction of the purity of this man who was dying at his side, and he saw himself sin stained and rushing toward death. He reached out his hand for help in this wonderful prayer. "Lord, remember me when You come into Your kingdom."

Did Jesus hear this heroic prayer? Did He listen to this man's dying plea? Yes! "Assuredly I say to you, today you will be with Me in Paradise."

How long does it take God to save a man? How long to snap the fetters and set him free? How long before a man is clean and unspotted in His sight? The answer is: It may be done instantly. In the quickness of a lightning flash I may be reborn, today, immediately, now. The robber is with Christ now and He will be with Him forevermore. He is no more a robber, but a new creation. Thanks be to God who loves us and longs for us to be with Him eternally.

Lord God Almighty, thank You for sending Your Son to show me the way. How can I resist the loving acceptance You show to all who turn to You? Amen.

September 26   Mount Ararat

Scripture Reading: Psalm 121

Key Verse: "I will lift up my eyes to the hills - from whence comes my help? My help comes from the Lord, who made heaven and earth." Psalm 121:1-2

On a summer vacation trip a few years ago, my family and I passed through twenty-five states by car. One of the great experiences given us was crossing over so many noted mountains including the Rockies, Alleghenies, Smokies, Blue Ridge and others. Naturally, my mind turned to the Bible. I thought of Mt. Moriah, with Abraham climbing up to sacrifice his son of promise, Isaac. Mt. Gilead, Mt. Calvary, Mt. Zion and others often filled our minds as we explored our own mountain ranges. But, no other mountain filled our thoughts as much as Mt. Ararat.

Mt. Ararat will forever be associated with Noah and the great act of judgment of the flood. As Ararat rises above all the mountains of the Bible so, standing upon its summit, we can survey the whole panorama of divine revelation which reaches its climax in the coming of Christ and the mercy of God as revealed at Calvary.

The first timeless truth we discern is that God is a God of righteousness and that judgment and punishment follow sin. It is recorded, "The Lord saw the wickedness of man was great in the earth and that every intent of the thoughts of his heart was only evil continually." It was this state of man which brought the flood upon the earth, a judgment which inflicted God's punishments but also, by purging away a corrupt generation, prepared the way for the coming generations.

We see such things on a local or national basis occasionally. Abraham Lincoln said, in his second Inaugural Address:

"Fondly do we hope, fervently do we pray that this mighty scourge of war may speedily pass away, yet if God will that it continue until all the wealth piled up by the bondman's 250 years of unrequited toil shall be sunk, until every drop of blood drawn with the lash shall be paid by another drawn with the sword, as was said 3,000 years ago, so still it must be said, 'The judgments of the Lord are true and righteous altogether.'"

The Civil War shed more men's lives than any other war in the history of this nation, but the flood the Lord sent in Noah's day was to punish and judge all of humanity.

The second truth which we discern from Ararat's lofty summit is the truth of God's goodness and mercy. God discerned the heart of Noah was right toward God and did not neglect this one in the face of the overwhelming stench of evil. No, God spoke to Noah and used him as a tool to save both a remnant of mankind, Noah's own family, and a remnant of the created animal kingdom. God will preserve His own today as well.

In Noah, who walked out of that ark on Ararat's peak, we meet the kind of man God can use for His great and wise purposes. In the first place, Noah was a godly man. Noah was distinguished by his courage and faith. Picture the discouragement of constant mocking through 120 years of preparing the ark, yet Noah did not swerve from his course of obedience. Such is the man through which God preserved the world. He still works through godly, courageous and believing men. We too can serve the cause of righteousness, if we will obey His voice and do His will.

Dear Father, give me courage, faith, and the will to obey Your Word today and every day. For Your Glory I ask it, Amen.

September 27

Israel in the Light of Prophecy

Scripture Reading: Isaiah Chapter 35

Key Verse: "And the ransomed of the Lord shall return, and come to Zion with singing, with everlasting joy on their heads. They shall obtain joy and gladness, and sorrow and sighing shall flee away." Isaiah 35:10

The present plight of the Israelites is a most unhappy one. They are beset on every hand by enemies. However, in 1948 there happened an event of world importance. It is perhaps the most significant prophetic event of the past 2,000 years. That event was the coming into being of the State of Israel. For the first time in 2500 years the Jewish people are gathered into a nation. For the first time they have a government and are able to fly the Jewish flag of white and blue with the star of David on it. And for the first time in 2,000 years the orthodox Jews are filled with a longing for their Messiah.

We Gentiles ought to be greatly stirred. Remember, Jesus said, "Now learn this parable from the fig tree: When its branch has already become tender and puts forth leaves, you know that summer is near. So you also, when you see all these things, know that it is near, at the doors."

If this is the birth pang of the Jewish Nation, and if this is the beginning of their prophesied return to Palestine, if this is indeed the budding forth of the fig tree, then mark it well, the Israelites are in for a time of great trouble. The world is also in for a time of great sorrow. We can look for World War III, the ten-toed confederacy and the coming back of our Lord and Savior to catch His bride away.

It is the preparation for the Day of the Lord, the end of the days of the Gentiles and the beginning of the clock of Israel, which according to Daniel 9:24 must tick again for seven years.

What was the purpose in the first place in the mind of God when He formed Israel? He designed that Israel should be a repository for His truth in the earth, a channel for the incoming of a personal redeemer, and a national witness to Himself before the other nations of the earth.

History shows that the first two have been fulfilled while the third has only partly been fulfilled. Now I say to you that the Lord has a glorious future for the Jewish people, proven by God's covenants, which cannot be annulled. If the church is the Bride of Christ, remember Israel is the wife of Jehovah. Read the book of Hosea for a true prophetic picture of Israel and God's love for her.

Some question whether Israel has any right to Palestine. In Genesis 12:7 we read, "To your descendants I will give this land." Genesis 13:15, "All the land which you see to you and your descendants forever." God has indeed given the children of Israel the title deed to this land, and woe to any who try to supersede the word of the Lord.

They have the pledge of God for this land, so that they might return there to suffer Jacob's trouble, and then to accept their Messiah who will sit upon the throne of David and rule with a rod of iron.

How can we apply these truths to our lives? How can we honor and support what God is doing in the panorama of history in and through the Jewish nation? Let us wholeheartedly obey His simple command. "Pray for the peace of Jerusalem, may they prosper who love you." And let us remember the promise that "He that blesses you, I will bless."

Almighty and Wonderful God, thank You that I am seeing what people have longed to see for thousands of years, the unfolding of the prophecies of the last days. I do pray now, for the peace of Jerusalem. May Your will be done. Amen.

178

Scripture Reading: Mark Chapter 1

Key Verse: "And as He walked by the Sea of Galilee, He saw Simon and Andrew his brother casting a net into the sea; for they were fishermen." Mark 1:16

Had Andrew, brother of Simon Peter, not performed certain non-spectacular services, he would have done nothing. Had he not been willing to be just Andrew, neither his name nor his place in life would have been important. However, Andrew is very important to us, because most people find themselves in likeness to him more than to most other folks who populate the Bible. Not many possess the dynamics of Peter, nor the brilliance of Paul, nor the oratory of Apollo. No, most of us more resemble Andrew.

Andrew was a follower. He did not despair because he did not have the gifts of his brother. He did not quit because he was not great. He did what he was capable of doing.

There is a mistaken notion among many of God's people that when the Holy Spirit fully and completely controls us, we are going to do auspicious things. This is not necessarily true, for each of us has his place in the Body of Christ. As Paul taught in 1 Corinthians 12, not all have the same office in the church. Did it ever occur to you that not all of the twelve apostles were equally famous? Each had his place, but their places were not equally visible to the world.

Now Andrew suffered what might be termed the misfortune of being Simon Peter's brother. Yet, we must not forget that had it not been for Andrew, who brought Peter to Christ according to the gospel of John, Peter would never have been known to us. Having brought Peter to Christ, Andrew was largely eclipsed by his brother's prominence. He was not among those who went with Jesus to Gethsemane, or to the Mount of Transfiguration. He was not chosen to be the spokesman for the Christians at Pentecost.

Yet, Andrew did not allow a feeling of insignificance to take hold. If he had, Andrew would have lost the usefulness God intended him to have in his own right. While Andrew did not have Peter's gifts, he had his own. He became an introducer. Three times we see Andrew introducing someone to Jesus. What Andrew could do, he did with great faithfulness and success as the record of his service reveals.

Yes, Peter could move multitudes, but it was Andrew who moved Peter. Barely a believer himself, Andrew set out to tell others.

And again, at the feeding of the five thousand, we find Andrew making introductions between a lad with a small lunch and Jesus. Andrew knew it was neither the lad nor the lunch that could save the situation, but what the Lord could do with the lad's yielded lunch.

And finally, we see Andrew with Philip bringing some inquiring Gentiles before Jesus just before the shadow of the cross falls across His path.

Andrew's conquest lay in the realm of willingness to be who and what he was.

He did not try to be his brother, nor did he despise being what he could be and doing what he could do.

Remember, rewards are for faithfulness and not for fame. They are for service, and not for so-called success. May God grant us the attitude of Andrew.

Dearest Father, Strengthen me to be faithful, brace me for service in the part of the Body in which I find myself placed, and inspire me to be what You designed me to be. Like Andrew, grant me boldness to simply tell others what I have found in Christ. Amen.

September 29   Do We Need the Church?

Scripture Reading: Acts Chapter 20

Key Verse: ". . . the church of God which He purchased with His own blood." Acts 20:28

There are multitudes of church members who feel no thrill when words like this are read in their hearing. They do not believe that the church has any exalted claims upon their loyalty or their love.

Christ died for us who are not perfect, and what is the church but the sum of all of us? Despite her faults and weaknesses, the church is necessary to your best life and worthy of your loyalty, your love, and your loftiest service.

The outstanding representatives of Christianity, the genuine prophets of the Christian era, have treated the church with peculiar reverence. Take Paul as an example. He was intense in his personal Christian life, had profound insight into the needs of men, yet his attitude expresses amply that his Christian experience was not for himself alone. It was to be enjoyed in a fellowship that included rich and poor, learned and ignorant, advanced and backward. And so, he became an organizer of churches.

Wesley, Booth, Augustine, and Williams, all substantiate in their writings that the history of Christianity is for some reason the story of an organized movement of the church. Consider the relation of the church to the Lord Jesus. He founded it and gave it its truths, forces, and ideals. His personal position as the Head of the Church gives it its foundation as the core of His work and His purpose, the Great Commission. They of like faith drew together naturally for the love of the founder of the Church that drew men to Him, drew them to one another.

You see, beloved, if men and women content themselves with a life apart from the Body, it is because they lack something that was powerfully present in the experience of the first disciples and later church leaders.

To quote from Wesley's diary, "The Bible knows nothing of a solitary religion." Your life needs the church and the church needs you. As you contribute your life to God through her, she will be strengthened. As you give your devotion to God, her love will be purified. And as you give your energies and enthusiasm, she shall be enlarged.

We say "my church" as we say my family, my home, my wife. I can meet with other Christians in united service, in great worship gatherings, or forward movements of the church, but my love, my service, my time and money must be given to my own. It is where my church family meets to worship God and love each other, where the Holy Spirit brings power and unity for the progress of the Gospel.

We have been providentially placed under the care and nurture of our local body. It offers me more work than I can do, more privileges than I can attain, more blessings than I can enjoy.

The church cannot live without power, so I must become a Spirit-filled Christian and pray that the Holy Spirit descend upon it that it may become a church after God's own heart; a church of passion, and of power, a church with the Shepherd's heart, full of the love of God, on fire for souls and victorious over sin.

Dear Lord, sometimes I diminish the importance of the church in my life and find excuses for not being faithful. Let me follow the example of Christ and regard the church with the reverence and importance it deserves. Amen.

September 30   It is Time

Scripture Reading: Hosea Chapter 10

Key Verse: "Sow for yourselves righteousness; reap in mercy; break up your fallow ground, for it is time to seek the Lord, till He comes and rains righteousness on you." Hosea 10:12

It is time. The Scriptures say, "You will seek the Lord Your God, and you will find Him if you seek Him with all your heart and soul." And it is knee-time in our world today. It is time to seek the Lord.

Hosea tells us very practically how we may accomplish this seeking after the Lord. If the Lord is to rain righteousness upon us, we must prepare the soil of our hearts. God will not waste His rain upon briars and thorns and weeds. Fallow ground is unproductive ground. Do you know why? Yes, that's it; it is because it is undisturbed.

And that is a great deal of our trouble today. Unless we allow our hearts to be stirred with the plow of conviction and brought to the place of repentance, they grow hard and become covered with weeds and thorns, crowding out God with the cares of this world. So there is a preparation that we must make in our own hearts before God will send rain.

The season of refreshing sent from the Savior will come when we get right with one another and with God. God will give the increase and the crop will come, but we have some farming to do first, my friends. No farmer can ever raise a crop without disturbing and preparing the soil, planting the seed, cultivating and irrigating the soil.

We must first investigate ourselves and take stock; make an inventory of our priorities and our heart for the Lord. Then, we must put in the plow to break up the soil. Pray with earnestness for the Lord to reveal any area in your life in which He would like to disturb the soil a bit. He will surely be faithful to show you. Is there a misunderstanding? Is there lack in a relationship? Go and seek reconciliation. Forgive that grudge that you have been harboring, and make restitution for any error you have committed against another. Acknowledge your pride, accept criticism with kindness, and remove any ill-feeling. "As much as it depends on you, live peaceably with all men."

Breaking up the ground is hard work, beloved. It requires effort and sacrifice. But like the farmer who sweats throughout the day to cultivate his fields, we can be assured that the resulting harvest will make our hard work worth the price.

While you are cultivating, try also to kill the weeds of worldliness that want to creep in around the edge of your field. Our hearts are exposed to so much of the world, in all the media surrounding us. Make sure that you have not allowed compromise to sneak into your life undetected. Take it before the Lord, beloved. Is that show you so favor one of the pure, lovely, and noble things Paul recommends you think on? Is that music really drawing you closer to Him?

God's time is now, beloved. Now is the time to break up the fallow ground. Now is the time to sow righteousness and prepare to receive the showers of His rain.

And when the showers come, you will reap joy indescribable which comes from an abundant spiritual life. You will reap joy that will change your want into wealth, timidity into courage, weakness into strength, and pessimism into glowing hope. It is surely time.

Father, please help me accept and deal with the weeds in the soil of my heart. Strengthen me with Your Spirit, Father, and please send the rain of righteousness down on me. Amen.

Classic Christianity
A Year of Timeless Devotions

AUTUMN
Daily Devotions for October,
November, and December

Based on the Writings of
The Reverend L.A. Meade

Revised and Edited by
Patricia Ediger and Cara Shelton

The Rev. Lawrence A. Meade

1917
Grand Ledge, MI

1928
With Mrs. Meade

1962
Bakersfield, CA

As the Rev. Meade began his second ministry, that of pastoring individual churches, God began to develop a new gift in him. His vision for reaching communities for Jesus, for expanding and extending the reach of the gospel through God's people, lead him to seek out churches ready to grow and step out in faith in order to follow God's plan to reach their city.

He continued faithfully ministering for the Lord until 1962, when sudden illness forced him into retirement. After a year's rest, however, Lawrence found himself once again looking for a way to be active in service to his Heavenly Father. Soon, he heard of a small group of believers in a town not far away. They wanted to form a church, in a community sorely needing one. Were they willing to step out on faith, to embrace a big vision? Yes, they were.

And so, at 70 years of age, the Rev. and Mrs. Meade packed up and moved again. They arrived in Lake Isabella to find a small but sincere group of believers ready to work hard and desiring to reach their town for the Lord. The first thing they would need would be temporary facilities from which the church could evangelize, and where they could meet on Sunday mornings. When the owner of the local bar was first approached, he was a bit surprised. But, soon the Baptist Church was meeting, and growing, in the bar. In three years, the church had a building of its own, and was regularly filled to its 200 person capacity. During this last pastorate, the Rev. Meade celebrated fifty years of active service in the ministry. In 1965, health issues once again caused him to retire.

In 1971, just as he was welcomed back by Pleasant Valley Baptist Church as Pastor Emeritus, our Papa was called home to heaven. It is not an exaggeration to say that God used Papa as the means for thousands to come into the Kingdom, and many, many more to find their way back to Him. Papa was a modest, friendly servant of the Lord, and we can almost hear the Savior say, "Well done, thou good and faithful servant. Enter into the joys of thy Lord." We miss his booming baritone whenever a good rousing hymn is sung, his agile wit and amazing memory, and his bold example of Christian living. Thank you, Papa.

October 1 The Man Who Was No Good

Scripture: Philemon Chapter I

Key Verse: ". . . who once was unprofitable to you." Philemon 1:11

A good many years ago in the city of Colossae there lived a young chap who dreamed dreams just as you or I. Tradition says he was sold into slavery because of debt, and he soon became so wretched that he decided to make a break for liberty. So, one night he slipped out of the slaves' quarters and into his master's room where he armed himself with his master's gold. Thus armed, he stole out through the window, hugged the deepest shadows and made for the open country, then for the anonymity of Rome.

One night, I imagine, a stranger out of whose eyes looked the peace of a great discovery, watched the haunted young man. To test him, he made on the dust of the pavement the sign of a fish which was a password among the early Christians. The young chap understood at once and it half angered him. "No, no," he replied. "I'm not a Christian."

"I am sorry you are not. But I have a friend in town I would be glad for you to meet. He's a much traveled man. His feet mark all the Roman roads. He's a fighting man. There isn't a square inch of his body that does not wear a scar. And he's a very learned man. You could rub enough learning off his coat sleeve to make you a scholar. However, I'm sorry to tell you that he is in jail just at this time, but if you care to meet him I will be glad to introduce you."

Therefore a few days later this runaway slave, partly because he was homesick but more because he was heartsick, went to see this man who since has become an acquaintance of all centuries. His friends knew him as Brother Paul. We know him as St. Paul. Soon Paul introduced this slave to Jesus Christ and the former slave became a Christian. A little later, in proof of the genuineness of his Christianity he showed up again at the jail. "Brother Paul," he said. "I am not what you think I am. I stole the money with which I came to Rome. Now that I have been converted don't you think I ought to go back and straighten matters up?"

Paul looked at him tenderly and said, "Yes! I think that would be fine. But remember, if you go back you might have to remain a slave the rest of your life."

"I have thought of that, but I would rather wear a ball and chain around my ankle than 'round my conscience."

"Good!" said the preacher, "But tell me your master's name that I might write him a letter that would help you."

"His name is Philemon. He lives in Colossae."

"I know him well," said Paul. Then, having written a brief note, he gave that note to this chap who had been notoriously no good. He gave it to a slave who had a thousand opportunities to duck down a back alley and forget it all, but this he refused to do. Therefore we can still read that letter in an old book called the Bible if we are so minded. This beautifully tender letter reaches its climax in these words, "I appeal to you for my son Onesimus, whom I have begotten while in my chains, who once was unprofitable to you, but now is profitable to you and to me."

We do not know what became of Onesimus, but of this one thing I am sure, he has enriched in some measure all the subsequent centuries. At this very hour he is reaching from that long-gone yesterday to put into our hands this priceless letter and he is telling us how we too may experience the transforming power of Christ. May we make his lesson ours.

Please transform me too, Lord. Amen.

October 2   The Gospel of God's Grace and Comfort

Scripture Reading: Isaiah Chapter 42

Key Verse: "A bruised reed He will not break, and smoking flax He will not quench; He will bring forth justice for truth. He will not fail nor be discouraged. Isaiah 42:3-4

To a careful reader of the prophecy of Isaiah, there is a change of message beginning with chapter 40. In the earlier chapters, we found messages of warning and judgment with an occasional word of hope. Beginning with chapter 40, we have messages full of assurance and hope with only an occasional glimpse of darker truth. In the first part of the book, Isaiah was addressing a heedless people headed for exile. Here, he writes to a people upon whom judgment has fallen making them humble and submissive. No wonder then that multitudes of the saints of God love quoting these chapters of Isaiah, for they are filled with comfort and strength for the weak and weary soul. The God of the Bible is the God of the weak, the humble. He has a partiality of kindness for those in need.

These two metaphors, the bruised reed and the smoking flax, are very suggestive of spiritual truth. Here is the picture: a slender reed, growing by the margin of some pond, has its sides crushed and dented in. The head is hanging by a thread, but it is not yet snapped or broken off from the stem. And the Master declares that He shall not break that reed. Then again, we have a little wick of flax put down into a pot of oil to form a light. The light has gone out, but the wick continues to burn, perhaps with more smoke than fire, yet there is a feeble spark remaining. The Master says He shall not quench this smoking flax.

In the case of the reed, we see Christ as the arrester of incipient ruin. The reed has suffered an injury which is neither complete, nor irreparable. In the reed, a process has begun which if continued would end in destruction. In the flax, however, a process has begun which if continued ends in a bright flame. In the reed, we see the beginnings of evil, which may still be averted, while in the flax we see the beginnings of incipient and incomplete good.

To all who are in need, whatever that need may be, this text comes with its great, triumphant hopefulness and gathers all into one mass. The most abject, the most ignorant, the most godless, are all capable of restoration. There are no hopeless outcasts to Christ, none beyond the Savior's reach of love and the healing, saving blood of Jesus.

Do these metaphors not suggest weakness? What is weaker than a broken reed, or a barely smoldering wick? Look at our lives in any way you wish and our weaknesses will be revealed. How weak we are in knowledge of Him. How weak we are in faith. How weak we are in gratitude, and how weak we are in resisting temptation. And, yet, He does not cast us out. Thank God that in His mercy, despite our weaknesses, He stands ready to encourage and stimulate and lead us on to victory in Him.

How long is this blessed preservation to last? The text says that He will faithfully bring forth justice. He will never fail. He is faithful. Just sit down this blessed day, and ponder this truth: Your Savior loves you. He cares. He cares enough to die to save you. He cares enough to keep you, protect and forgive you. And you can rest in His blessed name and eternal power. Soon, every knee will bow and every tongue confess His name which is above every name. Until then, He will faithfully bring forth justice.

Praise Your Holy Name, Lord. Thank You for Your unfailing mercies. Praise You for Your compassion, and Your gentleness. Amen.

October 3   My Grace

Scripture Reading: II Corinthians 12: 7-10

Key Verse: ". . . My grace is sufficient for you . . . ." II Corinthians 12:9

Many a man who cursed fate for some ugly thorn that has ripped his heart has discovered the true God through his calamity and afterwards given thanks for the gracious chastisement that saved his soul. God knows how foolishly our weak hearts cling to the seeming instead of the real, and it is well that we should learn to sing with Adelaide Proctor "Shadows fall on brightest hours and thorns remain, so that earth's bliss may be our guide and not our chain."

What Paul's thorn was is not explicitly divulged. Scripture exercises kind reserve here, so that all who are afflicted may share in the divine comfort which came to him. Paul begged that his thorn be removed. There is no hint that he complained. He prayed, and affliction should drive us to God, not from Him. Paul's prayer was definite and repeated. He says "Concerning this thing I pleaded with the Lord three times, that it might depart from me." Some pray for everything in general and get nothing in particular. Others call upon God but do not stay at Heaven's gate until the answer comes. Not so with Paul. His cry is urgent and persistent.

As in the garden, our Lord three times offered His agonizing prayer, and with sweat and anguish upon His brow, implores that this thing may be taken away. Yet, as the cup did not pass from Christ, so the thorn was not removed from Paul. Paul's prayer was truly and gloriously answered in a way which brought blessings otherwise impossible both to himself and millions of others. God said to Paul, "My grace is sufficient for you."

There have been times, perhaps, when some dire agony has wrung from our hearts the cry, "Does Jesus care? Why has this trouble come? Why has it not been removed?" He does indeed care. He is touched with the feeling of our infirmity.

"My grace is sufficient for you." What a sublime and satisfying answer. To have had the thorn removed was poor compared to having its presence sanctified. Paul wanted the thorn away, whereas Christ wanted to show how roses may be gathered of thorns. God's choicest flowers often bloom on bitter stems. It is a true paradox that God sometimes answers prayers by seeming to not answer them. He reads between the lines and sees the thing that is bigger than our words. Monica begged God that her son would not go to Rome with all its temptations, yet God allowed him to go and there in the very place which had been dreaded, young Augustine is converted to Christ. God not only answers prayers, He guides lives.

"My grace," how gloriously the grace of Christ shines from the pages of the New Testament. Gaze at the matchless character of Christ, then gaze at Calvary. See that triumph of self-sacrifice. No wonder John wrote, "we beheld His glory, the glory as of the only begotten of the Father, full of grace and truth." And that grace both by imputation and impartation may be mine.

"My grace," who but the absolutely divine Christ could say this? His grace is exhaustless, absolutely adequate and infallibly unfailing. Divine grace, in all its fullness, freshness and freeness gushes to us from that precious pronoun "My". Tomorrow we will explore the sufficiency of this wonderful grace.

Dearest Lord, thank You that no matter what I am going through today, Your grace is sufficient for me. Amen.

Scripture Reading: II Corinthians 12:7-10

Key Verse: "And He said to me, 'My grace is sufficient for you.'"
II Corinthians 12:9

God did not tell Paul that His grace was nearly enough, or over-abundantly enough, He said it was sufficient for him. The supply has exact correspondence with the need, never too much, never too little, but perfect adequacy. The grace is never too soon, never too late, but timed to the tick of the clock and to the beat of the heart.

Grace for tomorrow's need will never come today nor will grace for today come tomorrow. There is a story of an old-time martyr, a Christian in his cell awaiting the sunrise and burning at the stake. The prospect was terrible. How could he endure the ordeal? He picked up the candle and held his finger in the flame and with a gasp of pain he withdrew it. How could he possibly undergo the torture of his whole body? Yet at sunrise he went to his death with irrepressible exuberance. Amid the circling flames he testified to the all-sufficient grace of Christ and sang with a heavenly ecstasy shining on his face. When the real emergency came, sufficient grace was given to make him more than a conqueror

Moody was once asked if he had enough grace to be burned at the stake. Moody said, "No, for I do not need it. What I need just now is grace to live in Milwaukee for three days and hold a mission."

As the ceaseless rolling river, as the morning sun shoots its arrow of light, so through the ages in Him are fountains that never run dry, a sun that never languishes, an ocean that is ever full. His sufficiency is simply the expression toward us of His infinite fullness.

"For you." A bygone preacher has reverently dared the remark that there is a touch of beautiful ludicrousness in this text in the contrast between the first word and the last. "My grace," well there is absolute infinity; "for you," and there is the infinitesimal. As though the mighty ocean should say to the little laddie playing on the sand, "Little boy, my ocean depths are sufficient to fill your bucket." As though a tiny fish swimming in the Amazon should say, "I must not drink too much water lest I drain the river." Oh have no fear, burdened Christian, "His grace is sufficient for you," and not just for your present trial but for you, yourself, making you equal to all the trials that may come.

God does not pledge Himself to be ever-altering our circumstances and removing our burdens in answer to our prayers. Our truest blessings often come through the things that seem most grievous to us. Christ's way is to make us equal to our circumstances rather than reduce our circumstances to what we short-sightedly think they ought to be. Yes, pray for the removal of the trial. But more, be prepared to accept God's will and His blessing within His will. Trust Him. He will not just bring you through, He will lift you up.

Thorns and trials are blessings indeed if they bring the opportunity for the grace of Christ to perfect our character. Some flowers must be crushed before their full fragrance is released. Some metals must be flung into the fire before they reach full value and purity. So it is with saints. We must sometimes be laid low before we look high.

Dear Lord, take my trials, my circumstances, my present and my future, and use them to make me more like You. I trust that Your grace will be sufficient for me, too. You are truly all I need. I love You, my all-sufficient King, Amen.

Scripture Reading: II Corinthians 12: 7-10

Key Verse: "And He said to me, 'My grace is sufficient for you.'"
II Corinthians 12:9

Dr. Phillip Brooks says: "Do not pray for easy lives, pray to be stronger men. Do not pray for tasks equal to your power, pray for power equal to your tasks. Then the doing of your work shall be no miracle, but you shall be a miracle. Every day you shall wonder to yourself at the riches of life which have come to you by the grace of God."

Let us continue to study the last phrase of our text, "For you," for underneath all our care is Christ's care for us. Henry Moorehouse returned home one morning carrying a parcel, a present for his wife and was greeted by his little handicapped daughter. She asked that she might have the pleasure of carrying the present to the room where Mother was. "But you know dear, you cannot carry it," he said thinking of her weak state. "Give it to me and see," she challenged him. So the parcel was handed her and then she said "Now I'll carry the parcel and you carry me." So it is with us. If I must carry a burden, Christ will carry me. Underneath us are the everlasting arms of an all-sufficient grace which never fails.

"My grace is sufficient for you." Oh what a wonderful promise. Do you notice that the promise is in the present tense? "My grace IS sufficient." His grace is sufficient NOW. I need grace for each moment as it comes and His grace is as constant as my breathing.

Now, is the grace of Christ really adequate in the extreme adversities of human experience? A missionary was asked to call and see an invalid. He was blind and lying upon a bed, for every joint in his body was immovable. But his mind was full of vigor and his heart full of grace of service. For twenty-nine years he had lain thus, fed only with liquid foods. For twenty-two years he had been blind. Is it possible that such a one could do anything to help others? Listen! Seventeen blind children are supported by his efforts in India and ten more in China, a blind woman in Korea, a blind boy in the Sudan, a blind boy in Fiji, and a blind woman in Jaffa. Three hundred pounds a year is received in answer to prayer by that faithful sightless, silent, paralyzed disciple in that little shut-in room in Melbourne.

Yes, "My grace is sufficient for you." Here is the source, "My grace." Here is the supply, "sufficient." Here is the sustenance it brings, "sufficient for you." The source is infinite, the supply is proportionate, and the sustenance is individually adequate. In the words of the old hymn:

> He giveth more grace as the burdens grow greater.
> He sendeth more strength as the labors increase.
> To added affliction, He addeth His mercy
> To multiplied trials, His multiplied peace.
>
> When we have exhausted our store of endurance,
> When our strength has failed e're the day is half done,
> When we reach the end of our hoarded resources,
> Our Father's full giving is only begun.
>
> His love has no limit, His grace has no measure,
> His power has no boundary known unto men,
> For out of His infinite riches in Jesus
> He giveth and giveth and giveth again.
> (Annie Johnson Flint)

Thank You Father, for the grace You give to me moment by moment. I trust You Lord, Amen.

October 6   Remember

Scripture Reading: Leviticus Chapter 17

Key Verse: "For the life of the flesh is in the blood, and I have given it to you upon the altar to make atonement for your souls; for it is the blood that makes atonement for the soul." Leviticus 17:11

Justification is one of the great words in the study of the Bible. It means a new relationship between man and God. This relationship has been strained and severed by sin. Justification means that God looks upon the forgiven person as right and just, and that one goes forth free from the guilt of sin which had held him in subjection and slavery. Justification is more than acquittal. It is more than forgiveness. It is standing in the presence of God as if you had never sinned, freely justified by His grace.

The way of justification came to us through the sacrifice of Christ on the cross. Justification does not precede salvation, but it is an intimate part of the redemptive process.

Today let us especially think of the price of our salvation. As our text makes clear, blood is that price. Under Old Testament law, a sacrifice was brought as a sin offering. But, that cleansing wasn't complete. The sin offering must be offered again, and again, and again. It didn't make any permanent changes. The Old Testament sacrificial system detailed in Leviticus is only a stop-gap measure until the true Redeemer comes to offer a perfect sacrifice, once and for all, His blood to cover our sin.

Here is the great subject of the mystical transfusion of blood in the process of our salvation. The transfusion of blood from one person to another is a most wonderful discovery whereby the fresh life of a healthy body is imparted to a needy person in order to restore expiring life. The spiritual parallels are clear.

The efficacy of the blood of Jesus is complete. As a patient lays in a weakened condition, so the sinner is weak and helpless. Help must reach him from an outside source, or he will perish. He is without strength to save himself.

Outpoured blood is a symbol of life given, as the blood Jesus spilled at the cross signifies the outpouring of His life. Only the blood of Jesus, the anointed One, was not just human blood but royal blood, the blood of Messiah. Thus, when Jesus died He shed the blood not of a poor, despised Nazarene, but of the Sent One of God, the King Eternal, and the God-Man. This is why His blood can cleanse us from all sin.

The crimson stream from Jesus' side never ceases to function as a channel of freedom. It is for believers as well as sinners. It is for past sin, as well as future sin. His blood makes the vilest sinner clean. And as the surgeon takes charge of a transfusion to the body, so the Holy Spirit, the Great Physician, with wondrous skill causes the virtue and efficacy of the cross to pass into sinful, needy lives to bring restoration, justification, and life.

Some folks these days are a bit squeamish about mentioning the blood of Jesus too much. But we must remember. Remembrance begets gratitude for the awful sacrifice. Remembrance fosters holiness as we appreciate the price of our redemption. And remembrance inspires a blessed anticipation as we look forward to the day we will meet Him face to face. Remember.

Precious Lord, I don't remember nearly often enough the price with which I was bought. I come before You now completely humbled by the sacrifice You willingly made for me. Thank You, Lord, amen.

October 7　　Whoever Guards His Mouth

Scripture Reading: Proverbs Chapter 21

Key Verse: "Whoever guards his mouth and his tongue, keeps his soul from troubles." Proverbs 21:23

Getting the best of your tongue! What a job that is for all of us. Polonius asked Hamlet what he was reading, and his reply was, "Words, words, words!" And yet, how great is the power of words. It is impossible to calculate the injury wrought by an ungovernable and unconverted tongue. The iniquity of the tongue is a proof of the fall of man.

"Words, words, words," how mysterious their spell. How mighty their power and how irrevocable their influence. A man's words are the index of his character. Words are the transcript of the mind. But the most wonderful of all, the most mysterious, most inexhaustible in their meaning, most inspiring, arresting and comforting are the words of Scripture. The Bible says that a word in season is good, that a wholesome tongue is a tree of life, and that life and death are in the power of the tongue.

This power of words is confirmed by human experience. We have heard words that thrilled us to the center of our being, words that made the heart glad and healed our wounds like oil. We have heard words of counsel and warning, of exhortation and advice. We have heard words that have made us uncomfortable and unhappy, words that rankled, rasped and fettered. We have also heard words that provoked us to wrath, words that James said, "sets on fire the course of nature; and it is set on fire by hell."

Our Lord not only pronounced a judgment upon words, but He gives the reason for our own accountability for the words we speak in Matthew 12:36, "But I say to you that for every idle word men may speak, they will give account of it in the day of judgment." You see, words reveal the thoughts and uncover the heart of man. "Out of the abundance of the heart the mouth speaks. A good man out of the good treasure of his heart brings forth good things, and an evil man out of the evil treasure brings forth evil things."

How important that we heed this statement and think of our responsibility for our words. Wounds inflicted by the tongue may never heal. Words provoke, break friendships and homes, disrupt churches, divorce husbands and wives, and set nation against nation. In the Old Testament, the portrait of the noble man is that of a man who will not take up an evil reproach against his neighbor, and in the New Testament we are shown that love covers a multitude of sins.

My dear mother was afflicted with deafness in one ear. While yet young, I heard my mother say to a certain woman given to tale-bearing, "Now my dear, if it is good you wish to tell me, put it in this ear for it's my good ear. If it is of evil, speak it if you must, but put it in that ear, I'm stone deaf there."

What is the cure for the tongue? Only and always the love of Christ. For, if the love of Christ reigns in our hearts and lives, instead of delighting in dragging out, exposing, and exaggerating the faults of others, we shall do what we can to cover them with the mantle of charity. Live in fellowship with Christ, and your tongue will speak words of purity and truth, of encouragement and hope and faith.

Dear Lord, I confess I do not always hold my tongue when I should and neither do I always speak when and what I ought. Please teach me to speak only the words that I would be pleased to own before you on that day when I must give account. In Jesus' name, amen.

October 8   The Unpardonable Sin

Scripture Reading: Matthew 12:31-32

Key Verses: "Every sin and blasphemy will be forgiven men, but the blasphemy against the Spirit will not be forgiven men." Matthew 12:31 "Therefore they could not believe." John 12:39

Jesus said that it was possible to so sin in this world that it cannot be forgiven in the next. And because this thing is possible, it is mighty important that men and women who are liable to get to this fearful condition of soul know something of what Jesus meant.

In Genesis God says, "My Spirit shall not strive with man forever." God told Jeremiah three times not to pray for certain people because there was no hope for them. He said that Ephraim is joined to his idols, let him alone. Suppose God said that of us or someone we love?

Paul speaks of some men whom even God had given up to lasciviousness. Pity the man if the time should come when God would say "He is joined to his sin, let him alone." Let him alone, conscience. Let him alone, minister. Let him alone, Holy Spirit. In Proverbs we read, "Then they will call on me, but I will not answer." In John we read, "They could not believe." Not "would not," but "could not." They could not repent and therefore could not be forgiven.

In Hebrews there are two very solemn passages. In the sixth chapter we read of certain people for whom repentance is impossible. In the tenth chapter we see that if a man continues to live in willful sin after he has received knowledge of the truth there remains no longer any sacrifice for that man's sins. It is important to remember that no penitent man will ever be rejected, no matter how deep the sin, for his very penitence proves that he is within the reach of grace. The unpardonable sin is not an act, but a condition of the soul.

Look for a moment at the testimony of nature. It is the testimony of nature that if a man will not do a thing, the time comes when he cannot do it. Bandage your arm to your side and leave it that way long enough and you will lose the capacity to use that arm. Put a bandage to your eye, leave it long enough and you will lose the capacity to see. Harden your heart long enough by refusing to hear the call of God and the time will come when your heart will have lost forever the capacity to feel and believe. As John said, "Therefore they could not believe."

Only God knows when a man has hardened his heart beyond reach. Until then, He will call, plead, offer and welcome. His desire is that all men be saved.

What does this powerful truth mean to us today? First, let us examine ourselves to be sure we have asked forgiveness of the Father and through Christ come into right relationship with Him. Then, let us think of those dear ones who have up to now rejected the call of God. Let us pray diligently for their awakening. Let us pray for nothing less than their salvation. Let us prostrate ourselves before God for their souls. Let us travail and fight the spiritual warfare necessary to free them from their deception. It is up to God to know the moment of their loss or gain, until then let us persevere in love and prayer.

Holy Father God, I bring to You the following people who seem to be rejecting Your forgiveness and mercy: _____. Lord, please soften their hearts to the truth, and bring faithful Christians into their path who will testify to You. Let me boldly proclaim You in any divine appointment You might arrange. May they have the veil removed from the eyes of their hearts to see the truth and accept Your mercy. For the sake of the glory of Jesus' name, amen.

October 9 The Law and the Christian

Suggested Reading: Galatians Chapter 3

Key Verse: "But that no one is justified by the law in the sight of God is evident, for 'the just shall live by faith.'" Galatians 3:11

Now, the Christian is either under law or under grace. He cannot be under both. It is not partly by works and partly by grace that we are saved. The least bit of law working in grace and we spoil it all, for grace and law are opposites. There are three grave errors concerning the relation of the law in salvation, errors present in Paul's day and ours.

The first is Legalism: that we are saved by the keeping of the law and by our own effort. We have the entire epistle of Romans to refute that. Romans 3:20 says "By the deeds of the law no flesh will be justified in His sight."

The second error is Anti-Nomianism, (anti = against, and nomos = the law, thus "Against the Law"). This error teaches that since we are saved by grace we are now free from the law and can do just as we please. In short, we become "lawless." This is a grave error for we Christians who are free from the law of commandments come under a higher law, the law of love and gratitude. Good works are as a result of our salvation and not an effort to obtain salvation. We are given the epistle of James to refute this error. He says in 2:24 "You see then that a man is justified by works, and not by faith only." These passages sound like a contradiction, but remember, Paul is talking about how a sinner can be justified in the sight of God, while James is telling how a man (a saint of God, already justified in God's sight) may be justified in the sight of his fellow-man. It is how we prove to our fellow-man by our works that we have already been justified by faith. Man cannot see our faith, but they can see our works. The people of the world will never know or believe our testimony of salvation until they can see it in our lives.

The third error, far more subtle, is called Galatianism because it was so prevalent in the early Galatian churches. Galatianism is the teaching that we are justified and saved by faith alone, but then after we are saved we are kept by the works of the law and by our behavior. "Saved by grace and kept by works." This is a subtle deception of the devil, by which having delivered us from the law, would put us back under the bondage of the law for our ultimate salvation.

To this Paul cries "Oh, foolish Galatians! Who has bewitched you that you should not obey the truth?" Listen to him! "Are you so foolish? Having begun in the Spirit, are you now being made perfect by the flesh?" We serve Him not because of fear or judgment, but out of love and gratitude to Him.

It is by His grace that He has redeemed us and delivered us. We rest in a person, the Lord Jesus Christ. We read in Hebrews 10:12 that "after He had offered one sacrifice for sins forever, sat down at the right hand of God," resting in a perfect work of redemption.

Holy and Almighty God, thank you for sending Jesus to release me from the shackles of the law. It is as though you sent a lovely garment from heaven to cover my muddy, grimy life. The garment's crimson lining is the precious blood of Christ. The outside shines gleaming white and is His righteousness. As I raise my arms in complete surrender to my Lord, His garment settles over me. Now when you gaze at me, you see not sin, because I'm covered by the blood of Christ, but only the dazzling white of His goodness and His righteousness. I am fully accepted into your presence, forever and ever, amen.

October 10 A Revival in a Bewitched City

Scripture Reading: Acts 8:1-25

Key Verse: "Then Philip went down to the city of Samaria and preached Christ to them." Acts 8:5

The martyrdom of Stephen created a crisis in the early church, and Saul of Tarsus consented to this beastly act. While he did not throw the stones, he held the coats of those who did. Saul saw Stephen die. He saw that face, and despite the blood and cruel bruises he saw, as it were, the face of an angel.

But Saul just became meaner than ever, throwing Christians into jail and persecuting them in order to wipe them out. It's the same today. A woman gets converted and asks for prayer for her husband. Soon, he gets so mean she can hardly live with him. Why? He's under the conviction of the Holy Spirit. And so, under Saul's persecution, the people were scattered.

This dispersion was actually a blessing, a means of spreading the Good News. For, everywhere the believers went, they took Jesus Christ and scattered the seeds of Christianity. We see that persecution in the hands of Saul became the beginning of revival fires for Samaria.

Among those who were scattered is a fellow named Philip. He was not a preacher or an apostle. He was a deacon, one of those recently elected to serve the poor and see to the welfare of widows. But now, due to the persecution, Philip finds himself in Samaria. He does not assume the role of a poor displaced victim. He looks around to see where he could advance the Kingdom of God and begins to preach the gospel. He soon found himself in the center of a wonderful revival in Samaria.

So to this bewitched city under the spell of sorcery and witchcraft, God sends a deacon. Not an apostle, not a preacher, but a layman. We can carry Him into the city, like donkeys carrying Christ into Jerusalem, for it doesn't take a seminary degree to tell the simple Good News of the Gospel. It is God from whom all power and goodness comes.

What were Philip's qualifications? He was a man full of the Holy

Spirit, driven by the indwelling life of Christ, obediently proclaiming Christ. Conviction of sin even hit poor old Simon the sorcerer, and he believed.

When the apostles in Jerusalem learned about the great awakening, they sent Peter and John down to investigate and they found that the people were lacking the Spirit. The apostles prayed and laid hands on them and they received the Holy Spirit. The people were baptized into the body of Christ.

When Simon saw all this manifestation of power, he wanted it too. But he wanted the power of the Holy Spirit for personal gain, much as he once used his sorcery. Peter knew that the power had come as a gift of God and no man should receive the Spirit in order to exalt himself. So he sternly rebuked Simon who immediately repented.

There is much here for us to learn. The most severe circumstance may be an opportunity for the advancement of the Gospel. A Spirit-filled church is a church where "Simony" cannot exist. Simon had to get right with God or get out. Let us all be like Philip, using whatever we have for the glory of God and to the blessing of others in the spirit of love and co-operation.

Dear Father, I want to learn from this truth. Please help me to look around in every circumstance to see how I might contribute to the Kingdom of God. I will listen for Your direction and obey, leaving the miraculous results to You. In Jesus' name, amen.

October 11   The Church Militant

Scripture Reading: I Corinthians 12:12-31

Key Verse: "For as the body is one and has many members, but all the members of that one body, being many, are one body, so also is Christ." I Corinthians 12:12

The church was in the heart and mind of God before the world was created and it was what He meant when He gave His Son "to be head over all things to the church, which is His body, the fullness of Him who fills all in all." Ephesians 1:22-23.

The church is one, even as a family is one. A father is the head of his family even though the children be scattered to the ends of the earth. Similarly, there is one spiritual family in Christ and of that family, He is head and the church is His body.

Admittedly, God chose imperfect instruments for His work in the church. A large percentage of Christians are living continuously below their privilege. They have come out of Egypt and, like those of old who kept longing for the leeks and garlic of Egypt; they have retained their worldly lusts and appetites. It is one thing to get a drowning man out of the water, and another to get the water out of the drowning man. Just so, it is one thing to get a sinner out of the world, but still another to get the world out of the sinner. It is only when the Christian surrenders to the will of God, shedding his concern for the things of this world, that a true reflection of God can begin to be seen in Him. It is then that the radiant Christian experience which is the rightful heritage of every child of God becomes evident in his life.

Though the church is imperfect, its Head is not. Praise God that we are bound to Him. We are a part of His body, and we are to be a part of a local body of believers as well. But isn't the church imperfect? Oh, yes. But, we don't follow each other or look to each other. We look to the Head of the body; we follow only Him, our Lord Jesus Christ. Our Lord Jesus Christ positively identifies Himself with the church on the occasion of Saul's conversion. When Saul called out "Who are you, Lord?" the Lord announced, "I am Jesus, whom you are persecuting." Now at that moment, Saul was certainly aware that he had been persecuting the church. But, that the church and Jesus were to be identified as one, he had not known until that moment. As Saul persecuted the church, he had persecuted its Head.

Jesus gave His life to found the church. "Christ also loved the church and gave Himself for her." It was not for the Kingdom, or for Christendom, but for the church He died. The church shines forth the light of the world, and light reveals and chases away the darkness. The church is also the salt of the earth, and salt is a preservative power. It delays putrification. It gives life and saves life. As salt is given to save and preserve the meat it enters, so the church is not in the world to save herself, but to pour out her life for the salvation of others.

What now, dear ones? What is all this to us? Are we a functioning, alive, vibrant part of the body of Christ? We are also a bride, you know. The Bride of Christ for which He has promised to return. We are to be about the business of the Bridegroom, doing His will until He comes again.

While Jesus tarries, He expects us to carry on, speaking for Him, preaching and teaching for Him, reaching out in healing and in love for Him. We are His body, His hands, His feet, and His voice on earth. Let us be about the business of Him who called us.

Dear Lord, may I be faithful to do my part as a vital part of this body and never think that I won't be missed. There is no part of a body that is not missed. Let us be whole. In Jesus' name, amen.

October 12   Self-Made Fool

Scripture Reading: I Samuel Chapter 26

Key Verse: "Then Saul said, 'I have sinned . . . Indeed, I have played the fool and erred exceedingly.'" I Samuel 26:21

This is the confession of King Saul. He is referring to a series of acts he has committed against David. But, the same confession might have been used as a final summing up of Saul's life, an autobiographical epitaph, if you will. The pathos of it all is that the role of a fool is self-chosen.

Saul was not sent into this world to play the part of a fool. He was intended to be a king, but he chose the role of fool. He is not the type of fool that makes us laugh; we weep bitter tears over him, for he pictures so many even in our day. God has given his history to warn, to plead, and to lead away from the path of sin. How plainly God shows us the end of sin, its price, and its folly.

Oh, there was much to admire about Saul. He was a man of splendid physique, princely in his bearing. And, Saul was a modest man. When Samuel came to anoint him, Saul protested that he was of the smallest tribe, and the smallest family in that tribe. Saul also was in his prime, in the springtime of his life. But another thing about Saul is that he had a great friend. He had Samuel to advise him, to pray for him, to help him, and to encourage him. But Saul was not Samuel's choice. He was God's choice from all of Israel at the time. God set His seal upon him.

What use did Saul make of his opportunities? What return did he make for the investments that God made in him? "I have played the fool," Saul confesses. He rebelled against God. He turned from following after the Lord.

But, hear me; the tragedy of Saul's life was not that he was such a terrible sinner. Why, certainly he did sin, and sinned deeply. But, there were others who had sinned as well, David for instance. No, the tragedy of Saul's life was that he never could be brought to face his sin, confess it, and turn from it.

After Saul and the army destroyed the Amalekites, he was commanded to destroy everything, sheep, cattle and all. Samuel came to see Saul, and confronted him about keeping some of the sheep, which he could hear bleating. Saul offered excuses, placing the blame on others, only confessing when Samuel finally cornered him. Saul offered many confessions, but always because of his desire to get out of trouble and to save his own kingdom, not because he was repentant. And, hear me; many live this "foxhole Christian" life today, calling on God only when they are desperate to save their own skins.

So, what was the outcome of Saul's foolishness? He became a godless man. He became a wretched man. Saul had no peace in his heart, no hope for tomorrow. But, listen beloved, he did not go to his ruin alone. When I was a small boy, I would go to the woods with my father to cut great trees for our home. Yet, when the large trees fell, often others in their path would perish also. Just so, Saul's sons fell with him, as his foolishness affected all within his sphere of influence.

The Scriptures tell us that "the fear of the Lord is the beginning of wisdom." May the epitaph of our lives reflect on the presence of His wisdom in our lives as we submit ourselves to Him.

Heavenly Father, I realize that all wisdom comes from You. I know that You are the author, architect and engineer of all. I want to live my life victoriously as a testimony and a witness for You and for Your glory. In Jesus' name, amen.

October 13   Which Are You at Calvary?

Scripture Reading: Matthew 27:33-40
Key Verse: "Then they crucified Him." Matthew 27:35

As we gather around that green hill far away to visualize afresh the tragedy that marked the crossroads of the ages, let us remember that each one of us is represented in one or another of the groups that met at the cross. It seems that God so arranged it that every sort of man or woman is typified in the different groups that watched Him die. Study these groups and you will find your crowd there.

Consider first the soldiers. They spat upon His face, pressed the crown of thorns upon His brow, and watched the blood flow down. They mocked Him and nailed Him to a tree. But they only administered the wounds that the sin of all the world had caused. It was you and I who spat upon Him, who crowned Him with the thorny wreath. It was your sins and mine that nailed Him to the tree. "He was wounded for our transgressions, He was bruised for our iniquities; the chastisement for our peace was upon Him, and by His stripes we are healed." The Lord indeed laid on Him the iniquity of us all.

When you refuse Him, when you live on in sin and spurn the Word of God, and reject the pleading of the Spirit, you are pressing the thorny crown upon Him. You are spitting on Him, smiting, crucifying Him.

The Scriptures also tell us that the soldiers gambled for His seamless robe. They gambled for His vestments while the crucified Christ looks on. Well, the world plays its games today at the foot of the cross. No matter where you are, you are facing Calvary. Men sit before this eternal fact and gamble away health, time, talents, reputation and soul, while the Crucified One looks on.

We next read about those who passed by wagging their heads. They did not actually crucify Him, they only passed by reviling Him. It is fashionable today to pass by Calvary wagging the head. Indifferent souls use the name of Jesus as a curse word; they jeer at the Prince of Glory.

The word records three things of these passers-by. They misquoted the claims of our Lord and shouted, "You who destroy the temple and build it in three days, save Yourself!" He had not said that. He said "Destroy this temple and in three days I will raise it up." Then, they minimized His death. "Come down from the cross!" They did not believe the Word of God which says "The Son of Man must suffer many things." So it is today with critics and blinded souls. They make light of Calvary and see no need for the atonement. At Calvary, the passers-by mocked His deity. "If You are the Son of God, come down from the cross." Today many deny His deity. They see a great teacher, an idealist, the crystal Christ, but not the Calvary Christ. They offer praise for His words while denying the deity that makes those words truth.

Oh, my friend, are you in this class of passers-by, wagging your head, minimizing His death, belittling His sacrifice and questioning His deity? It is a dreadful thing to be a passer-by at Calvary. Let us stop here for today, examine ourselves. Ask God to reveal to you any wrong attitude, ask God to forgive you for the times when you take Him for granted, and go out joyfully to the day knowing who your Savior is and serving Him with gratitude.

Precious, Holy Lord, thank You for this reminder of what You did for us at Calvary. Bring to my attention any way in which I treat Your great sacrifice lightly through either omission or commission. Lord, forgive me and help me to serve You today by loving others as You love us. Amen.

October 14   Which Are You at Calvary? II

Scripture Reading: Matthew 27:41-50
Key Verse: "Then they crucified Him." Matthew 27:35

Today let us consider a third group at the cross. They were the chief priests, scribes and elders. One would have expected them to be quiet and dignified at least, but sadly, even the priests joined in the cry of the rabble. Who were these men who stood at Calvary and taunted the Son of God? They were men who studied the Scriptures and prayed in public, attended the House of God, gave tithes, and lead clean, moral lives. For all of that, they joined the enemies of Christ at Calvary.

Today there are those who draw near with their mouths but their hearts are far from Him. No group of men and women have caused more pain to the heart of Jesus than the Pharisees who go through all the motions of religion, but their lives are a hollow mockery of faith.

Another group at Calvary was called "the crowd" that great throng that stood withholding. They did not revile, nor wag their heads; they just looked and did nothing. Most people come under this classification. When Christ is preached and the cross is held up, they do not revile or insult the Lord. They just look on respectfully and then do nothing about it. But that's all any man has to do to be lost, just nothing. These folks were impressed at Calvary. The darkness and death of Christ stirred them, and the solemnity of this greatest hour of history hushed them with an awful silence, but they only smote their breasts and went away.

So it is today that men and women sit under the teaching of the gospel and as the realities of the cross and sin and salvation, judgment and hell are made vivid before them, they are impressed, moved, stirred. But they walk out the door and say it was a good sermon. They only smite their breasts and go away.

Your Bible tells of another man who smote his breast, but he followed it with a prayer, "God, be merciful to me a sinner." And he went home justified because he offered confession and a plea for mercy.

But there was one at Calvary who was saved beyond a doubt, the penitent thief. And note, of all the throng that witnessed the death of our Lord that day, he was the only one, the lowest character of all, who was saved and he only asked to be remembered. How gracious was our Lord's reply, "Today you will be with Me in Paradise." The first recruit for heaven was a criminal. Surely Christ came into the world to save sinners.

Finally, there were those who loved Him, His mother, and John the Beloved. I thank God He was not utterly forsaken. Oh, I ask you, do you love Him? What does the cross mean to you? Love demands something from us. Who is it that loves Jesus anyway? The Scriptures tell us, "For this is the love of God, that we keep His commandments."

Where do you stand at Calvary? There are only two groups there at the cross. There are those who rest upon His finished work, and then there are those who reject the provisions of His love. Where do you stand, my friend? To which group do you belong? Which prayer do you need to pray today?

Holy Father God, I confess that I am a sinner and accept the sacrifice you paid for me on the cross with deep gratitude. Please come into my heart and be the Lord of my life. In the Holy name of Jesus, amen.

Dearest Father, I am thinking of _____ right now and ask that You send the Holy Spirit to woo them to You. Please don't stop working in their lives until they see clearly the wonderful gift of salvation You offer to them. Amen.

October 15   The Larger Life

Scripture: Ephesians 5:8-21

Key Verse: "And do not be drunk with wine . . . but be filled with the Spirit." Ephesians 5:18

"Be filled with the Spirit" is a command, and it should be obeyed. We are commanded, even expected, to live a spirit-filled life, to be filled not with the wine of the earth, but the new wine of the kingdom. If I asked you, "Do you obey the command to be not drunk?" You would probably say yes, and that is obedience. Now I ask "Do you obey the command to be filled with the Spirit?" What is your answer? If your answer is yes, you are in obedience. If it is no, it is disobedience.

In Ephesians, you see, the believers were saved but did not have the Holy Spirit's fullness. It is just so with many today. Years ago in Scottish banks there went unclaimed $40 million pounds in deposits. There were some dear folks who owned a share in these deposits who died in the poor house, unaware. Some lived in dire need while they had money for the claiming, but didn't know it was theirs. Think what vast unclaimed deposits remain in our Lord's treasury while children have died Spirit-poor. The Spirit is our birthright, ours for the receiving.

Do you have the idea that the blessing is only for a favored few, those with a special work and not for ordinary folk? That is a lie from the father of lies. Mothers in their homes with pressing duties need the fullness of the Spirit as surely as the apostles, the washerwoman as well as the pastor, the tradesman as well as the evangelist. We all need the Holy Spirit's presence in order to live a Christ-glorifying life in whatever station God has placed us.

Why is there backsliding, backbiting, envy, strife, discord, unrest, and criticism in some churches today? Why? Because of the lack of the Holy Spirit, for if He had His way we would show His fruits: meekness, gentleness, kindness, longsuffering, and joy.

Now let us turn to the practical side. How is this filling obtained?

When God spoke of being filled with the Spirit, He really meant something, for every word in Scripture is laden with truth.

In Acts 15:8-9 we read "So God, who knows the heart, acknowledged them by giving them the Holy Spirit, just as He did to us, and made no distinction between us and them, purifying their hearts by faith." This is God's work. It is an act of God. God cleanses us from sin, God gives us the Holy Spirit, and then the filling of the Spirit is to empower us for the work of the Lord.

How is the fullness of the Holy Spirit received by the cleansed and consecrated believer? By availing ourselves of it in prayer. God commands us to be filled, and it is up to us to be ready to receive. Then, thank God, and believe. It is yours to keep believing, it is God's to keep you filled.

Oh, dear ones, do not be like Hagar in the wilderness, sitting alone with an empty bottle and a dying, thirsty heart. Call out for God, for Him to fill you with His Holy Spirit. He will fill you from the fountain that never ceases, and you will never thirst again.

"If you then, being evil, know how to give good gifts to your children, how much more will your Heavenly Father who is in heaven give good things to those who ask Him!"

Dear Father, I do want my life to be Spirit-filled, Spirit-led, and Spirit-controlled. Please fill me with Your Spirit, Lord, and use me to glorify Your name. I receive the fullness of the Holy Spirit into my life and thank You for it. Amen.

October 16   With Painted Face

Scripture Reading: II Kings Chapter 9

Key Verse: "Now when Jehu had come to Jezreel, Jezebel heard of it; and she put paint on her eyes and adorned her head, and looked through a window. Then as Jehu entered at the gate, she said, 'Is it peace, Zimri, murderer or your master?'"

This face at the window gripped the attention of Jehu at once. No man could pass her face by and utterly ignore it; Jezebel was far too striking for that. As surely as they glimpsed that face, they could not fail to recognize something of her coarseness and cruelty. But Jezebel was also strong and intelligent, capable and forceful. She is the most hated woman in the Bible, and this fact alone is evidence of her strength. For we do not hate weaklings and fools; we pity them. We hate giants and tyrants.

Jehu calls Jezebel "that cursed woman." The evil genius of her day, Jezebel is the Lady MacBeth of the Old Testament. She has all the ambition, the brilliant dashing courage of that ill-starred Queen. She also has all her flinty cruelty and stoniness of heart. Here is a woman whose life ended in a ghastly tragedy, yet everyone feels that in dying that death, she but reaped what she had sown.

How did Jezebel become the monster that she was? Well, it might be tempting to say she was born a monster. We like to think, after all, that people who so greatly sin are somehow constructed of baser ingredients. But such is not the case.

Jezebel was born into a heathen palace, and was nurtured in an atmosphere that was foul and filthy. She was trained in a religion that infected its devotees with moral leprosy. The gods to whom she was introduced were gods of filth and lust, with no power to make men good. And this early training cast its blight over Jezebel's entire life.

Then, Jezebel's second handicap was that she made an unfortunate marriage. Her husband's name was Ahab, a nominal follower of the Lord. In reality, however, his religion counted for a naked nothing. The big difference between Jezebel and Ahab was that while he was weak and wicked, she was strong and wicked. Had Ahab been a man who was strong in the faith of God, the story might have been different for Jezebel, and for the nation.

It is not common to see a man who will hold on to his faith when his wife is out of sympathy with him. I have seen a little butterfly of a society girl whose moral weight was about that of a soap bubble quench the zeal of a man and turn him away from both the church and the Lord. Well, not only did Jezebel influence her husband, but she dominated the court and the nation as well.

She was so active and aggressive that she fairly swept the nation off its feet. But God did not leave her without a witness in that day. She knew better, oh, yes. Her pastor was Elijah, who came to the palace to warn the guilty pair. Both Jezebel and Ahab refused to face the facts; blaming Elijah instead of their sin. They blamed the physician, rather than the disease.

It was not lack of light, you see, that was the ruin of Jezebel. It was her refusal to walk in that light. And today each one of us needs to examine our hearts to see, are we walking in the light that God has given each of us. The field is ours, and the harvest of tomorrow we determine today by our choices in life. Walk in the light of His love, beloved, and have no regrets in the harvest time.

Dear Father God, please strengthen me to make choices that will be glorifying to You, and will make my life an investment in Your Kingdom. Amen.

October 17　　　　Who's That Knocking?

Scripture: Revelation Chapter 3

Key Verse: "Behold, I stand at the door and knock." Revelation 3:20

There is a lovely painting of Christ standing at the door to our heart, gently knocking. It is a true moment this artist captured; for the Scriptures plainly state that our Lord does just that. When someone knocks at the door to our homes what is our first reaction? Is it happy anticipation of a friend's visit or dread that perhaps it might be the landlord coming for the rent?

You know, our Christ would have every right to knock on our doors to demand rent. Years ago a landlord went to collect rent from one of his tenants and the tenant locked the door. The landlord forced it open. The tenant barricaded himself in the attic and when the landlord forced that open he emptied the contents of a shotgun into the landlord's body. You say, "I wouldn't do a thing like that." But listen to me; you crucify Christ afresh by your rejection. He has a right to your time, your money, and your love, doesn't He?

We of the North used to call Stonewall Jackson a rebel, but listen to the testimony of his life. After the second battle of Bull Run, communication was disrupted and people were anxious to get word from the front. A great group was gathered outside the post office at Lexington, his home town. Word came that a letter had been received from General Jackson and the preacher to whom it was addressed hurriedly opened it. It read, "Dear Pastor, I remember that this is the day for the collection for foreign missions. Enclosed please find my check." Signed, T.J. Jackson.

How much do you give your Lord? We have electric gadgets, fashionable clothes, homes, - nearly anything we want, but when Jesus knocks at our door we barricade ourselves in the attic and throw a nickel down through the crack, feeling righteous that it is not a penny.

He has the right to collect, yes; He has the right to be the landlord at the door. But Jesus does not come to us demanding anything. He comes to give. Jesus knows we cannot save ourselves, so in His love He comes to pay our debt to God. He comes bringing along the very thing we owe and offers it to us without money or price.

The Scriptures say that Jesus knocks for still another reason. He knocks because He wants to come in and sup with us. Supping in Christ's day was a sacrament as well as hospitality. When a man of that time and place partook of a meal containing salt or blood with another, he became a covenant brother with him, bound as closely together as though of the same mother.

Lastly, Jesus knocks at your heart's door because He wants to go with us along the journey of life, and when we have finished the course He wants to take us to His home. You will remember how when the Wise Men visited Jesus, Scripture says "They returned unto their own country another way." Well, we will be able to return another way, the way Jesus has prepared for us. We shall not pass this way again.

So, I ask the question again. When you hear the gentle knock at the door to your heart, do you run to the attic because it might be the landlord coming for the rent, or will you fling open the door to your heart with happy anticipation of the visit of a friend and brother bearing gifts? Beloved, don't miss the blessing He has for you.

Dear Lord Jesus, I've been afraid to open the door to total commitment to You for fear of what You want of me. Now I see that You come to give. I happily open the door to my heart for You, and I pray that _____ and _____ will open their hearts to you also. Amen.

October 18

Taking the Stew Out of Stewardship

Scripture Reading: Matthew 25:14-30

Key Verses: "For the kingdom of heaven is like a man traveling to a far country, who called his own servants and delivered his goods to them. And to one he gave five talents, to another two, and to another one, to each according to his own ability; and immediately he went on a journey . . . For to everyone who has, more will be given, and he will have abundance; but from him who does not have, even what he has will be taken away." Matthew 25:14, 15, and 29

A little girl was marking words whose meaning she did not know and her mother noticed that she passed by the word "stewardship" without marking it. Her mother said to her, "Do you know what that word means?" The little girl replied, "Yes, it means that I've got it but I must use it for someone else." The word had the right meaning to her loving heart. To many today the thought is "I've got it and I'm going to use it for myself."

The master in the story is the Lord Jesus Christ. The servants are the apostles He's teaching, but in a broader sense, He is referring to the visible church. The talents are primarily the gifts received for His followers and dispensed by the ascended Christ or opportunities in stewardship which Christ has given to all who come in contact with their Lord and His Word. The "going away" of the Lord into a far country is the withdrawal of Christ as a visible presence from the earth. And the return of the Lord after a long time is the second coming of Christ when the final reckoning of judgment shall be held.

So let it be clear, we are the servants in the parable. He is the master who called His own servants and delivered His goods, and there we have it. All we have is His. We originated nothing. He is the Creator, Owner, All the goods we have are His goods, and we are to enrich the owner by their use and service of these talents.

In the parable of the talents the unprofitable one was only one out of three. Who is the one? Is it you? Is it me? He is the one who does not live to enrich His Lord. He does not care or plan for the support of Christ's work. He feels the stew of stewardship and wants to keep out of it.

A young fellow was seen on the street with a magnificent diamond which he had never worn before. Admiring friends gathered around and many were the exclamations of wonder and delight over the jewel. Said one, "It must have cost a thousand dollars. Where did you get it?" The proud possessor of the ring replied, "Yes, it cost more than a thousand dollars. My father gave it to me. He recently died and in his will he gave me the money and said to erect a stone to his memory. And boys, here is the stone." Such brash self-interest may seem exhilarating at the time, but we are sure to reap the bitter harvest later on.

Our Heavenly Father made us stewards of the riches of His grace and His wealth. He desires, as expressly stated in His last will and testament, that we erect a kingdom here on earth for the glory of the Lord Jesus Christ with part of the wealth He left us.

Have we obeyed His will? Instead of obeying, some of us may have been using our Lord's money to buy useless baubles with which to decorate our own persons, like the gaudily dressed heir mentioned before. "We earned it," we say. But, beloved, it came ultimately from the hand of God, we are simply stewards.

Loving Master, how easy it is to look at our blessings as toys to be used for our amusement rather than tools to be used for Your kingdom. Please help me to be a good and faithful steward of all that You have entrusted to me. Amen.

October 19

Unconscious Spiritual Deterioration

Scripture: Hosea Chapter 7

Key Verse: "Gray hairs are here and there on him, yet he does not know it." Hosea 7:9

These words describe Israel's true spiritual condition following the reign of Jeroboam II in Hosea's time; falsehood, theft, and adultery were rampant in the land. Kings, princesses and their people rivaled one another to indulge in the deepest iniquity. The thief robbed from within Israel, the spoiler from without, and sin was consuming their strength both spiritually and nationally. They were rapidly hastening to national extinction, yet of all of this they were totally unconscious.

They imagined that they were as strong as at other times, they dreamed of years of prosperity before them and like Sampson, shorn of his power, they didn't realize the Lord had departed. They little reckoned on the destruction that was soon to overtake them in the mighty sweep of the Assyrian army carrying them off into captivity.

This is a very dangerous picture of a very common case. Unconscious slipping away from God, ordinary backsliding we used to say, comes silent and unaware. Oh, others remember the fellow's fervor, zeal, and love for the Lord. Somehow, that Christian distinctiveness has rubbed down. He lost his watchfulness over his speech. He lost his relish for the people of God. He even lost his delight in the ordinances of the Lord. But, he doesn't see it. He can point to his past history, and he can point to his present standing as being all right. And he goes on unaware of his own spiritual deterioration.

Why is there this unconscious element characterizing backsliding? Because we are all inclined to look more favorably upon ourselves than on others! We mark the external changes in our neighbors more exactly than we do those that manifest themselves in our own life. Two friends, separated for many years, meet on the street. "Why, how changed you are!" they each exclaim, but neither had taken note of changes in himself. The Bible tells us it is not otherwise in spiritual matters.

So how shall we prevent this unconscious spiritual backing away from God? By trying ourselves fairly by the standard of God's Word, and laying ourselves open to the inspection of the Lord Himself. The great preacher Matthew Henry once said that "apostasy from God generally begins at the prayer closet." In public a man might try to play the hypocrite, but in secret face-to-face with God, he can't. This is why so many find it so difficult to have daily time with the Lord. Like the bankrupt merchant who fears to look into his books and strike a balance, we are afraid to know the certainty of our own spiritual poverty.

The grand, sovereign cure for spiritual drifting is personal devotions. The mariner does not just leave himself to the wind to go where he will, no, no! Hourly, he calculates from the compass his position. Each reckoning may not reveal much, but he does not imagine that the calculation is of no consequence! He understands that it is the small corrections that keep him on course. Surely the loftiest attainment as a believer is simply to serve God in daily life as He directs. And this cannot be done apart from Him.

Dear Father, forgive me for the times I believe the lie of busyness. No matter how busy or how demanding my schedule, I know I should bring every day before You. Please guide me; keep me on course. I don't want my life just to be a series of accomplished chores, but to be a history of Your working in my daily life. In Jesus' Name, amen.

October 20   The Beggar

Suggested Scripture: Luke Chapter 18

Key Verse: "As He was coming near Jericho, a certain blind man sat by the road begging." Luke 18:35

It was the last time Jesus was to go through Jericho, for he was on His way to Jerusalem, and to Calvary. That night He would sleep at Bethany, with the cross but a week away. A long line of beggars was sitting just outside the city gate, no doubt, just as they have done for centuries.

At the sound of the approaching crowd, they lift their voices in a wail. Bartimaeus is among them. He asks what the crowd is, for he cannot see, and someone stops for just a moment to tell him that it is Jesus of Nazareth passing by. This name wakes strange hope in Bartimaeus, which can only be accounted for by his knowing of Christ's miracles done elsewhere. It is a witness to the notoriety of Jesus, which had filtered down to the city gates where the beggars sat.

Pouring out of a hungry heart there comes a cry, "Jesus, Son of David, have mercy on me!" Note well, beloved, that he was a beggar but he did not ask for alms. His need was deeper. His need was greater. When he is told to be quiet, Bartimaeus only cries the louder, "Son of David, have mercy on me!" And Jesus stops to care for the need of a poor, blind beggar. Bartimaeus needed sight. He was born blind. He needed what the whole world stands in need of today, for humanity is blind to all the highest facts of life which only can be found in Jesus. And Jesus met his need.

Now, there are three things we need to understand about Bartimaeus. First, he needed Christ. He could not see without Jesus. Neither can you. The things of God are not intellectually discerned first, they are spiritually discerned and it is not what a man can weigh with his intellect that will save him, it is the acceptance of Jesus. The world says, "to see is to believe," but God's way is to believe, and then you see.

Secondly, Bartimaeus knew he needed the Savior. That is the

experience of every man away from Christ, though he may not acknowledge it. The pleasures of the world have not satisfied him. Sin has only mocked him. Troubles have only crushed him, and he has an ache in his heart.

And finally, the only thing he could do was to step out into the darkness. Bartimaeus could not see, but he found the way to Jesus. He could only feel, and when he stepped out into the darkness, Jesus gave him sight. Whittier puts it beautifully when he pens, "The steps of faith fall on the seeming void, and find the rock beneath." Oh, whenever God has a man's will, whenever He has his absolute surrender, whenever He has his acceptance of Christ by faith, the man who has stepped out into seeming darkness finds the light.

We all know those who need to step out on faith to find the light. If they will only let Him into their lives, He will be their strength in weakness, their friend in sorrow. He will be theirs in life and death and in eternity. He will be a friend who will be all the world to them. His is the only name in which they can pray and God will hear.

And yet, some still hesitate. Remember to tell them, won't you, that Jesus of Nazareth still passes by.

Dear Lord, so often I am concerned about not being an offense, and thus I do not speak of Jesus. I humbly ask for boldness to simply point out to those in need that Jesus is still passing by, and He still meets needs. Please bring to me an opportunity to speak of Christ today. Amen.

October 21 He did not Give Glory to God

Scripture Reading: Acts Chapter 12

Key Verse: "He did not give glory to God. And he was eaten by worms and died." Acts 12:23

Here is the epitaph of a man, but it is all the more impressive because of what immediately precedes it. The people had shouted, "The voice of a god and not of a man!" It was a moment in time, a destiny-deciding moment, when Herod could have dismissed the praise of the people and attributed any glory to God; but he did not. He accepted the praise and glorification of the people as though he were a god. This was quite a poor choice, as the Scriptures say that an angel of the Lord struck him and he was eaten by worms.

The pattern of Herod's choices and those of his family are consistent with this defining moment. These Herods, descendants of Esau, came to power in the century before Christ and they showed the animalism which had characterized the brother of Jacob who sold his birthright for a mess of pottage.

Let us tour the family burial plot, for it will serve to remind us of the history of this notorious lot. Over here lies Herod the Great, who slew the innocents of Bethlehem, murdered his three sons, drowned his brother, and had his queen strangled to death.

Here, next to Herod lays his son Archelaus, banished by Augustus after nine years of misrule. And here is another Herod, Antipas. This is the one who tried to please his wicked wife Herodius by beheading John the Baptist. Over there is Herod Agrippa, the one before whom Paul preached but did not persuade. They are a bad lot, all of them. And, Herod the King, as he is called in Acts, was no exception. He was the grandson of Herod the Great, a favorite of Emperor Caligula. When he was given the kingdom over the Jews in Palestine, in order to please them, Herod instituted persecution against the Christians. His first victim was James the brother of John who was killed by the sword.

He was not the first martyr, that distinction belongs to Stephen, but he was the first of the twelve apostles to drink the martyr's cup.

This world is a battlefield between Christ and the anti-Christ, and we might be tempted to despair if we did not have the great assurance of God and the luminous pages out of the book of the past.

We see the hand of God acting through the mid-wives of Pharaoh's time, refusing the edict to kill all the baby boys. We see the hand of God acting within the breast of Pharaoh's own daughter, sparing the life of Moses. What but the power of God was evidenced in the warning of Joseph to take the child Jesus into Egypt? Then came that wonderful word of victory at last. The angel of the Lord appeared unto Joseph telling him to go back to his country for they who sought the young child's life were dead. And there it was, a helpless child against a cruel blood-thirsty tyrant. But when we read the final word, Herod dies; the Child lives.

And for your encouragement, my friend, who is struggling in the battle, remember that Herod was smitten by the angel of the Lord. Remember that Pharaoh sought in vain to destroy the destiny of God's people. Remember that Haman who got a decree to kill the Jews was hanged on the gallows he built for Mordecai, his enemy. Never doubt the final outcome of the question of good versus evil, no matter how dark the present may seem to be.

Almighty God, thank You for keeping and protecting me from the plans of evil men. May I glorify Your name today, and shine Your light in the darkness. In Jesus' name, amen.

October 22   The Anger of Man

Scripture Reading: Numbers 22:22-40

Key Verse: "And when the donkey saw the Angel of the Lord, she lay down under Balaam; so Balaam's anger was aroused, and he struck the donkey with his staff." Numbers 22:27

Anger is common, yet it is also potentially dangerous. It blasts the flower of friendship, destroys peace and concord in the home, incites to crime and violence, and turns love and affection to hatred. Truly, "The wrath of man does not accomplish the righteousness of God."

The Bible, like a great mirror, shows by personal illustration and explanation how anger brings havoc to human life. The first angry man to appear in the pages of the Bible was Cain, who became the first murderer. Christ warned men against being angry with their brother, and the reason is evident in Cain's life; anger opens the way for crime and violence. This is how anger works, first in the heart, then in the face, and finally in the deed.

The folly of anger is also illustrated in the life of the prophet Balaam, one of the most gifted and eloquent men of the Old Testament. As the Angel of the Lord stood blocking his path, protecting him from speaking against God's will, Balaam became enraged at his terrified donkey and fell to beating it with his staff. The donkey, first seeing the Angel with drawn sword and then being beaten by its master, thrust itself against the wall crushing Balaam's foot. What a picture of a man venting his temper upon brute creation because he was confronted by adverse circumstances.

As with most cases of anger, the donkey was not the real problem. The Angel of the Lord was there to rebuke Balaam and judge him. Balaam should have been angry with himself, for he was the source of his own trouble and sorrow. Flares of anger are always followed by remorse, but too often remorse is too late to save relationships, reputation, and respect.

What, then, is our remedy? "Grievous words stir up strife but a soft answer turns away wrath." The remedy is to not allow the anger of another to be contagious in our own life. When a man is angry, a wise friend can do a great service by using a kindly answer or no reply at all, saving a quarrel.

Further, we must stop excusing our own angry outbursts. You don't just have a bad temper, beloved, you have a recurring sin. Instead earnestly endeavor to conquer your anger. Cultivate patience by consciously stopping the hurtful words. Pray for His strength to set a new path, a new habit of response. Best of all, yield your own will to the keeping power of the One who said, "To whom you yield, that one's servant you are." Anger is not the fruit of the new man, but the old nature. We are called upon by Paul, "Do not let not sin reign in your mortal body, that you should obey its lusts. But yield yourselves to God."

Thus, the apostle said, "Be angry, and do not sin; do not let the sun go down on your wrath." Do not give place in your life to anger. Allow Christ to so control your thoughts, words, and actions that, as your Counselor and Friend, His presence will give the needed strength for victory over the tempter and your temper.

Dearest Father, I confess that sometimes I allow anger against my fellow man to intrude into my mind and reside in my heart. Even if the angry words do not actually leave my lips, there are times when I harbor that feeling in my heart. Please forgive me. I yield control of my anger to You, Lord, and ask that You help me resist the tempter in this area. Amen.

October 23   A Universal Liberation

Scripture Reading: Matthew 28: 16-20

Key Verse: "Go therefore and make disciples of all the nations, baptizing them in the name of the Father and of the Son and of the Holy Spirit, teaching them to observe all things that I have commanded you . . . ." Matthew 28: 19-20

Jesus was always compassionate towards the multitudes. He was thinking of them when He gave the Great Commission. It was for them as well as for us that He agonized in Gethsemane and died on Calvary. This challenge of the multitudes is a militant challenge for every Christian in the world.

The question naturally comes, how shall we reach them with the gospel? Not just by talking about it, nor pleading with one another, nor discovering the great need, nor scolding ourselves. No, there are four steps to the devotion of one's self to the challenge our Lord gave to us in the Great Commission.

The first thing necessary to liberate the multitudes from the bindings of sin in this world is "conception." We must get some real conception of the gigantic proportion of the task as a whole. If we are not doing our best to reach these countless multitudes, we are failing at the very heart of the most solemn task ever committed to man or angels. We must see the multitudes with the eyes of Christ. Can we grasp the right conception of the value of one boy or girl to God? The task is so vast, it seems truly impossible, but Christ would not give us a command so close to His heart if He did not know it could be accomplished through Him. We do not have to reach them all. We simply have to reach all that we can. There are millions of us, soldiers of the cross, all marching to His command to not leave a single soul within our reach untouched by the gospel.

Secondly, this conception must be backed by a conviction concerning the needs of the multitudes. There they are: an endless numberless human mass, needy, hungry, sick, hopeless, baffled, and lost. Among them are wickedly brilliant men, richly selfish women, and hopelessly rotten children, all needing God who can transform every life. Whole families of them are falling into Christless graves. They have hearts He can satisfy, needs He can supply, emptiness He can fill, hunger He can appease, and a moral and spiritual catastrophe He can avert. In this mass are children, boys and girls, and young people. They are normal, needy and approachable. They need the gospel message and are open to it.

But look again and you see death stalking every street, clanking along every boulevard, thudding along every highway, hanging around every corner, grinning at every window. Its muffled tread, its stealthy march is ceaseless. To die without Jesus is to be eternally lost.

They are not as antagonistic as we are apathetic. We are content enough to sit together in heavenly places, but unwilling to walk in unholy places. If our message is what we profess it to be, if it is what we believe it to be, if it is what its fruits through history prove it to be, we should carry it in all haste to these neighbors and friends of ours all about us. We dare not gamble with their lost souls. We must hang indifference on the scaffold and place the deepest interest upon the throne.

Won't you seek to see the world through the eyes of our Lord today?

Lord, fill my life so full of You that You overflow into every conversation with joy and praise, honoring You before each person who touches my life. Help me to obey Your great and final commission to make disciples. I can surely do something toward fulfilling this command. Please show me what that is. Amen.

October 24   The Universal Liberation II

Scripture Reading: Matthew 9:35-38

Key Verse: "But when He saw the multitudes, He was moved with compassion for them, because they were weary and scattered, like sheep having no shepherd." Matthew 9:36

We have seen that when it comes to the liberation of the multitudes from the binding ropes of the world, we must first realize the scope of the task and the value God places on it. It was Christ's final command as He left us for Heaven. It was of enormous importance to Him. Then we must have the conviction to pick up the task and believe that Christ will make the impossible not only possible, but a blessing to us in the process.

A wealthy Mr. Davis once told of a dream where he asked Jesus where He was in this world of hate and shame, "Are You hiding? Are You indifferent? Are You preoccupied?" Then the Lord answered and said, "Come with me." The Lord took him to hell, a great divide where a beggar stood on one side and Davis stood on the other begging for a drop of water for his tongue. Then, Jesus took him back to earth to Davis' beautiful mansion, and there at the doorstep lay the beggar. And there, He pointed out, was the place where that great gulf began, at Davis' very own doorstep. Davis could have avoided that gulf, but he did not. He could have fed the man, but Davis gave crumbs, crumbs from the table. God forgive us for our lack of conviction about this task He gave us, for it is not God who is indifferent or preoccupied.

Now, a right conception of, and a true conviction concerning the multitudes should set us on fire with compassion for the unreached souls. Compassion led Brainard to write, "I cared not where nor how I lived, nor what hardships I went through if only I could win souls for Christ." It led Vassar to say, "My business is not to preach, but to go over the hill to seek for the sheep that are lost."

Compassion led David Livingstone, worn out by forty-nine attacks of Yellow Fever and surrounded by countless difficulties to write, "Nothing earthly can make me give up my work in despair. I encourage myself in the Lord and go forward." And as Jesus beheld the multitudes he wept over them for their souls' sake. Without compassion, your convictions will dissolve into the air, aimless and useless.

There is a fourth and vital component to our completing the task set before us. It is the cap-stone of them all. It is a word without which all our conception, conviction and compassion fail to bring forth fruit. That word is consecration, consecration to God. Faith gives power to consecration. Jesus said, "If you have faith as a mustard seed, you will say to this mountain, 'Move from here to there,' and it will move." Doubt will never reach the multitudes, but faith will.

With our lives, our talents, and our goods consecrated to God and the task, and our eyes fixed upon Jesus, we would win a host for God. The salvation of these multitudes depends on what they do with Jesus. Moral essays will not reach them, social reform is not sufficient; a milk and water gospel will not change their hearts and lives. Jesus alone, His message, His blood, His gospel, this alone will suffice to liberate the lost everywhere. Do not, at the end of the age, go empty-handed. Must you meet your Savior without one soul to greet Him? No beloved, let us bring all of the multitude we can. What a day of rejoicing that will be!

Lord, I want everyone I know and as many as possible of those I don't know, to be with You in Heaven some day. Please make my life count for You and the Kingdom of God. Let me win souls for You, dear God. Amen.

October 25   Blood Work

Scripture Reading: Leviticus Chapter 17

Key Verse: "For the life of the flesh is in the blood, and I have given it to you upon the altar to make atonement for your souls; for it is the blood that makes atonement for the soul." Leviticus 17:11

From Genesis to Revelation we see a scarlet stream of redemption. The Word of God is a different book; it is a living Word wholly distinct from others for one reason, it contains the blood of Christ circulating through every page and in every verse. This scarlet stream imparts the very life of God. Without the blood of Christ, the Bible would be like any other book, and of no more value, for the Bible teaches plainly "that the life is in the blood."

Life, that mysterious something which science has never been able to quite fathom, is said by God to be in the blood of the flesh. And while this is true of all flesh, it is particularly relevant when referring to the blood of the man Christ Jesus. In His blood was not only life as we think of it physically, but also eternal life as well.

Scripture teaches in Acts 17:26 that natural man is related by the blood of Adam, that sinful and polluted blood which causes us all to be born spiritually dead in trespasses and sin. All men have this common origin, with Adam's blood coursing through their veins. This blood carries the sentence of death, and for this reason all men die a common death with no exceptions. The blood poisoning of the first sin was so potent that even yet all who are related to Adam by human birth still succumb to its poison

Here is a marvel of divine Chemistry. In Revelation we read that the saints of God washed their robes white in the blood of the Lamb. Now, it is impossible to wash your clothes white in human blood, but God's chemical laboratory of redemption has found a way. His sinless, supernatural blood alone can accomplish this great feat. When Satan comes before God to accuse us, all we need to do is point to the blood that was shed for us, and it is enough, "It is the blood that makes atonement for the soul."

It was on Calvary's cross that God's blood bank was opened, and into it went the blood of the Lord Jesus Christ. It suits every type, for Jesus is the Divine Universal Donor. It is free for all who submit to its transfusion by the Holy Spirit. It does not deteriorate, and it never fails. All that needs be done to receive it is to apply by faith. Then, as a believer, you are saved by His blood from the poison of sin.

And so every born again believer is made a member of the body of Christ. The one thing which unites them and makes them relatives and brothers is the incorruptible blood of Christ which reaches every member, white or black, preacher or layperson, Roman Catholic or Plymouth Brethren. All believers who have trusted the finished work of Christ are brothers by blood, members of one family, and body.

We may differ in function, as the cells of a physical body differ in function. We may differ in location, or structure. It doesn't matter. The blood is fluid, touching every cell, supplying each bit of tissue with nourishment and constantly cleansing of that which is not necessary. All of us are one through the blood of Jesus. Have you recognized this unity of the body of Christ? We are one in Him, and we have one common interest, to exalt our Head, the Lord Jesus, and to love one another.

Thank You, Jesus, for shedding Your precious saving blood for me on Calvary. Thank You for Your great undeserved love. Praise Your Holy Name, Lord, for You are worthy, the spotless and blameless Lamb of God. Amen.

October 26   The Coming World Dictator

Scripture Reading: Revelation Chapter 13

Key Verse: "Then I stood on the sand of the sea. And I saw a beast rising up out of the sea." Revelation 13:1

The Bible frequently and very definitely states that there will come, in a time of world crisis, a man who shall assume world dictatorship. In the study of the wicked trinity; the Anti-Christ, the false prophet, and the Red Dragon, we find that they do not come to save the world, but to damn the world. If it were not for God's elect being preserved by His infinite power, these wicked ones would destroy all men.

How different than our precious Lord Jesus Christ, who said, "I did not come to judge the world, but to save the world." There is the pure and priceless in God the Father, the Son, and the Holy Spirit, and there is the cheap counterfeit of the evil trinity in all its deception and malevolence. Jesus teaches us that the devil comes to steal and kill and destroy. We can count on it, so let us not be deceived by cunning and pretty words, threats and lies.

Some Bible teachers instruct that the time of our being caught up to Christ will be before the appearance of the Anti-Christ, some during his reign, others that we will endure his entire reign. Since Noah and other faithful and Godly examples have been removed and kept safely apart from judgment falling upon the earth, it would be consistent that we be raptured, or caught up to Christ, ahead of this time of tribulation. However, as Christians, we have the assurance of God's loving care in whatever circumstance we find ourselves in. "For He who is in you is greater than he who is in the world."

We see by God's word that the Anti-Christ is a person, he comes out of the revived Roman Empire, he utters blasphemous charges against God, he wears out and oppresses the Jewish nation, and he alters the calendar. This man of perdition's power will be supreme for three and one half years; he assumes a fierce countenance, practices the occult and will exercise a strange and mighty power over the minds of men, a power given him by Satan.

He will be ingenious in solving world problems through economic devices which he uses to restore economic prosperity for a time. He will come in the guise of a peacemaker, but the peace will not last. The anti-Christ will be a military strategist and will wage war successfully. His crowning act of infamy will be when he sets himself up as God and demands worship from mankind, giving all mankind a mark of identification without which they cannot buy or sell. But thank God, his end comes.

Oh beloved, the first words of the angels are always, "Do not be afraid." Let us not fall into the clutches of fear, for fear is not of God. Our Savior is greater than all that can befall this world. Why does God speak of such things in His Word? If a kindly father's children were safely in a lifeboat, would he not still point out others that were in danger of drowning so that they might be offered a hand into the safety of the boat?

Let us think of what most assuredly lies ahead in the future, and offer the lifesaver of Christ to all we know and help to tell even those we don't know. Let us give freely of our hope to all we meet, our finances to missions, and our prayers to the salvation of those not yet saved. It is what our kindly Father wants.

Dearest Father, there is a terrible time ahead. We see the storm clouds gathering faster and faster. But through Jesus I have no fear. Please bring all who are within the scope of my influence to a saving knowledge of You. In the name of Jesus, amen.

October 27　　Precious Children of God

Scripture Reading: Romans Chapter 8

Key Verses: "The Spirit Himself bears witness with our spirit that we are children of God, and if children, then heirs - heirs of God and joint heirs with Christ." Romans 8:16-17.

God is here addressing Himself only to believers, for only believers are indwelt by the Holy Spirit. And the Spirit ministers to us in many ways. "The Spirit Himself bears witness with our spirit." He does not witness to our spirit but with our spirit, showing us that the child of God, having had communicated to him the life of Christ, is necessarily conscious of the glorious fact of filial relationship to God. We know that we are born-ones of God.

Believers will find themselves calling God, Father. It is a fine thing for us, to cultivate Biblical addresses in prayer, Father, our Father, my Father, or Righteous Father. Jesus did. We love to call Him Father because the Holy Spirit has put within us the deep consciousness of being born of God and belonging to His family.

If we are born-ones of God, then we are heirs. This is said of no angel, cherub, or seraph, that he is an heir of God. If we would only meditate deeply upon these facts: I am born of God, and I am one of His heirs, then earthly things will shrink to nothing. When we fully comprehend our position in Jesus, it will change the way we live our todays and plan our tomorrows.

We are heirs of God and joint heirs with Christ. Think of it: that we, guilty, lost, wretched children of Adam, have become joint heirs with Christ, the eternal maker of all things, the well-beloved of the Father, the Righteous One, the Prince of Life, the only God. We are heirs of all things. It is utterly amazing that He could love us so much.

Later in the eighth chapter, Paul speaks of the Holy Spirit's ministry in the realm of prayer. How eloquent are some addresses to God, but not so with Paul or Stephen and the real saints of God. Eloquence really has little to do with the matter. So, the Spirit Himself makes intercession, with "groanings that cannot be uttered." He helps us in our weakness. He cares enough to search our hearts.

"Groanings," what a word! How ignorant we are of the infinite concern of the blessed indwelling Spirit for us. And God, who searches our hearts, knows what is in the mind of the Spirit because He makes intercession for the saints according to the will of God. It is God the Father who is searching our hearts. He knows the mind of the indwelling Holy Spirit concerning a saint, in order that He might supply it and in order that He may cause all things to work for our good.

Remember that in the plan of salvation, God the Father is the source, Christ is the channel and the Spirit is the agent. All are working according to the Father's plan, and according to our needs which He discerns, according to dangers which He foresees, and according to all the desires He has for us. His providence is limitless and for good.

We are called by Him; we are God's heirs and precious children. We are already before Him justified and glorified, though not yet manifested so, as an embryo is not yet manifested as the man he will be. It will be so in time and already is so in the eyes of God who sees the past, present and future together in one glorious panorama. Live this day with the knowledge that you are God's precious child.

Dearest Father in Heaven, thank You for seeing me as I will someday be instead of how I am today. And thank You for forming me into all that I can be. Amen.

Scripture Reading: Psalm 27

Key Verse: "*One thing have I desired of the Lord, that will I seek: that I may dwell in the house of the Lord all the days of my life, to behold the beauty of the Lord, and to inquire in His temple.*" *Psalm 27:4*

David was a man after God's own heart, and David was a man whose heart was set on God. Here he expresses his greatest desire: to be in the House of God, the place of public worship and fellowship with Him. In the twenty-third Psalm, he made the same great statement, "I will dwell in the House of the Lord forever." Oh, would to God all of us felt this strongly about the House of the Lord.

David was desirous of seeking God. Why? Because he deeply wanted to see God, and to behold the beauty of God. David first desired to worship God, to worship the Lord in the beauty of His holiness. But also notice his second desire. He yearned to inquire in His temple. Now that is spiritual growth and education. David aspired to learn more about His God, and to know Him. He sought true wisdom and knowledge. And truly, the next time we enter the House of our Lord, we should enter yearning to worship, aching to know God better.

For David to enter a place of worship and have the concentration to focus his worship, to seek the Lord in that public place, shows how seriously he took his search for God. It is those who seek that shall find, for God has promised, "Those who seek me diligently will find Me." When we attend church, is our concentration on the Lord?

I have a few suggestions that might make the time spent in service more profitable to those who truly desire to seek God's face. First, we need to recognize that such intense communion with God as David speaks of requires complete concentration. Arrive early, so that you can prepare to participate both in worship and in the inquiry into God's Word that is about to occur.

After you are seated, purpose to remove the obstacles that would seek to distract you. Consciously set aside the worldly cares and interests that intrude on your thoughts. Avoid needless talking. Do not be consumed with looking around, but rather with looking inward. Be thoughtful and silent. Time spent in God's House is the most precious time in your life. Pray humbly, kneeling if possible. Remember, you are in the awesome presence of your God.

And what might you pray? Well, tell God you have come to meet Him there that day. Pray for the preacher, that he may be filled with the Holy Spirit and that he may speak boldly and truthfully from Scripture. Pray for yourself that all wandering thoughts be banished, and that your heart would feast on the truth. Pray that the burdened souls in the congregation may find peace and those who do not know God might find Him.

Fasten your thoughts firmly on the service. Sing the praises of your God and King. Meet Him in that holy place. Then concentrate on the words of the pastor. Do not miss a word; you have no time for vain thoughts. Look for something in the sermon, and purpose to find it. God would certainly have you learn something in service, and you can trust Him to provide it if you will listen. Purpose in your heart, also, that you will not be the cause of distraction to others, but that in every action, every thought, you will say with David, "I will offer sacrifices of joy in His tabernacle, I will sing praises to the Lord . . . your face Lord I will seek . . . Wait, I say, on the Lord."

Dear Lord, thank You for Your patience with me. Please help me to center my thoughts, my heart, my purpose on You daily. Help me to seek You in weekly service, and in my daily walk. Amen.

October 29 — The Call

Scripture: Jeremiah Chapter 33

Key Verse: "Call to Me, and I will answer you, and show you great and mighty things, which you do not know." Jeremiah 33:3

From Genesis to Revelation, God calls upon His people to pray. Like the scarlet thread in the rope of the British Navy, so God has tied up all blessings, all power, all real success, all true spirituality, and all real fellowship with the Father, in this great rope of prayer.

After all, prayer is the first sign of conversion, the birth cry of the soul. It is a refuge in trouble, strength in weakness and armor for our spiritual battle. Prayer provides comfort in sorrow, and a guide in darkness. It is the Christian's vital breath and native air. And, hear this, neither men nor devils can take prayer away from the believer. Persecution may drive us from the House of God. The preacher's voice may be silenced and the Bible plucked from our hands. We may even be locked in prison for our faith. Yet the avenue of prayer is open.

Daniel was in the lion's den, Shadrach and friends found themselves in a fiery furnace, and Paul and Silas were in the inner prison. Nevertheless, all these continued in prayer. Prayer is the gateway to God that hell itself cannot close. Jonah, through his own disobedience, found himself in the belly of a great fish. Yet, the avenue of prayer provided a means of communion with God when he was ready to seek it.

Prayer is so vastly beyond the utterance of mere words. It is the relation and constant attitude of the soul to God, which includes submission and surrender, whereby we are in harmony with the will of God. It is the desire of the soul for God. It is the confidence of the soul in God, both dependence on Him and the utter distrust of self and self-will. And, it is the fellowship of the soul with God, the delight of His presence, and freedom of communication with Him at all times.

So, listen to God as He cries out in Jeremiah, "Call to Me . . ." This is the call of God to you and me. This is a generous invitation from God to man. Out of eternity, the mighty Creator calls. Here, too, is a command. Not to obey is to sin. The sin of prayerlessness is a shame indeed. We cannot ignore God's call. Think, oh just think, of having contact with the God of heaven! The God of glory and a poor sinner like me, in communion through prayer.

Also, He offers us a contract, "I will answer." Here is an unbreakable promise from the immutable God. And, the scope of the promise is wide, "I will show you great and mighty things you do not know." Who knows the extent of God's revelation? Wide indeed is the contrast between His great and mighty things and our own poor, feeble asking.

So we are invited to this personal communion with God. We can come to Him, and we can continue in prayer. That means much more than having frequently recurring times of prayer. It includes the idea of clinging closely to God, remaining constant to Him in continuous devotion and steadfast earnestness. This continuance in prayer will make God's presence very real, bringing a peace which calms the soul.

What a sense of encouragement and confidence should fill our hearts with such an appeal from such a God. What a revelation of truth awaits the man or woman who prays. What a generous invitation this is from our dear Heavenly Father.

Dear Heavenly Father, I come before You to answer Your call. So, now, boldly I come to lay the concerns of my heart and life before You in expectation of your great and mighty answer. Amen.

October 30   What Shall We Have?

Scripture Reading: Matthew 19:16-30

Key Verse: "We have left all and followed You. Therefore, what shall we have?" Matthew 19: 27

A rich young ruler, interested in Jesus and in eternal life, came running to ask, "What good thing shall I do that I may have eternal life?" Jesus asked him a few questions, then put the young man to the test saying, "If you want to be perfect, go, sell what you have and give to the poor, and you will have treasure in heaven; and come, follow Me." But when the young man heard it, he went away sorrowfully, for he had great possessions.

Then Peter speaks up. Doesn't it seem as though it is always Peter who asks the questions? And what great answers he receives! Here is the question. "See, we have left all and followed You. Therefore, what shall we have?" In other words, Peter is saying that the young ruler is not willing to leave all and follow Christ, but they have done that. Now what shall they get?

None of the disciples was a rich man, but it meant as much for Peter, James and John to leave their nets and fishing boats as it would have meant for the rich young ruler to leave his money and follow Christ. Actually his question was fitting and appropriate. He wanted to know what was to be the end of their faith and discipleship. He knows there is something more in store for them, so he plainly asks, "Lord, what shall we have?" In the great answer Jesus spoke, first of all to the twelve disciples, then in general to every faithful and self-denying follower of Christ in every age.

Jesus said, "Assuredly, I say to you, that in the regeneration, when the Son of Man sits in the throne of His glory, you who have followed Me will also sit on twelve thrones, judging the twelve tribes of Israel." Here Jesus says things are to be restored to the original plan and order that God had for creation and for man, a state of glory and happiness, founded upon regeneration.

That is what the world needs, what you and I need today, regeneration, a new birth. The regeneration of the world will come some of these days, not through the efforts of man, and not through political revolution. It will come when Christ Himself comes to fulfill and establish all righteousness. What a day that will be!

Next we hear the general promise for all who have preferred Him and His gospel to the things of this world. The promise is that they shall receive a hundred fold of what they have given up, fathers, mothers, family, lands and houses, and in the world to come, eternal life.

You see what things He offers here in this world and then what the believer will have in the world to come. The Christian has in this life, beyond all the blessings this world gives him, the kindly light of a great hope for the future where he enters into the fullness of eternal life. The Christian need not fear death as a great unknown. We have the assurance of a home with our dear Lord.

We have a living hope, a hope that neither money nor prestige, nor popularity, or effort can ever give of unending blessing in eternity. We have eternal life. We have an eternal future to spend with the Author and Finisher of our Faith. We have forever in His company to sing His praises. That is what we shall have, beloved. That is what we shall have.

Dearest Lord, thank You for the gift of my salvation. You bless me so much in this life that I wouldn't want any other lifestyle. But I know You have promised even more when we are with You in paradise. Thank You Dear Lord, for saving my soul. Amen.

October 31   True Worship

Scripture Reading: John 4:19-26

Key Verse: "The hour is coming, and now is, when the true worshipers will worship the Father in spirit and truth; for the Father is seeking such to worship Him. God is Spirit, and those who worship Him must worship in spirit and truth." John 4:23-24

The Master was here leading a sin-scarred, hardened woman step by step from sin to self, and now to salvation and service. The Samaritans had rejected all Scripture save the Pentateuch and by doing so had rejected a large part of God's revelation of mercy. They had put themselves in the position of those who worshipped an unknown God. Like so many today, they had a religion of encrusted forms and ritualism, ignorant and cold. In this moment of revelation, Jesus reveals the mode of true worship to this Samaritan woman. God must be worshipped both in spirit and in truth.

Now to worship the Father in spirit is to worship Him in the innermost soul, to pay unto Him the homage of reverent thought and feeling, of utmost trust and love. And this spiritual worship is not to be compared to a formal worship dependent on place and ritual. It is not that spiritual worship will reject all outward rites, but it will use them only as helps and expressions of inward spiritual service. Worship is a matter of the heart.

And to worship the Father in truth is to worship Him in conformity to and fellowship of truth. It is to render Him the honor and service which His own nature prescribes. It is worship that seeks to know and understand the worshipped. Thank God, the Samaritans were to welcome the full and final revelation of God in the person of His Son and to serve and worship Him in the light of that revelation. Worship, you see, is also a matter of the mind.

"God is Spirit," said the Son of God, and therefore is not confined to mountain tops or within temple walls. We do not worship a God bound by creation, by time or by space. His love is perfect, His power boundless, and His knowledge infinite. No wonder the Psalmist cried, "Where can I go from Your Spirit or where can I go from Your presence?"

Yes, only worship offered in spirit and truth corresponds with the nature of God: pure, guileless, sinless, perfectly holy, and righteous. But how can our worship be true and heartfelt in spirit? The answer is found in the revelation that came to this woman of Samaria. When she sought with a sincere heart and repentant spirit to find God, He said to her, "I who speak to you am He."

True worship brings to your heart and soul the presence of Jesus. True worship will lead you and me to shut out all else and let the light of His countenance shine in. And in truly worshipping Him, we will become more and more Christ-like. Our worship will be true and real and reverent in proportion as it expresses itself through Christ-likeness. Anything less than this is insincere and mechanical and God will not accept it from our hands, or our hearts.

True worship becomes a highway to God that extends through us to others. Jesus went about doing good, and so will we. Jesus bound up broken hearts, and so will we. He proclaimed liberty to the captive, and hope to the hopeless, and so will we. He taught the truth of the Scriptures, and shone the light of the truth into a world of darkness. And when we worship Him in spirit and truth, His light will shine through us as well.

Dear Lord, may my worship be acceptable to You, Father. As I seek Your face, Your light, Your presence, please reveal Yourself to me. I wait upon You Lord . . . amen.

November 1

New Creation

Scripture Reading: Genesis Chapter 1

Key Verse: "In the beginning, God created the heavens and the earth." Genesis 1:1

Our world was not just the result of a fortuitous combination of atoms. It was created by God. All things were empty and void, until God took hold and made this world into something beautiful, functional, and reflective of the glory of its Creator. Man, too, needs this touch from God so that empty lives can be made beautiful, of service to God, and reflective of the image in which man was made.

For in the creation account in Genesis we find a perfect pattern of the new life wrought by the redemptive work of Jesus. God's work in the restoration of the world from its chaotic state parallels the work He undertakes to restore a fallen soul. As the earth was dark and God said, "Let there be light," this is also the first step God takes in saving a soul. He sends forth His light of truth to put the sinner under conviction that he is lost and needs a Savior. Truth, to the moral and spiritual nature, is exactly what light is in the material world. Only in the light of truth can a sinner see himself, and thus see his need for a Savior. And only in Christ our Savior can we find the light of the truth. The darkness was only driven out of the world by the light, and sin can only be driven out of a life by the light of the world, Jesus.

In Genesis 1:2, we see that "The Spirit of God was hovering over the face of the waters." The Holy Spirit is often the active agent, the executor of the God-head. He brooded over the darkness of the formless earth, and He is the seal of the new believer to fill with His presence. He convicts the unbeliever, and indwells the new believer.

Also, as God provided the firmament as a fixed division separating vapor from liquid, so too God provides a dividing line between the soul and its sins. God aids the seeking sinner, who in the light of truth has seen himself and his need for a savior, to see that his sins can be taken away by Christ. Christ can produce in him a separation between the sinner and his sins.

Note that God begins the day at night. When God marks time, He marks it thus, "So the evening and the morning were the third day." God always works from dark to light, from sin to holiness, from sorrow to joy, from weakness to strength. The world began in darkness, and through the workings of the Spirit of God, light came. So it is with our individual lives, also, from the darkness and sorrow of sin, into the light and joy of salvation.

God's work culminates on day six, when God concluded creation by making man in his own image, giving him dominion and lordship over the entire world and everything in it. In the new life, this corresponds with the enthronement of our dear Lord Jesus Christ as Lord of all in our lives. After the new birth, we are not immediately made perfect, but rather the enthronement of Christ extends the boundaries of His perfect love throughout the whole of our life, until we are like Him.

We cannot forget, however, that God's work of six days was followed by a seventh day, a day of rest. God rested from all His work on the seventh day, and He blessed it and sanctified it. So we, too, await that ultimate rest with God when we shall be forever with the Lord, rejoicing in His presence and praising His name eternally!

Father, I have such a burden for _____'s eternal soul. Please, Lord, shine the light of truth on them, and soften their heart, I pray. In Jesus' name, amen.

November 2   Rainbow Glory

Scripture Reading: Revelation Chapter 4

Key Verse: "And He who sat there was like a jasper and a sardius stone in appearance; and there was a rainbow around the throne, in appearance like an emerald." Revelation 4:3

Every Bible-literate Christian is deeply conscious of our God's great and everlasting mercy every time he looks at a rainbow. When God made His covenant with Noah, in Genesis 9, it was a covenant on His terms, for our benefit.

It was the first covenant made with man in distinct terms. In it God bound Himself to a certain course of action, that He would not destroy the world anymore by means of a flood. It was a covenant of forbearance, an act of pure grace, a revelation of the nature of God in nature.

This covenant throws light upon the permission of evil, for here we see that His mercy triumphs over judgment. This reveals the nature of God as full of tenderness and compassion. Evil is permitted that greater good may arise, and that God might magnify His mercy. God's mercy then may lead men to repentance.

Beautiful in itself, a rainbow is calculated to attract attention. It is most fitting to teach the fact of God's constancy and to encourage the largest hopes from His love. God said He set "His bow," thereby separating Himself from nature. Mankind was to learn to recognize a presiding mind in all the phenomena of nature.

And God said, "I will look upon it that I may remember." Now God does not have any need of reminders, but rather this special sign appears to God as He looks down over the depravity of man. It is a marvelous thing to know that God will look upon His bow, for in this appointed sign of the rainbow, the eye of man can meet the eye of God.

So the rainbow is a fitting sign, a message from God. Because it always appears after a storm, it is God's reassurance to man. We do not have to be frightened by storms, for they are transitory and harmless. So, too, the verse of our text reassures us about the future. See the rainbow around God's throne? There are storms ahead of this world, dear friend, but they are transitory and nothing can harm the soul in God's care.

Again we look at the rainbow's composition. What is a rainbow but pure light, passing through vapor? Yet in the concentric bands we find order, wonder and beauty. Ezekiel says, in Ezekiel 1:28, "Like the appearance of a rainbow in a cloud on a rainy day, so was the appearance of the brightness all around it. This was the appearance of the likeness of the glory of the Lord." The Light of the world is beautiful and though we cannot see the Light itself, we can see the beauty of the Light reflected in lives all around us. Wherever we see order in worship, wonder at the revelation of His Word, and the beauty of His holiness recognized, there we find Him.

And as the light of the sun creates the rainbow as it passes through the drops of mist, so the beauty of the Light of the world should shine through the lives of believers everywhere. In eternity, at last we shall see the rainbow around the throne of God, and join in the endless praise of He who sets the bow of color in the sky, and the bow of grace in your life and mine. Oh, what a beautiful reminder of God's grace!

Dearest Lord, It is an awesome thing to realize that if I allow myself to decrease, and Christ to increase in me, that it is the Light that the world will see, not me. May it be so. Amen.

Scripture Reading: Matthew Chapter 3

Key Verses: "He will baptize you with the Holy Spirit and fire."
Matthew 3:11 "Then there appeared to them divided tongues,
as of fire, and one sat upon each of them." Acts 2:3

A very strange promise indeed, that Christ should baptize us with the Holy Spirit and fire. To be baptized with the Holy Spirit is a blessed and glorious occasion, but to be baptized with fire also is of great significance and full of meaning. One may define flame as a gas temporarily luminous because of chemical action. But when we speak of fire as combustion we mean one substance is uniting with another in chemical action and that while this is going on there is heat and light attending this action. This begins to solve the mystery.

On the day of Pentecost, when the Holy Spirit united with the believers, the symbol of this uniting was the symbol of fire which sat in a two-edged flame on each of them. It meant a new life for those believers, a new life of power and service.

When the Holy Spirit and the believer unite, there is a tangible, observable reaction and response. Those 120 who were baptized with the Spirit immediately began to manifest their fire. Their tongues were loosed to tell out what wonderful things the Lord had done. Everybody heard in their own language. It was a living human and divine flame sparking and crackling the hot tidings of God to a lost world.

And watch the fire burn in the early Church! On the first day 3,000 souls were saved, fear came upon every soul, and many wonders and signs were done by the Apostles. See the lame man healed and praising God? See Peter and John in prison, and the address to the Sanhedrin? See the fire? Peter, filled with the Holy Spirit said, "If we this day are judged for a good deed done to a helpless man, by what means he has been made well, let it be known to you all . . . that by the name of Jesus Christ of Nazareth whom you crucified, whom God raised from the dead, by Him this man is shown before you whole." And the Sanhedrin marveled at the boldness and they realized that they had been with

Jesus. They didn't know what happened, but Peter did. He had been baptized with the Holy Spirit and with fire; and they preached on, witnessed on, healed on.

Man works hard to produce enthusiasm, but the fire that Jesus promised comes not by works, but by yielding. Man produces fire by friction, by flint, or by refraction, today men work to produce fire by inventing new ways to stir up enthusiasm. There are Rag-time services, Vaudeville services, and Jazz services to draw a crowd and then give a message. Why is it necessary? Has the simple Gospel Story lost its power? No, God forbid.

The message of the Church must center not around jazz bands and social reforms, but on Jesus Christ. The Holy Spirit came to help us turn from idols, not turn ice cream freezers; to turn our face to God in prayer, not to turn picture wheels and supper wheels. The early church knew their crucified, risen, glorified, coming Christ by the presence of the Holy Spirit.

We can have this same Pentecostal fire burning in our hearts. It comes to a wholly yielded and cleansed heart when we honestly and truthfully say, "not I but Christ, I want only His will." Then the Holy Spirit's glow of a holy fire springs up within our believing heart.

Dear Father, fill me with Your Holy Spirit and fire also, that I may burst out with power and service for You. In Jesus' name, amen.

November 4   Preservation of the Saints

Scripture: Jude

Key Scripture: "Now to Him who is able to keep you from stumbling and to present you faultless before the presence of His glory with exceeding joy, to God our Savior who alone is wise, be glory and majesty, dominion and power, both now and forever. Amen" Jude v.24 and 25

Jude's picture of the apostasy of the closing days of this age is a dark one indeed. The sad thing is that it will only end in the Lord's return to earth to vindicate His insulted majesty by executing His judgments upon an apostate Christendom who once professed to be followers of the Lord.

Now Jesus told us that when He was here, so let's not get discouraged. He said the wheat and the tares would grow together until the harvest in the end of the age when the Lord Himself will separate the evil from the good. So let us take up the seven things that should characterize a true believer called to live in an apostate Christendom.

Each believer must be earnestly contending for the faith. Since the inception of the Christian Church, a multitude of its members have suffered persecution and death because of the preaching and the defense of the faith. The evil one's methods are many. Salvation by works is substituted for salvation by grace. Beautiful pagan ethics are substituted for the filling of the Spirit. The transformation of human society by a social gospel and national legislation is substituted for the coming of Christ and the establishing of His kingdom.

Remember the teaching and warnings of the apostles. They foretold that conditions would come when mockers would scoff and make light of the fundamentals of our holy faith. How we need to be filled up with the apostolic teaching and prophecy to discern the errors from the truth. To be forewarned is to be forearmed.

Each believer must be building themselves up in the faith. Dr. Dixon says that every church is divided into trees and posts. When you plant a tree it begins to grow. When you plant a post it begins to rot.

The life of a believer cannot be static; there must be growth, progress and advancement.

Each believer needs to be continually praying in the Spirit. To pray in the Spirit is to pray in the energy of the Spirit and according to the will and leading of the Spirit of God. Our prayer life began when we first turned from self and sin and yielded to Jesus Christ as Savior.

Believers must keep themselves in the love of God. Yes, we can maintain the attitude of love in a world filled with hate, controversy and warfare by not allowing these things to take us out of fellowship with our ascended Lord. We must be faithful and uncompromising in sincere love for our enemies.

Also, believers must use every legitimate means to reclaim the apostate and save the sinner. Jude says "And some have compassion . . . but others save with fear, out of the fire." Soul-winning is set before us as a task that demands the wisdom, grace, and power of God. None but those who have been clothed with the garments of Christ's salvation and who love the sinner, yet hate his sins, dare engage in it.

The Epistle closes with a most gracious benediction. It is the upward look of the child of God to his Lord who is able and willing to keep us to the end. Hallelujah! What a Savior!

Dearest Lord, thank You for providing me with all I need to be faithful to You. Yet with all of that You still promise to be the one who "keeps" me. I need only be willing. I am willing, Lord. Amen.

Scripture: I John 5:1-5

Key Verse: "And this is the victory that has overcome the world, - our faith." I John 5:4

I agree with those who say that theologians have spoiled faith. They have defined the life out of it. They have analyzed it until, like sugar, whose component elements when they are separate are bitter to the taste, faith for multitudes has lost its primal sweetness.

The fact is that faith is one of those elemental forces in human life, like love and hope, which can only be described in terms of what they do to life. It can be illustrated better than defined. Jesus never defined faith, He illustrated it. See Him gathering that little group of untutored men, and with faith launch a spiritual movement that turned the world upside down, and then you will understand what He meant when He said that faith could move mountains.

Paul never defined faith, he illustrated it. See him growing from the harshness of his first persecuting temper to the beauty and grace of his latter years and you see what he meant by "Christ may dwell in your hearts through faith."

Only one endeavor is found in the New Testament to define faith. In Hebrews the author says that faith is the substance of things hoped for and the evidence of things not seen. It is a great definition, but even the writer was not satisfied, for he at once leaves it behind and goes on to describe faith in terms of what it does to life. "By faith Abraham . . . by faith Moses," and he illustrates through the lives of the great people of faith in the Bible what it did in their lives. For, there are two aspects to our experience, the outer circumstance and the confidence within.

As to which is more important we need not long debate, for even the experience of your life would testify today that the central matter is the confidence within. For one thing, what you give faith to is the object of your loyalty. If a man gives himself to a woman whom he loves, it is because he has faith in her. If a man gives himself to Christ as his

Lord and Master, it is because he has faith in Him. Faith centralizes life around its dominant devotion. Too many lives end like a broom, in a multitude of small straws instead of like a bayonet in point and power. It is faith that brings this focus.

The New Testament (especially Galatians, Thessalonians, and Corinthians, as these were written within twenty-five years of the Crucifixion) portrays the great faith of the apostles. They had not faith in formal creed, for no creed had yet been written. It was not faith in a New Testament for it was not yet in existence. It was not faith in an authoritarian church for the church was still unorganized. This faith antedated all and was of quite another kind. It was a personal faith. Christ had come. He had brought life. He had revealed what God was like. He told them how life ought to be lived to obtain the fullness and joy that was meant for them. Men had seen Him and fallen in love with Him and given themselves with trustful loyalty to Him. That was the central meaning of faith in the New Testament.

Faith makes God real to the soul. It overarches and undergirds life with the presence of God. Faith like that is victory. The deepest, truest, most abiding and reliable fountain of power for life is a vital faith in Christ.

Father God, I see that you have given me as a believer, all the resources I need to live a full and victorious life no matter what my circumstances. Thank you for the gift of faith. Amen.

November 6   Saul's Testimony

Scripture Reading: Acts Chapter 9

Key Verse: "Then all who heard were amazed, and said, 'Is this not he who destroyed those who called on this name in Jerusalem?'" Acts 9:21

Excepting only Christ's journey up Calvary's Hill, no journey has meant more to the salvation of souls than Saul's journey to Damascus. The claims of all other religions can be met by outward conformity, but Christianity demands the regeneration of the inner man. Saul's testimony is a startling example of the power of Jesus to change lives.

It had not been difficult for the early Christians to evangelize Judea. But it seemed that the most difficult work was in reaching the far-off ancient cities with their Jewish customs and Greek influences.

The ideal of Hebraism was that of the moral, the righteous, and the religious law. The ideal of Hellenism was that of culture, and freedom, and the perfection of the power of the individual. In Jesus' day, these opposing forces were evidenced by two groups, the Pharisees and the Sadducees. The Sadducees were at root Hellenists, denying the supernatural, while the Pharisees stood firm for tradition and the law.

Saul was a Hebrew of the Hebrew. So, Paul became a Pharisee, even a member of the Sanhedrin. Yet, this Pharisee was also in some ways a Hellenist. Greece had touched him with its culture, its refinement, its poetry and passion.

Soon there came a young man, full of the Spirit, full of faith and power. His name was Stephen. Now Stephen's martyrdom sermon was one of defense against Hellenism. Stephen's fight was with the Sadducees. Yet, Saul consented to Stephen's death, and continued on to persecute the church of Christ with passionate zeal. As the persecution drove believers out of Jerusalem, Saul obtained letters from the high priest allowing him to track down believers in Damascus, and bring them bound to Jerusalem.

But Saul never arrived in Damascus. To this man there came a bright light from heaven, the voice of Christ, and blindness. To this man, so full of himself, came absolute emptiness and uncertainty, "What do You want me to do?" Saul became an empty vessel, emptied of self. Next came the command, "Arise and go into the city and you will be told what you must do." But this was not the same man who had set out. He was becoming "a chosen vessel" of the Lord.

Blinded, humiliated, led to a home to wait for a destiny he did not understand, the revelation of the living Christ dealt immediately with Saul's heart. After Ananias visited Saul at God's behest, Saul regained his sight, and was filled with the Holy Spirit. Saul had become a filled vessel, ready to be used of Him. This man who had tormented the believers with such zeal now "immediately preached the Christ in the synagogues, that He is the Son of God."

What a message of hope to us today. There is no one out of the reach of God's amazing power of regeneration. Every mocker or persecutor can be changed in a moment into a child of God. Is there one today for whom you have almost lost hope, beloved? Let the testimony of Saul bring the light of renewed expectation to you today. Commend that one to God just now.

Dear Father, You know my heart. In the areas of my life where I need Your correction, I submit to and ask for a Damascus Road experience. Transform me, Lord, that I may be Your useful servant and please reveal Yourself to _____ as well. Amen.

November 7   Naaman the Leper

Scripture Reading: II Kings Chapter 5

Key Verse: "Naaman became furious, and went away and said, 'Indeed, I said to myself, He will surely come out to me, and stand and call on the name of the Lord his God, and wave his hand over the place, and heal the leprosy.'" II Kings 5:11

In everyday English, we call this act of Naaman's "getting mad." This man of our text, with superb lunacy, after making the long trip to see the prophet, turned and went away.

Naaman was a wealthy man, a military hero, and a mighty man of valor. But, he was a leper. He was unclean.

Well, in Naaman's home, he had a slave girl who evidently had a Godly upbringing. She had convictions and she was not afraid to speak them out, "I wish that my master were with the prophet . . . he would cure him of his leprosy." This child's simple testimony is the kind of testimony that is everywhere needed and that is sure to be blessed; it was a testimony of faith, given at the right time, and in the right spirit.

Naaman eventually arrived at the prophet's home and he waited at the gate with his attendants and a valuable present. Naaman had thought about how it would be; Elisha would come out to see him personally. Elisha would pray over him. Yet, Elisha is reserved, will not even come out to receive Naaman, as common courtesy might have suggested. Elisha simply sends him a curt message of direction, "Go and wash in the Jordan seven times . . ."

Naturally enough, the hot-headed soldier begins to explode. His pride is touched. He has not been received with due deference. So he flounces away and would have sacrificed his hope of cure to his passion if his servants had not brought him to common sense by their cool remonstrance. He said, "I thought he will surely come out to me." But no, that proud "I" and the haughty "me" must be broken down before God's saving power can be enjoyed. Elisha desired to conceal himself, and to make God's power prominent. He wanted to cure Naaman's soul.

The simple message of the Gospel of Christ cuts at the roots of all preconceived opinions and self-efforts of men. Naaman, or any other man, may wash as often as he likes in the "Rivers of Damascus," but there is no regenerating virtue in them because there God has not put His promise. All our own works are Godless, and therefore utterly powerless to save us.

Then Naaman went down and dipped himself seven times in the muddy Jordan. When? After he had reasoned with his sensible servants. He was willing to do any great thing, but he stumbled to believe that this simple thing was the remedy for his great need. It isn't until he believes the message of grace, and makes a personal application of God's promise that he becomes a new creature through the obedience of faith. This great change was followed by an open confession, "Behold, now I know that there is no God in all the earth but in Israel."

Naaman's story reveals to us, as in a mirror, what human nature would like the gospel to be. It reveals how men stumble at the very characteristics of the gospel which are its glory and the secret of its power. Men must put away pride, preconceived ideas, and believe that Christ's death is all-sufficient. If my hands grasp hold of anything else, they cannot grasp the cross.

Dearest Lord, thank You for the gracious, elegant simplicity of the Gospel. May I, like the young servant girl, present a faithful testimony for You, at the right times, and in the right Spirit. For the sake of Your Glory, amen.

November 8   A Militant Message

Scripture Reading: Romans Chapter 1

Key Verse: "For I am not ashamed of the gospel of Christ, for it is the power of God to salvation for everyone who believes." Romans 1:16

The gospel message is so militant that it blazes! It is the most militant message that ever fell on the ears of man. Many messages have sounded and resounded through the corridors of time, but the gospel is the one great conquering force of the centuries. It has witnessed the decay of time. It has heard the scoffing of the ages. It has been rebuffed by the ridicule of enemies. Yet, the gospel has so endured that it has won victories everywhere it has gone. The militancy of the gospel makes the courage of such men as Hannibal, Alexander, Caesar and Napoleon appear as the fear of children. No wonder Paul here acclaims it as "the power of God unto salvation."

The imperative need of this day is a more militant spirit in our work for Christ. By "militant," I mean war-like. Like it or not, we are engaged in a spiritual battle. We have a militant foe. God has given us the weapons of warfare. Militant Christianity can, under God, enable us to transcend today and transform tomorrow.

Listen to Paul, "I am ready not only to be bound, but also to die at Jerusalem for the name of the Lord Jesus." See him; bound in chains, thrown in dungeons, beaten, conspired against, falsely accused, forsaken. Yet he goes militantly and triumphantly on and on, for Christ's sake. It was this militant spirit that made him the top preacher of the ages. He did not stroll, he marched. He did not play, he fought. He did not retreat, he charged. And he did not do it in the spirit of Paul; he did it in the Spirit of the Lord.

View the message of the gospel from any angle and you find that it burns with militancy. It challenges us to deny ourselves, forsake the world, surrender to Jesus, take up our cross, and follow Him. It points out clearly that if any man would save his life he must lose it. The power of the gospel fathoms man's deepest need and is the one remedy for his lost condition.

The power of the gospel lifts from death to life. Ten thousand burning stakes and dying beds tell us it is so. The voice of the redeemed who have gone on before defy earth and hell to dispute it. It is the very importance of the battle that increases the magnitude of the struggle. We are to wrestle with evil as good soldiers of Jesus, and conquer in His name. The battle is not easy, but the outcome is sure.

The conquest of the gospel in untold numbers of lives saved shows that its power can break any chain, set free any captive, release any prisoner, dispel any darkness and save any soul. The gospel goes beyond feeding the poor, comforting the widow and clothing the orphan. It goes to the root of our world's problems, and gives pardon and mercy to the sinner.

The gospel's course will never be obstructed. The confusion, chaos, crime and infidelity of this day are just the groanings and travailing of the struggle for men's souls. Christ has broken the shackles that hold us, the gates of death have been torn off their hinges that we may be free.

And now, it is up to us to say with Paul, "I am not ashamed of the gospel of Christ, for it is the power of God to salvation for everyone who believes." Onward, Christian soldier.

Dear Lord, I am so grateful for Your priceless gift of salvation. Help me to go out in Your power to spread the good news of the gospel of Jesus Christ to a needy and dying world. For Christ's sake, amen.

November 9 Isaiah's Gethsemane

Scripture Reading: Isaiah Chapter 64

Key Verse: "Oh, that You would rend the heavens! That You would come down! That the mountains might shake at Your presence." Isaiah 64:1

This is the cry of a heart breaking under an intolerable load of grief. It is the prayer of a man who is overwhelmed with the misery and sin of the people. Their guilt, sin, and misfortune had gathered itself into one great burden and he sees that there is no hope or help but in God. This is Isaiah's Gethsemane.

What is the condition of the people that Isaiah is in such a frame of mind? Israel had backslidden from God, her sins had polluted her and she was unclean. There was a general corruption, and the people's thoughts and affections were not toward God. And as a result of all their sin, God had poured out sorrow and judgment upon them. Their houses were in ruins, their cities were a wilderness, and their temple was desolate. Worst of all, the people were in captivity, trampled under the heel of the oppressor. So, Isaiah calls to God.

He asks a great thing, not that God would look down but that God would come down. Isaiah knew that then they would have order instead of chaos, peace instead of war and reverence instead of lawlessness. "Oh, that You would rend the heavens! That You would come down!"

Isaiah's confession for his nation is piercing, "But we are all like an unclean thing, and all our righteousnesses are like filthy rags; we all fade as a leaf, and our iniquities, like the wind, have taken us away. And there is no one who calls on Your name, who stirs himself up to take hold of You." In Israel there was not a prayer warrior to be found. No one called on the Lord, no one. So Isaiah asks a great supplication, only let God appear in His majesty and might. What a change would come!

Isaiah remembers the times past when God came down, when He manifested Himself to His people. Oh, how the mountains shook! Isaiah does not ask for that which has not happened. Revivals have burned and blessed before, so why not now?

Yes, why not now? Do we not see coldness and indifference among believers today? Yes, and in answer to prayer and confession of sin, God will work again. If God has blessed in the past, it is good proof He will bless today. He is the same yesterday, today and forever.

In a time of revival among believers, cold and torpid Christians are set on fire for the Lord. Ritualism gives way to reality, unbelief gives way to belief, forms of godliness give place to power, prejudice is uprooted by brotherhood, and God's adversaries tremble at His presence.

Two men were once talking about a little village church in Chester, England. Most of the members were gone as the older ones had passed on, and some families had moved. One man said to the other, "If one more family leaves, we will have to close the doors and give up." "No," said the other man, "I tell you that one breeze from Calvary is enough to put life in the whole place." Yes, one breeze from Calvary will put life and power and blessing into all our lukewarm churches and Christians alike. What was true in Isaiah's Gethsemane, is true today.

Yes, Dear Lord, I pray with Isaiah from my heart that You would come down and manifest Yourself that the nations would tremble! Send, Lord, for Thy glory, a fresh breeze upon us today! In Christ's name and for His sake, Amen.

November 10   Victory is Ours

Scripture: Revelation Chapter 1

Key Verse: "Fear not, I am the first and the last. I am He that liveth and was dead and behold, I am alive forevermore and have the keys of hell and death." Revelation 1:17-18

In our text, John writes in the Spirit on the Lord's Day, approximately sixty years after our Lord had triumphed over death in resurrection. John fell at the feet of the Master as if dead because he could not behold His grandeur and His glory with finite eyes, the Master put His hand upon him and told him, "Fear not."

Fear not. It seems as though Christ was always telling His disciples to "fear not." How many times that phrase occurs in the New Testament! In fact, "Fear not" is the watchword of our Christian experience. The first words of introduction to our Master that we hear are when the angel declares, "Fear not, for behold I bring you good tidings of great joy which shall be to all people. For unto you is born this day in the city of David, a Savior which is Christ the Lord." It is repeated frequently through the ministry of Jesus, till at last the women came to the tomb where the angel appears and says, "Fear not, for I know that you seek Jesus which was crucified. He is not here, for he is risen."

How our world needs to hear this message, "Fear not." Seldom, if ever, was the world in such a grip of fear as today. Never before were there so many people who are in need of food, and clothing, and comfort, and hope. Here in our land, we stand confused; not knowing whether this technology we have shall be used for man's good, or for his destruction. All about us we see the future in a blur of nervous tension, not knowing what a day will bring forth. But the world is still the same, "Fear not." "Fear not" for a bomb cannot kill the soul. "Fear not" because we have the victory over death, over sin, and over fear itself.

Now the rest of our text tells us why we should banish fear. I like these next words, "I am the First and the Last." You put that on the lips of anyone excepting only the Eternal God, and they do not fit. He is the only one about whom it could be written. He is the Alpha and the Omega, the beginning and the end.

And, "I am He that lives, and was dead, and behold, I am alive forevermore." You need not doubt that! You can trust the efficiency of the Roman soldiers. There was too much at stake for them to have been inefficient in the action of execution. Undoubtedly, they killed Him. When they pierced His side, and blood and water poured forth, we may be sure He was dead. Then, they placed a Roman seal upon the tomb and placed a Roman guard in front of it. You may be sure they did not place it upon the grave of a living man.

But on Sunday, He was gone. The grave clothes were loosed and laid aside and the stone was rolled away. The many appearances of our Lord attest to the fact of His resurrection. In a sense, we worship at a tomb, but there is no other tomb like this one. The great pyramid took 2.3 million blocks of stone and the labor of thousands of men to build, yet it houses the remains of one Pharaoh with no message of life. Yes, we worship at a tomb because it is empty and in it we see our victory. He was dead. Today, He is alive.

We worship a risen Christ, and He holds the keys to death, but He is also the way of life. Our destiny is in the hands of the keeper of the keys. "Fear not!"

Oh Lord how I rejoice today in Your mighty victory over death and sin. I am so thankful that the keys to my future are firmly in Your loving hands. Thank You that I truly can say from the depths of my soul that I "Fear not." Amen.

November 11   Spiritual Victory

Scripture Reading: Philippians 2:5-11

Key Verse: "Let this mind be in you which was also in Christ Jesus." Philippians 2:5

The question is, does the Christian life which we profess find a place in the life we live? Do we possess the holiness of Christ? Holiness is a condition for growth into maturity. A rosebud is perfect in its bud but is perfected in the full-grown flower. A baby is perfect, having every member and faculty, but is perfected in manhood or womanhood. Holiness is not freedom from progress, judgment, ignorance or unprofitableness. Holiness is freedom from the realm of sin and the power of sin. Spiritual victory is found in this submission to the nature of God.

Where do we find this holiness? Only in Christ Jesus. He is the only one who can make us pure as we grow in His ways and example. Sometimes we become discouraged because we are not what we expected to be. Sometimes we are discouraged because we are not what others are. We are each on our own spiritual journey, with its own timing and plan designed by God. Don't some babies walk before others? Yet aren't they equally as loved and precious to the Father? We cannot keep our eyes on others. We must keep our eyes only on Jesus. He knows we are learning and He understands when we fail. We have only to ask His forgiveness and He opens His arms wide to us in love and perfect acceptance.

Are we trying to be holy and good on our own? The Scriptures tell us that no one is good, not a single one. We can separate ourselves from other people, become hermits alone or in community, but this won't make us holy. Our first step is to ask Christ to help us. It is His power that transforms us, not what we can do ourselves. Then, we must realize that steel must be tested. If an infant is kept swaddled in his cradle, he will never learn to walk. He must try and fail with his loving father helping him up and cheering him on.

Let us submit ourselves to His plans, His ambitions for us, His affection and His life. It will be what we were designed for. We could choose no more fulfilling way than His way.

Our Christ walked in humility, faith and obedience. We can have all the other graces. We can do all the service, be ever so surrendered and humble, but if we are not obedient to His commands we will fail to reach the maturity of faith that Christ is leading us to.

Moses and the Lord met one day. "What is that in your hand?" "A rod." "Cast it on the ground." Poor Moses was surprised. It was only a stick yet it was all he had. God transformed it into a serpent, a supernatural manifestation. Then God told Moses to "reach out your hand and take it by the tail." Oh dear, there's hardship here. The serpent was hissing and crawling, it was probably a frightening sight, yet Moses obeyed and picked it up. Then it was transformed into a stick again. Now Moses stands at the water's edge and lifts the stick. The waters separate under the power of God. The whole family of the Lord is preserved by the great power that came upon a simple stick in the hands of an obedient man.

God is calling us to lay down our will, our plans, our purposes. He is calling for an absolutely surrendered and emptied life. Wait before Him for the transforming power of God to be made known in your life. Remember, in His hands we are safe. God will preserve your going in and your coming out. Let the Lord be your shepherd.

Dear Lord, my Shepherd, help me to grow and mature every day in my faith with You as my example. Amen.

November 12   Throwing Stones

Scripture Reading: I Samuel Chapter 17

Key Verse: "Who is this uncircumcised Philistine, that he should defy the armies of the living God?" I Samuel 17: 26

See David? He is the youngest son of Jesse of Bethlehem. He is only at the battlefield between the Philistines and the Israelites to bring food to his brothers and bring back news of them to his father. And see Goliath? A champion who had never been defeated, Goliath strutted up and down taunting and aggravating the Israelites, challenging them to meet him, defying them. Finally, see Israel. Dismayed and greatly afraid, not one man among them had the courage to face Goliath. In the end, David would win the victory over Goliath, but that was not the only victory he would have that day.

His brother Eliab hears David say that he would fight Goliath and angrily rebukes him, making fun of him. Now, David could have gotten angry in return. But David did not quarrel. He gave a soft answer.

Yes, he tempered himself and kept his cool. For not many minutes later, when it was life and death before Goliath, David had to be calm and steady, tensed and set for the strike. What would have happened if David had not had self-control? Well, David's first victory, over his own tongue and temper, prepared the way for the second victory, over Goliath. So today, we must keep ourselves cool and in God's hand for the striking time. The first victory we must win in any battle is fought against our self.

Then, David's second victory was over his brother. For, Eliab sought out the splinter in David's eye, and was not aware of the beam in his own. The very things he charged his brother with, presumption and wickedness of heart, were most apparent in his own scornful reproof. While David's thoughts and feelings were on the great national disgrace and his plan for its removal, Eliab thought only of a flock of sheep. Above all, this was not time to quarrel. It was a time of war, when every enemy and every force was needed to bring victory. It was a time for united action. And the day in which we find ourselves is also a day for united action.

In this incident, Eliab's envy was silenced by David's meekness and truth. David used weapons against his brother which were as effectual to silence him as the sling to slay the giant. He won victory over Eliab by his forbearance. Every believer today would find these same defenses to be handy. Speak truth in meekness, and practice forbearance.

Finally, David had victory over the giant Goliath. Now, Goliath had a mighty spear, but David did not dwell on that. What paralyzed the soldiers liberated David. It is no small thing to fling a stone so that it strikes that small open spot. It takes wisdom and patience to wait for just the right time. It takes faith to refuse the armor of the king, trusting instead in the protection of God. God used David just as he was, with a sling and five stones.

David won the victory over Goliath just as he had the other great victories of that day, because he had something better to trust in than Saul's armor. He had faith in his great God. It was for His sake, and His honor, that David went forth. It is the same today.

Dear Father God, I forget sometimes that I am in a war. I speak before I pray; I act before I think. Please do not allow me to dishonor You by my hasty actions. Rather, let me bring glory to You as You work through me, just as I am. Thank You, Lord. Amen.

Key Verse: "Now as he reasoned about righteousness, self-control, and the judgment to come, Felix was afraid and answered, 'Go away for now: when I have a convenient time, I will call for you.'" Acts 24:25

Felix was a black sheep. He was such a rascal that he was conspicuous even in a day when this was a prevalent characteristic among politicians. Born a slave, Felix had in some way managed to win his freedom. Not only that, but by ingenuity, ability, and rascality, he had worked his way up to position and power. But in spite of his lofty political position, he was still a moral pygmy. Within, Felix was still in bondage. Tacitus, the historian, tells us that Felix ruled in the spirit of a slave, with cruelty and lust.

Why did this renegade want to hear of Christ?

Well, he may have been prompted by curiosity. He knew something of Paul, having met him face to face at court. Evidently, Paul's handling of the situation had won Felix's admiration. Felix might even have sent for Paul out of desire for personal gain. If Felix indeed had tried to capitalize on the church, he would not, unfortunately, be in a class entirely by himself. We might, of course, give Felix the benefit of the doubt; he may have called Paul simply because of an insatiable hunger for God. Such longing has stirred the heart of many men as sinful as Felix.

After all, his motives are not of supreme importance. The proprietor of a store had pasted behind the counter where only the salesmen could see, "It is not what the customer comes in after, but what he goes out with, that matters." So it is with church attendance. And surely, this was Paul's hope as he faced Felix.

Paul's sermon was meant to search Felix's soul. We must bear in mind that Paul did not get to finish his sermon. The physician-preacher had hardly finished diagnosing the disease before the patient walked out on him. But, in the fragment that we have, Paul spoke of righteousness.

Righteousness is simply right living. The call of Paul, and the call of this and indeed every hour, is for righteousness. We need to be right; right with God and then right with our fellow man.

And then, Paul spoke of self-control. He spoke of temperance to a man who was dressing his soul in chains. He spoke of self-mastery to one whose passions and appetites were scourging him as a whip.

And finally, Paul spoke of judgment to come. Judgment is not just a faraway day. Every time I stand at the forks in the road and take the lower instead of the higher, I undergo judgment. My sentence is that ever after I find it easier to take the lower and harder to take the higher road. When I face light and refuse to see it, I am judged in that I lose in some measure my capacity to see. When I hear truth and refuse to respond to it, my sentence is that I become a little duller of hearing.

And the Scriptures say that upon hearing the word of God through Paul, Felix trembled. Felix knew Paul was right. And yet, he sent him away. The sermon was never finished, because Felix was afraid to listen. What about you, beloved? Is God calling something to your attention today? Listen to Him. Do not wait for a more "convenient time."

Dear Father God, I ask that You would point out to me the areas in which I might be afraid to see or hear Your truth. Help me to be willing to follow You on the higher road, the path of righteousness. Help me to face the hard decisions and make the right choices. Thank You, Lord, amen.

November 14   What About Faith?

Scripture Reading: Romans 3:21-31

Key Verse: "But without faith it is impossible to please Him."
Hebrews 11:6

Many of us in this generation seek adventure, excitement and thrills. There is a limit to all of these in the world, but there is no limit to adventure and thrills in the spiritual realm, for divine power works miracles through hearts and hands consecrated to God. How exciting! And consider this, the days in which we live call for heroes. Are you eligible? There was never a greater need for a faith that risks for God, that can face this dark age and live victorious lives.

In order to have faith there must be three preliminaries. First, someone must have made a promise. Then, there must be good reason for believing in the integrity and sufficiency of that one. Lastly, there is a need for the comfortable assurance that it can be counted as already done. It will be so. It is the same as actual possession. Faith then is the faculty of realizing the unseen.

These three conditions are fulfilled in Christian faith. As to God, we are sure. His voice has spoken to us through the Scriptures. The speaker is infinitely credible for several reasons. His words have consistently come true in past generations accompanied then and now by the miraculous. The maxim of the world is "seeing is believing," but with the child of God the reverse is true, "believing is seeing."

Faith comes primarily by the study of the Word, by believing prayer, by opening our hearts to God and by putting away anything that hinders our growth in faith.

Faith "greatens" men. Run through the roll call of heroes of the faith and you will realize that their claim was not because of natural genius or ability. Faith lifted them up and placed them among the exceptional. This it will also do for you and me, for it mightily affects our ordinary human life. With most men you can determine nearly how they will act under a given circumstance. But a Christian? Never! Why? Because his faith is making real much of what the world around is taking no thought. The martyr may be tempted with flatteries and seared with threats, but he does not move. It is inexplicable. But the reason is that the eyes of the young martyr are open on a world his persecutor does not see.

Faith is not careless of time, but is mindful of eternity. Faith does not underrate the power of man but magnifies the One Omnipotent. Faith is not callous toward present pain but weighs it against future joy.

There are great difficulties before us all. Stormy seas forbid our passage, mountains bar our progress, kingdoms defy our power, and lions roar against us. What seas, mountains, kingdoms and lions do you face?

Yes, all these menace our peace, but faith has conquered all these before and it shall do it again. We truly can do all things through Christ who strengthens us. Do not look at the wind and the waves but at His character and power. See before you your mighty Captain. He that is for us is far more than can ever be against us. Get alone with God. Steep your heart and life and mind in His precious and exceeding great promises. Be obedient to the voice of God and walk in all the light you have. And as you walk in the Spirit so shall you be deemed worthy to join this band whose names and exploits run over from this book into the records of eternity. He says to you—drop into my arms, I will catch you.

Dearest Lord, in this day, when I want to control everything around me and be "in charge," help me to lift my eyes higher to the unseen plane and respond to the things of God above. In the name of Jesus, amen.

November 15   Message Between Two Holidays

Scripture: Deuteronomy Chapter 6

Key Verses: "Hear, O Israel: The Lord our God, the Lord is one! You shall love the Lord your God with all your heart, with all your soul, and with all your strength. And these words which I command you today shall be in your heart." Deuteronomy 6:4-6

Today we stand between two holidays, two national, memorializing, and significant holidays of our culture. One is Armistice (Veteran's) Day, that day of silence and respect. The other is Thanksgiving, the day of gratitude and remembrance. Perhaps it is fitting that the two days should be thus contiguous in the procession of distinctive days.

There is a sense in which on Armistice Day we think of the human contribution to the making of a nation. At Thanksgiving we recognize the hand of God in our history. And while today we ponder the thought, we cannot but think also of the warning and exhortation God directly gave to another nation in another day.

The record of it is in the sixth chapter of Deuteronomy. While this exhortation was addressed to Israel just as she was about to become a nation, there is here a warning which applies to all nations, and a principle which still persists. This principle is printed in black-face type in the Word of God. When God is crowded out of the life of a nation, that nation has entered a path the end of which is oblivion.

In pioneer periods people are not inclined to forget God. The privation and struggle of their daily experience call for dependence on a power apart from themselves. But as life grows easier, the sense of dependence disappears.

The danger time in national life is always the day of prosperity. "When you have eaten and are full," said God to Israel, "then beware lest you forget." To forget the contributions made to our lives by parents and teachers, inventors and explorers, sailors, soldiers, schools and churches.

To live as if we had piled up all the stores of culture and as if we had filled the reservoirs of knowledge.

Yes, when a nation loses its memory it is in danger of losing its soul. Memory is ballast in national life. Governments are sane and governments are sober as long as they remember. When they forget, they unlearn history's lessons and become like children chasing toy balloons along the edge of a cliff.

So, as we stand between two holidays, let us as a nation and as individuals remember the veterans, those people and moments in history that have shaped our present and the future of our children. Let us partake of their knowledge and experience, let us teach it to our children, and let us never, ever forget the lessons of our forbearers.

Then let us look forward to Thanksgiving and recall what God has done for us. Let us do as God bids Israel and teach our children diligently to love the one and only God with all their heart, and to speak of these words of God when we sit and when we walk, when we lie down and when we get up. Let this command be always before us in our homes and in our minds, and in our hearts. Let us remember our blessings and who provides them.

So, today, won't you teach your children to remember both those who have gone before in our history, and He who goes before their future?

Dear Father, I can see by Your counsel and command to the children of Israel how fervently You desire that we love and remember Your graces to us. Please help me be an obedient steward of Your will and teach the children well. Amen.

November 16   That First Service

Scripture Reading: Acts Chapter 2

Key Verse: "But Peter, standing up with the eleven, raised his voice and said to them . . ." Acts 2:14

This religious service held many centuries ago was memorable and unique because it was the first real Christian service ever held and thus ushered in a new era. The same power that made this service victorious must characterize our services every day or all our efforts toward the saving of our sagging civilization will be in vain.

First, let us look at the congregation. It was filled with two groups, believers and unbelievers. I am persuaded that the same two groups ought to compose our congregations Sunday by Sunday. As for the believers, the record shows that "they were all together." Not only were they present, but they were present with the thrill of a boundless enthusiasm. Those who looked on were compelled to ask in wistful perplexity, "What does this mean?"

If your church was entirely present next Sunday what high expectations would be born of seeing the sanctuary filled, with almost as many on the outside seeking to gain entrance as there were already within? Thousands would ask again, as they asked long ago, "What does this mean?"

If believers were present, unbelievers were present in even greater numbers. Why, in spite of their deep prejudice against this Christian movement, did so many attend this service? Those who drew these outsiders within the hearing of the gospel were the church members themselves. Nothing attracts folks so well as other folks who have themselves been drawn. Those who are deeply committed to any cause intrigue those who have not found their passion in life.

Next, look at the message Peter brought. When he spoke he was not alone. A consecrated minister, plus a consecrated congregation, plus Almighty God proved a compelling power for the proclamation of the Christian message.

Simon's sermon speaks to the question of the people, "What does this mean?" First of all, it is a correction. The enthusiasm and joy of the believers was so intense the crowd wondered aloud if they were drunk. Simon Peter puts the notion to rest declaring it is a divine intoxication they are experiencing. Intoxication of the flesh will leave you with an aching head and an aching heart. If you want life to thrill with meaning, purpose and power, be filled with the Spirit.

He declares that what God is doing now before their very eyes, He is doing through Jesus of Nazareth who they had rejected and crucified. Since Jesus was now in action in their midst pouring forth the Holy Spirit, He is not dead. He is their Lord and King. So, Simon's sermon was a correction, and explanation, and a conclusion. What was the result of these Holy Spirit empowered words? One version of the Scriptures states that "they were cut to the heart." As a result, 3,000 of Peter's hearers repented and turned to the risen Christ.

What does this lesson say to us today? Let us not seek the outward and the passing, but the inward and abiding. We don't need flashy, attention-drawing services. We need the Word of God. We need consecrated hearts. We need the presence of the Lord. Oh that you and I might know Him, find Him, and let Him fall afresh on us today.

Dearest Lord, please fill me with Your Holy Spirit as the believers were filled on the day of the first Christian service. May I radiate Your glory and love to all who are around me and testify by my lips and by my actions to Your wonderful gospel of love and mercy. Amen.

November 17   The New Commandment

Scripture: John Chapter 13

Key Verse: "A new commandment I give to you, that you love one another as I have loved you, that you also love one another." John 13:34

Everything conspires to make these words impressive. First, they are words from the lips of Christ, our Savior, the One whose name is above every name, who spoke as never man spoke, and whose words will outlive the stars. Next, He is speaking to His followers, the little company of men trained to carry out His work. These men are to disciple the nations, and teach them to observe all things which He had commanded. They are the nucleus of the church against which the gates of Hell will never prevail. Also, He is speaking on the last night of His earthly life. Death is looking on, the shadow of the cross lies across His face. The time has arrived for Him to go back to God. In this last hour, only the most momentous subjects can be touched upon. Even His language shows how deeply His own heart is moved as He calls these men "little children." He had usually spoken as their teacher, now He addresses them as a father speaks to his children whom He is leaving to fight life's battles in the midst of a cold and unsympathetic world.

"A new commandment I give to you, that you love one another as I have loved you . . ." There are no more important words recorded in the Gospels. You see, the disciples' love for one another is the badge of Christian discipleship and the crowning proof that men belong to Jesus. It is the message of a King, not a suggestion, but a command. Obedience to this law is the test of loyalty.

But, the tragedy of Christian history is that the new command has been continuously neglected. Everyone knows the Ten Commandments, many know the two commands given by our Lord, but, alas, the new commandment lies in the shadow forgotten, disobeyed, and ignored. Why is this?

Well, it is difficult to find the meaning of the word "love." Look in I Cor. 13. Love is one of the most indefinite and baffling of all words.

Love, like faith, is not defined in the Bible as much as it is illustrated. Love is sometimes a passion, an affection, a sentiment, a charity, a philanthropy, but love on the lips of Jesus was different from all these.

He did not leave us to grope in the dark. He said to the scribe, "You shall love your neighbor as yourself." To the disciples, He said, "Love one another as I have loved you." His conduct was the only sufficient interpretation of that word. Christians are to love one another after the style of Jesus. The love of Jesus is not filial or romantic love. Filial love seeks to protect, like a parent. Romantic love seeks to possess, as in courtship. But the love of God seeks to perfect. That explains Calvary!

This commandment is also new in that it was not intended for Israel, as was the Levitical code. Nor is it for the world in general. It is for His disciples, as they listened to Him speak these words, and for you and me, professing Christians today. So, this is indeed a new commandment; our bond to Jesus Christ creates a new bond to one another. Here is a new standard of love: to love after the manner of Jesus. This is the only love that will save the world. Only the love of the Son of God, expressed through you and me, can thus serve God's eternal purpose.

Dear Heavenly Father, Please give me the grace to be a conduit of Your amazing love. Amen.

November 18   The Song of the Waiting Bride

Scripture Reading: Song of Solomon Chapter 2

Key Verse: "My beloved is mine, and I am his." Song of Solomon 2:16

In "The Song of Songs" Solomon sings in glorious terms of his beloved, but this book is more than a love story. It is a love story based on facts reaching beyond the life of Solomon to a prophecy of the holy relation that exists between Christ and His church.

It is also the Song of the Bride as she awaits the coming of the Bridegroom, when the nuptial vows shall be said and He shall be hers and she shall be His forever. In a deeper appreciation of the Song, we see some of the most sublimely beautiful, deeply spiritual, and richly instructive teaching in the entire Bible.

As the bride waits, she instructs us on the proper attitude of the church towards Christ who has gone away. In Scripture, we know, the marriage relationship is used as a type of the affectionate, confidential, and exclusive union that exists between Christ and believers. And, in the inspired drama presented in the Song of Songs, there is the most beautiful and instructive symbolism.

The Shulamite is constant, waiting in purity for her beloved to return to take her unto himself. Oh, what an attitude for the members of the church, awaiting her Lord. We await our coming King, and in His absence we watch and are ready, as He has bidden us, constant and devoted to Him.

This relationship is a relationship of separation. As 4:12 states, "A garden enclosed is my sister, my spouse, a spring shut up, a fountain sealed." The bride is separated unto the Bridegroom. Our lives, you see, are not a playground for the world, but a garden for Him in which the fruits of the Spirit bloom.

We also note that there is a conscious effort to guard against the loss of the harvest. "Catch us the foxes, the little foxes that spoil the vines, for our vines have tender grapes." There was caution that the harvest and fruit not be spoiled. So with us in the church today, we must be cautioned against the little foxes that can ruin our fruit-bearing for Christ. Be on guard.

Also, we see an attitude of mutual possession. "My beloved is mine, and I am his." Yes, He is ours in salvation and we are His in consecration. We are His workmanship created in Christ Jesus for good works. Think of the possibilities wrapped up in God's willingness to shape us and make us like Him!

Finally, we see the victory of the marriage feast. "He brought me to the banqueting house, and His banner over me was love." Our relationship with Jesus Christ is a feast, not a funeral! Thank God we feast in the very presence of our enemies, and not one of them is able to do us harm. We are under the protection of the banner of Jesus Christ, a banner which has for its insignia a cross on a field of blood-red. Oh, beloved, what blessed and holy relationship is this of the bride and her Bridegroom who has gone away to fit the mansion for her, and returns to take her unto Himself.

What blessed joy awaits those who are faithful to Him in His absence, and who watch and await His return! While we wait, let's make sure our attitude reflects the devotion, separation from the world, fruitfulness, mutual possession, and anticipation of victory that the Shulamite embodies. Let the song in your heart reflect that today, as you remember, "My beloved is mine, and I am his."

Oh Dear Lord, I do wait with eager anticipation the moment I see You face to face. Please purify the church, I pray. Sanctify us, Your bride, and soften our hearts yet further that we may long for You as the Shulamite did her bridegroom. Maranatha. Amen.

November 19   Revival, not Revolution

Suggested Scripture: II Chronicles Chapter 7

Key Verse: "If My people who are called by My name will humble themselves, and pray and seek My face, and turn from their wicked ways, then will I hear from heaven, and will forgive their sin and heal their land." II Chronicles 7:14

Everybody enjoys a revival of nature. Oh, spring is only too welcome after winter's cold. We also do not object to a revival in these physical bodies of ours. Have you ever been very ill? Boy, how good it is to get to feeling better again. And, oh, how I could cheer you, if with authority I could tell you of a revival in the stock market. If business was booming, stocks were climbing and production was good, you would not object.

So why, beloved, do so many object to talk of a spiritual revival? I think the first reason is that the present-day generation has possibly never really seen a revival, a "spiritual awakening." They don't understand that a revival occurs when the heart recovers its first rapture, when the soul recovers its first love.

The second reason for indifference to revival, I believe, is that the modern church is to a great degree an ease-loving church. Too often it is not willing to pay the price that revival costs. We would have to repent of our spiritual barrenness, and of the shameful way we have shunted God's cause into second place behind business or pleasure.

Fog is the thing that every seaman and aviator dreads. And, all believers today should be on the watch, too, for the fog of spiritual apathy and indifference that has settled over so much of the Church today. Only a spiritual awakening will ever lift us up out of it. More life in our singing, more life in our preaching, more prayer in our homes, and more scripture in our hearts—all these spring from and through spiritual awakening.

I am persuaded to believe that if we ask God for a real work among the Christians of this great nation, He won't give us a counterfeit. If we ask Him for bread, He will not give us a stone. If we ask Him for fish, He will not give us a serpent.

Oh, beloved, sin is the same as when it broke the heart of the Son of God. And the preaching of the cross is to them that perish foolishness, but to us who believe, it is the power of God unto Salvation. Hear me! A true revival is a rediscovery of God. The nation, and the church have forgotten God. We have gone to depending on men and money, dreaming of peace while the world plans war.

The one hope for the cure of this old world's ills is the recovery of our vision of God. Legislation is not enough. Preaching high ethical standards is not enough. Doctoring the outside of life, while the heart is rotten, is futile. And the great writer of our text paves the way to our only salvation as a nation, "If my people that are called by my name . . ." Pray, and He will hear. Repent, and He will heal. A rebirth of fiery earnestness and a rekindling of burnt-out enthusiasms mean a new passion for the saving of men and for the spreading of the gospel to the ends of the earth. Oh, it is a sick world, but there is a remedy. Are we willing to pay the price?

Dear Lord, I have not sought You as I ought on behalf of the Church. I confess that we are not the strong Bride of Christ that we should be. We do not stand up against wrongs, nor do we boldly lead the way in right. We are in desperate need of Your help, and Your healing, both in the Church and in our nation. Please forgive us. Fill us with Your Spirit, Lord, that we might bring glory to Your name, amen.

November 20   Five Beautiful Girls in the Dark

Scripture Reading: Matthew Chapter 25

Key Verse: "And at midnight a cry was heard: 'Behold, the bridegroom is coming; go out to meet him!'" Matthew 25:6

Ten young women were excited and awaiting the arrival of the bridegroom, that they might enter in with him to the bridal feast. Five of them were wise, and five foolish; five were prepared, and five tragically unprepared. When the midnight cry was made, there was a scurry of excitement and a great rush in making ready. But, the excited rush of preparation turned into a decided panic for the foolish young maidens who found themselves unprepared. They had lamps and vessels but no oil. They lacked the main thing; for of what value are lamps without oil? As useless as a watch without works.

There are five simple yet profound truths that spring from the words of this fascinating parable of our Lord. First, we must see that without question the five foolish maidens thought they were ready to enter in with the bridal party when it should arrive, but they were deceived. There is much deception in the world, for "the devil like a roaring lion goes up and down seeking whom he may devour." And, since Satan is the father of lies, deception is one of his favorite tactics. Don't rely on what the world says about your eternal destiny; follow God's Word so that when the Bridegroom returns, you may enter in to the celebration.

Secondly, not all persons are able to enter in with the Bridegroom simply because they want to. These foolish maidens wanted to enter. For this purpose they had left their homes and come to await the wedding party at the point where they fell asleep. When they awoke, it was to the fact that they were not ready. They frantically ran to the wise maidens, to the sellers of oil, and to the closed doors seeking entry. They wanted to go in, but they could not. Just so, despite the fact that our Lord's invitation to come to Him and be saved is universal and all are invited to come, yet all do not come to Him. The world would have us believe that all paths lead to heaven. The Word of God teaches otherwise. If one desires to live with the bridegroom, Christ, then one must accept Him and receive the oil of the Holy Spirit to be prepared for His arrival.

The third thing we should notice is that after securing oil, the maidens got to the door and knocked for admittance, but they asked too late and were refused entry. There is no doubt that God hears and answers prayers. Now is the time for answered prayer, there is an end to the time when we may accept Christ.

See also that those who are not ready will be shut out. What an irreparable loss. How terrible in retrospect was their false security, slumbering when they should have been preparing. What a picture of our world.

The glorious, wonderful news in this parable, however, is that those who are prepared will enter in with Him, "They that were ready went in with Him to the marriage." Just as sure as God is God, so surely will all who are His enter in with Him when He comes. Not because of any merit of ours, but because of the saving grace of God.

Oh, dear ones, the midnight hour of this world will come. Now is not the time to sleep and slumber, but to share the gospel with those around you, encouraging them to prepare to meet the bridegroom. Trim your lamps, beloved, and let their lights shine.

Dear Father, I do not know if the midnight hour of the world is upon us, or if it is yet a little ways off, but I do know that it seems very dark. Give me boldness, that through the working of Your Spirit I may be used to rouse the slumbering to wakefulness. Amen.

November 21   The Gospel

Scripture Reading: Romans 1:15-17

Key Verse: ". . . I am ready to preach the Gospel to you . . ."
Romans 1:15

What is the gospel? Is it an argument or an announcement? Is it a problem or a proclamation? Is it good news or good advice? Dr. Riddle, the great British theologian, says, "The Gospel is the disclosure, demonstration, and donation of the free, unmerited love and mercy of God, disclosed at Bethlehem, demonstrated at Calvary, donated at Pentecost, the supreme fact of history and the deepest wonder of experience."

Through His incarnation, Jesus revealed God to man. Through His atonement, Jesus reconciled man. Through His gift of the Spirit, He made possible a new life from above for those who sat in darkness and in the shadow of death. God with us at Bethlehem. God for us at Calvary. God in us at Pentecost.

In my mind, I see the gospel as a beautiful body, strong and healthy, virtuous and vigorous, a living thing, giving life. First we see an unblushing face. Paul lifts the trumpet to his lips with no uncertain sound, "I am not ashamed!" There is no blush on his face. Why? Because of what it does for mankind. This gospel confronts all men with the high challenge of being born again. It has won Saul the Persecutor, Peter the Braggart, Augustine, Bunyan, Tolstoy, Mueller, and multitudes of others beyond our comprehension.

On the unblushing face, I see testifying lips, for the gospel is the power of God. It is the preached truth that Christ died for our sins, was buried, and rose again the third day.

I see on the body of the gospel, a pointing finger, pointing the way to salvation. The first obligation of the gospel is salvation. And what can be compared to your salvation? "What shall it profit a man if he gain the whole world and lose his soul?" Hence the pointing finger of the glorious testimony would have us behold the greatness of salvation.

Thus, it reveals God as searching for man. God takes the initiative in salvation.

This salvation saves from the past. He takes the chapters of my life which I regret, its remorseful memories, evil hours, mistaken words and deeds, and blots them all out so that the record shall be white as snow. In this salvation, He casts our sins from us as far as the east is from the west and remembers them against us no more, forever.

But that is not all. This salvation is our guide for the present. "In all thy ways acknowledge Him and He will direct thy paths." And in the future, we need never be afraid of the end of the journey, of death, or judgment, or anything here or in the hereafter.

Black or white, rich or poor, He takes us all in the arms of His glorious provision, saying by invitation, "And the Spirit and the Bride say, 'Come! And let Him who hears . . . whoever desires, let him take the water of life freely."

Now look at this great body of the Gospel and see the believing heart. You cannot make it your own by your works, by religious observances, by prayers or philanthropies, but by simple faith. "For by grace you are saved through faith and that not of yourselves. It is the gift of God, not by works lest any man should boast."

Salvation is mine if I believe and accept it. It can also be yours and it can belong to all those you know and love. Won't you pray for them? Won't you tell them the wonderful gospel so they too might have salvation?

Dear Lord, Won't you show me who You'd have me share this great truth with today? I especially pray for _____ for salvation. Amen.

November 22   What Is Faith?

Scripture: Hebrews 11:1-34

Key Verse: "Now faith is the substance of things hoped for, the evidence of things not seen." Hebrews 11:1

As we look at this passage, we see there is such a thing as an unseen world. Really, we see little of the world in which we live and which influences us. We are conscious of this world by faith. Some things never have been seen and cannot be seen; for instance God, the soul, characters of the past and present around us (so great a cloud of witnesses) and the future in front of us. Faith takes the long view and takes into account this future world. The farmer does not see the rocky, barren field in front of him; he sees that field through the eyes of faith, waving with a golden harvest.

You need to apply your faith in the realm of conditions, for you cannot be what you should be unless you face conditions around you. There are social, national, and world conditions that must be set right. You must dedicate yourself to great causes if you are to realize the possibilities of your own soul. Faith gives you the power of endurance, confidence, and patience, and by faith you will succeed for God.

We need to apply our faith in the person of Jesus Christ. This world is being treated with all the panaceas of countless isms, fads and cults, and all the while the patient sinks lower. In the midst of all this, stands the Great Physician of the soul who is the answer to every need and the solution to every problem. In Him are hid all the treasures of wisdom and knowledge. But men will not receive Him, will not come to Him that they might have life. Since Jesus Christ is the answer to the world's need, and since by faith we receive Him, we can see that the world's misery is due entirely to what is covered in the scriptural phrase "Because of unbelief."

Because of unbelief: (Rom 11:20) Israel was broken off and set aside nationally in this present age of grace. Because of unbelief: (Mt. 13:58) the Lord did no mighty works in Nazareth. In Matt 17: 20 we read that the disciples could not cast out the evil spirit from the demon-possessed boy because of their unbelief.

If this is true, then the converse is also true. The way out is found in the Word of the Lord, "According to your faith be it unto you." So, here is the key and there is no other, your life will be in proportion to your faith. According to your faith, not according to your fate, not according to your fortune, your friends, your face or your fame, nor does it say according to your feelings. Feelings are our pet false measure.

It is not the quality of faith, or the quantity, but the object of your faith that really matters. The only faith that saves and satisfies is faith in Jesus Christ for He is worthy of absolute trust and only He can meet our need. Salvation comes by Jesus Christ because there is no salvation in any other.

Jesus Himself said again and again that your faith appropriates the blessing. To the centurion He said "As you have believed, so let it be done for you." To the woman anointing Him with oil, "Your faith has saved you." To the friends who opened the roof and lowered the paralytic into the presence of Jesus, when He saw their faith He said, "Be whole."

Do you live as the world does, by your own wits and resources? And all the while our Lord stands among us marveling at our unbelief saying, "Do you believe that I am able to do this?" Be not afraid, only believe. "All things are possible to him that believes."

Dearest Lord, take my steps and make them a mile, take my words and make them a book, take my life and make it a symphony of love for You. Amen.

November 23   Much Obliged Lord

Scripture: Psalm 100

Key verse: "Enter into His gates with thanksgiving, and into His courts with praise." Psalm 100:4

Fulton Oursler tells a story about his old nurse, whose habit it was to sit at the kitchen table before a meal and raise her eyes heavenward saying "Much obliged, Lord, for my vittles." Little Fulton asked, "What's a vittle?" She replied, "It's what I eat and drink." "But," mused Fulton, you'd get your vittles whether you thanked God for them or not." "Sure," she replied, "But it makes everything taste better to be thankful" She went on to teach him about gratitude by saying she was taught by an old preacher to look for things to be grateful for.

As the young boy grew to manhood he went through some very trying times. It was this memory of what his nurse taught him about gratitude that steadied him. One day as he was summoned to her death bed he wondered what she could ever find to thank God about in these circumstances. When she laid eyes on the boy she'd helped to raise, she lifted her eyes to Heaven and said, "Much obliged Lord, for such fine friends."

I dislike to mention it, but we can be a nation of fussers and complainers if we fail to train our hearts toward gratitude.

Let us compare our Thanksgiving with the first Thanksgiving. The house will be full of kids asking "When do we eat?" Dinner will be late, and everyone will be starved. Then the big moment will arrive and the whole family will sit down to a table sway-backed and bow-legged with every imaginable good thing to eat. After dinner there will be a race to see who gets the couch first. The women will be stuck with the dishes while the men turn the TV to the Thanksgiving Day football game. Complaints about the government, which is surely going to the dogs, and the price of gasoline they had to pay to drive here today head the list of topics. The lucky guy who got the couch will snooze and dream of better days.

Now, compare this with the first Thanksgiving. The scene is a village of seven log dwellings. The logs were felled and hewn by hand from the forest. An epidemic coupled with overwork and exposure killed forty-six that year, leaving fifty-six men, women and children to build these seven dwellings. The Indians of Plymouth showed the pilgrims how to grow corn by placing fish beside the seed as nourishment. The crop was bountiful and after carving out the fields, planting, staying up at night to keep the wolves from digging up and eating the fish, they were thankful for it.

In the autumn of 1621 Governor Bradford proclaimed the first official Thanksgiving on American soil. Five housewives prepared a feast of wild turkey, geese, duck, clams, lobsters, eel and fish, dried fruit, hoe cakes and Indian pudding. What's more, they invited their neighbors, the Native Americans of Plymouth, to feast at their side.

They had no transportation, save their legs, their only food came from the forest and the sea, they had no money, no amusements, and no means of communication with their relatives. But, they had great assets. They had initiative, courage, willingness to work, and a boundless faith in God. They had much to be thankful for.

Lord, at this Thanksgiving season, may I always remember to thank You for my blessings and the blessings of this nation. May I train my heart toward gratitude and remember to say with deep appreciation "Much obliged, Lord." Amen.

November 24   Dollar Day Religion

Scripture Reading: Daniel Chapter 3

Key Verse: "Our God whom we serve is able to deliver us from the burning fiery furnace, but if not let it be known to you O king, that we do not serve your gods, nor will we worship the gold image which you have set up." Daniel 3:17-18

Here in our text the three faithful young men, Shadrach, Meshach, and Abednego, refuse to obey the pagan king's decree commanding all the people to worship a golden image. For their obstinacy and refusal, they are sentenced to torture in the fiery furnace. But, calmly, they make their reply, insisting that God is able to deliver them from the fiery furnace but whether He will or not, they will not worship the golden image. In other words, their faith is higher and deeper than any circumstances; their loyalty to God will be determined not by what God may or may not do for them, but by their duty to Him. This is one of the noblest insights in the Bible.

While on vacation, I accompanied my wife on a few shopping tours. August sales were on, with Dollar Day Bargains. I watched the shoppers as they stormed the bargain counters, grabbing, searching, and seeking those bargains. As I sat there, I compared our faith (at least the religion of many of us) to this Dollar Day Bargain Hunt.

"Dollar Day Religion," that is just what too much of religion today is. Like a mob of eager Monday morning shoppers, we storm the counters of life seeking bargains. Many desire faith to be a kind of business arrangement with God, so much service for so much reward. This essentially pagan attitude crops out in a dozen different ways. For instance, a few years ago a book was published titled, "Why Not Try God?" in much the same category as "Why not try Parker's Pink Pills?" What they mean is, see what you can get out of God!

Oh, beloved, in our faith we need to depart from the similes of the commercial world and deal with personal relationships such as worship, friendship, love, marriage and the family. To Jesus, God is not the big boss, or the manager, He is Father. To His disciples, Jesus said, "I call you not servants, but friends." And friendship dies in the bargain atmosphere.

And, just as marriage begins with the vow, "for better or worse," so must we say to God in our confession of faith.

Jesus never made promises that we may imply as freedom from testing or adversity. Rather, His life shows us that Gethsemane and the Cross are the truest and strongest rebuttals of the bargain notion of religion. Of Himself, Jesus said, "The Son of Man hath no where to lay His head." He was despised and rejected of men, a man of sorrows, acquainted with grief. Yet, in Gethsemane Jesus was able to say, "Nevertheless, not my will but Yours be done."

George Tyrell once wrote, "To believe that this terrible machine world is really from God, in God, and unto God, and that through it and in spite of its blind fatality, all works for good to those who love God, that is faith in long trousers." True faith, dogged faith, faith in long trousers, strikes no bargains with God for service or faithfulness. Such faith has its own reward, the ability to say to the fiery furnace, or at Gethsemane, "Nevertheless . . . I will serve the Lord."

Dear Lord help me today to remained focused on You, and not allow the distractions and concerns of the day cloud my view on eternity. Amen.

November 25

Scripture Reading: Matthew 4:1-11

Key Verse: ". . . When the tempter came . . . ." Matthew 4:3

The tempter is sure to come, and when he comes then a critical hour has struck for the soul. Then everything, innocence, hope, joy and strength, depends not upon what the tempter does, but upon what the tempted does. The recording angel waits with uplifted pen to write and put on record what the tempted soul has done.

Always the tempter is coming. He misses no individual and skips no race or age. Just as seedtime and harvest, never fail to come; neither does temptation. That desert scene of our Lord is timeless and universal, for temptation is as eternal as human history, and as universal as human nature.

The temptation of our Lord took place at the beginning of His ministry. All His work as redeemer depended upon what Christ did in that moment when the tempter came. So too, the usefulness and strength and honor of life may depend upon what a soul does in the moment of temptation, and whether it gets the best of temptation or temptation gets the best of the soul.

The Bible has no high-sounding theories as to the source of evil and temptation. It declares plainly that the tempter, the originator of evil in man, is Satan, the devil. And if Christ was not too great to be tempted of the devil, then certainly neither are you or I.

Jesus plainly declares that man is the object of a hostile interest on the part of the Prince of Evil himself who goes about seeking whom he may devour. In the Lord's Prayer it really says "Lead us not into temptation but deliver us from the evil one." Christ wanted us to have a clear understanding of our enemy's reality.

If we follow the history of the temptations of Jesus we will find them somewhat parallel to our own. The first temptation of Jesus was a temptation of the flesh. The devil came to Him after He had

301

fasted forty days and nights and was hungry. It was then, at the point of vulnerability, that the devil said, "If you are the Son of God you should turn the stones of the desert into bread so You may eat." Such a temptation to a hungry man is very powerful. Satan knows the appetites of our nature and tempts us accordingly. These appetites of our nature have their proper and natural uses, but it is Satan's lie to say, as many are saying today, that it is never a sin to indulge in an appetite because God has implanted it in us.

That was the trap that our first parents fell into. The forbidden fruit, the tempter told them, was good to eat. It would satisfy their hunger and make them like gods. That was the pit that Esau fell into when he despised his birthright and sold it for a mess of pottage. "I am about to die so what good is my birthright to me?" That in substance is what every man who yields to the temptations of the flesh says. "God put the appetite in me, and I will satisfy it."

But that is not what the great souls said. It is not what Joseph said when he was tempted. It is not what Daniel said or John the Baptist or many, many others. They said rather, that the soul must live even though the body perishes. And Christ said, "Man shall not live by bread alone, but by every word that proceeds from the mouth of God."

Father God, please help me to be a great soul like Daniel who put the soul before the body. Do not allow me to be deceived, I pray. Please help me as I learn to resist the temptations of the flesh. In the name of Jesus, amen.

November 26

Scripture Reading: Matthew 4:1-11
Key Verse: "The devil took Him up . . . ." Matthew 4:5

The second and third temptations of Christ were that of power and position. In Satan's final and supreme effort to tempt Christ he took Jesus to the top of a high mountain and showed Him all the kingdoms of the world and the glory of them and said, "All these things I will give You *if* You will fall down and worship me." What a fatal "if."

God's word tells us that we can be stronger than temptation if we want to be. "No temptation has overtaken you except such as is common to man; but God is faithful, who will not allow you to be tempted beyond what you are able, but with the temptation will also make a way of escape, that you may be able to bear it." When we realize this, when we say to ourselves, "It can be done!" then temptation can be resisted and conquered. Our soul is on guard.

A second method of defense is to avoid exposing ourselves to temptation. You will never hurt temptation, but it will try to hurt you. And do not be ignorant of this fact, that there is such a thing as tempting temptation. There is such a thing as entering into temptation's territory. The Niagara Falls has a river above it, but it is not a safe place for swimming. So today, much of the entertainment world is not a safe place for character building. We must avoid the places; the persons, the books, and the sights which Satan makes use of to tempt the soul.

A disciple of Plato, Trochilus, had escaped from a storm at sea in which the ship was sunk and he himself had nearly perished. When he reached home, the first thing he did was to order his servants to wall up the two windows in his chamber that looked upon the sea, lest upon some fine day when the sea was calm and tranquil he should again be tempted to venture upon its treacherous waters. There are many windows looking out upon the sea of temptation which the soul would do well to wall up.

The word "Blitzkrieg" came into being by the lightning speed of war the German's waged upon their helpless enemies. Well, that's the only way to meet the temptations of our lives, with lightening speed. "Resist the devil and he will flee from you."

Still another important means of defense is to prepare in advance for the coming of the temptation. We are instructed in the Scriptures to put on the whole armor of God. Soldiers, who know the battle will come, as the tempter will surely come, do not leave their armor leaning against a chair in the bed-chamber. They fully prepare, and so should we.

Men and women do not fall suddenly. When a dam goes out it seems as if it had gone out in a moment of time, but it is usually only the last stage in a long process of weakening and degeneration. So it is when the soul gives way. Beware lest you leave your doors and windows unlocked. Lock them by prayer, Bible reading and faithful church attendance. It is said that Satan trembles when he sees the weakest saint upon his knees.

Above all, take the name of Jesus with you. Make Him your invisible companion every moment of every day. And you shall have God and His power at your disposal and "if God be for you, who can be against you?"

Lord God Almighty, You have already given every provision for me to be able to withstand temptation for You are faithful and will provide a way of escape. Thank You Father, for Your wonderful provision and care for me. Amen.

November 27

What Have We to be Thankful For in 1942?

Scripture: Psalm 92

Key Verse: "It is good to give thanks to the Lord, and to sing praises to Your name" Psalm 92:1

Throughout the nation today, Christians meet to give thanks to God for His gracious providence and protective power throughout another year. But well do we realize that since last Thanksgiving our nation has been plunged into a World War, with all its human atrocities and suffering, tears and tortures. There is no doubt about it. The world is now experiencing the worst tribulation it has ever known. Therefore, we may ask, what have we to be thankful for?

Think of the hunger and devastation in Europe. Gaze upon the scorched earth in devastated China. And think of Russia, O Russia, with its ruined homes, crushing poverty, and the homeless fleeing populations wandering blindly on, hungry, deprived of clothing, money, children, and loved ones. Gaze upon the forms of those innocent people whose homes have been bombed, searching in the ruins for loved ones they will never find alive. Stand in line with those half-starved, half-frozen people waiting for a bit of black bread. Did you ask what you have to be thankful for?

As mortal beings we should be thankful for bodily comforts. We are fed, clothed and sheltered. We have not yet felt the pinch of hunger, or lack of daily needs. Oh yes, we have no tires, no gas, little sugar, but did not our fathers live without these commodities?

So, what can we be thankful for? Well, first, we should be thankful that we still enjoy religious liberty. The people of Europe have been robbed of this inestimable God-given privilege. Cloisters and other Catholic institutions have been confiscated for non-religious purposes, and Germany has given up Christ for the "Furher." All Europe faces the barbarous treatment of a mad race of self-imposed would-be supermen who hate Christ, Christianity, and God's people the Jews. Yea, all people who evidence any faith in God and desire religious liberty are in jeopardy of prison camp. But, here we are still free to worship God according to the dictates of our own conscience. Our Bibles are still printed and may be carried and read. We may meet to pray, to sing, and to praise our God. We should be thankful.

Christians should especially thank God for His Church. We ought to be thankful for her radiant record, for her cloud of witnesses, for her martyrs faithful unto death, for her self-sacrificing missionaries toiling in obscure parts of the earth, and for her ministers laboring for the furtherance of the gospel. Yes, we ought to thank God everyday for the Church.

What else do we have to be thankful for? We should be thankful for our country. We have more privilege and more hallowed freedom than any other nation on earth. Thank God for the land of the free and the home of the brave, and, let us ever remember that it is righteousness that exalts a nation. Thank God for the knowledge that He is still at the helm. Jehovah reigns today, and every day. Furthermore, thank Him that we can call upon Him in the day of trouble.

And finally, thank God for the opportunity of service. I cannot help but be challenged by the way so many of our boys have given themselves in service for Uncle Sam. Genuine thanksgiving will always show itself in wholehearted service. So bow your head in gratitude to our Lord for His many blessings, and then rise to serve Him in this needy world.

Dear Lord, I am so grateful to You. I cannot imagine living life without the assurance of Your presence and Your help. Thank You, dear Lord. Amen.

November 28   Overstating Our Poverty

Scripture Reading: Matthew 14:13-21

*Key verse: "We have here only five loaves and two fish."
Matthew 14:17*

These disciples are obviously worried. They have come out to the lakeside for a bit of rest, possibly hoping to have a private conversation with their Master. But, their hopes are doomed to disappointment. The boat in which they are riding hardly touches the shore before they are besieged by a great multitude of troublesome people who take up the Master's time until the disciples have no moments alone with Him. The day wears on through ceaseless toil, the hours are hectic until eventide and still these troublesome people refuse to leave. By this time they are facing a serious problem, for they have been without food all day and are hungry. There are no markets and no money to buy bread, and to make matters worse, Jesus seems entirely unconscious of their plight. He is so busy teaching and healing He has lost all track of time. And so, the only thing they know to do is take matters into their own hands.

Now this is a very human story. Life is constantly bringing perplexing situations to us, both as individuals and groups. Our resources seem entirely inadequate for what is demanded of us. Having faced their poverty, the disciples proceeded to pass the following resolution. (Does this sound like a church board?) "We are in a desperate situation to which we are entirely inadequate. Be it resolved that there is but one course open to us and that is to send the multitudes away."

How modern all this sounds. They are, while willing, hopeless and helpless in the pressing demands of the hour. And why is this? It is because they have so grossly overstated their poverty. "We have here," they say, "only five loaves and two fish." "Really? Is that all?" someone asks. "Do you have no wealth besides this lunch?" "That is all," they answer. "But how about your Lord and Master?" asks the questioner. "Has He ever failed you? Why not look to Him?" Sometimes we just leave God out altogether. To every appeal that smacks of the impossible we cry, "Send them away!"

Will you refresh your mind with that story of Elisha at Dothan. Elisha's servant goes out in the morning, sees an enemy army and is overcome with fear and despair. He cries, "Alas my master, what shall we do?" And the prophet prays, not for deliverance but that the eyes of the servant might be opened to see the infinite forces of God. And then his fear turns to faith and courage. So it was with the disciples when they realized that they did not have to meet this trying situation alone. That day, that seemed destined for defeat, ended in victory.

The difference was made by the Lord. He had neither forgotten nor forsaken them or the pressing need. How simple was Christ's method. All sat down, all ate, all had enough. And it was brought about by Jesus and the disciples together.

And so it is in the meeting of every need, problem, and difficulty. God walks to His missions on human feet. He ministers through human hands. He speaks His message through human lips. He is the vine and we are the branches. The vine has no bearing of fruit except through the branches. But it is equally true that we are absolutely dependant on the vine.

As He took the loaves and fish and fed the multitudes, He will take your life and your gifts and use you to the glorious accomplishment of His purpose.

Dearest Lord, thank You that You are the source of all that is needed to accomplish Your work. I am not poor at all, but wealthier beyond belief, because I am a child of the King and heir to all You possess. Father, turn my focus to all that is possible in You, amen.

November 29   Songs in the Night

Scripture Reading: Job 35:9-11

Key Verse: ". . . God my Maker, Who gives songs in the night."
Job 35:10

Have you ever been sick, perhaps in a hospital, and the hours of the night seemed so long that dawn would never come? Well, these words were spoken to a man who was in terrible trouble and was also terribly sick. The night had settled down upon him and apparently there was not a star in the sky. His heart had lost its song. And when he bemoaned his condition, his friend asked him, "Where is God who gives songs in the night?" This was as much as to say, where is your God? Have you forgotten Him?

Well may the night of this world's sorrow and sin furnish the occasion for terror and alarm among those who do not know God. But, for those who have learned to lean on Him, it is the occasion for song. It takes the night to bring out the stars, but it is then that the heavens declare the glory of God and the firmament shows forth His handiwork.

Yes, there are times when those who fear the Lord do have to walk through the dark. But they do not walk there alone. Fanny Crosby, the famous hymn writer, saw through blinded eyes the glory of the King and her songs set the people of God around the world singing. Paul and Silas, with bleeding backs and manacled limbs, made the walls of their Philippian prison echo with song. Jesus, in the dark night of His betrayal, sang with His disciples a song of victory that has sent its echoes of gladness down the centuries, probably our Psalm 118.

The question is often asked, "Why must I endure these times of struggle?" Well, sometimes it is God's way of bringing to us the best that is possible for us. Michelangelo answered a student who had remarked about the waste of the marble under the heavy strokes of the great sculpture's mallet and chisel, "As the marble wastes, the image grows."

And there is much that needs to be cut away from our lives before the beauty of His image is seen.

And then, God lets us walk through the dark valley sometimes because it leads to the brighter way. Often it is the walk in the valley that brings us into closer fellowship with Him. It was certainly the bleak side Paul took, as he said, "That I might know Him and the fellowship of His sufferings." The times of testing develop in His children courage that only the hard experiences can give. A life of ease does not grow strong character. Children reared in ease and idleness do not become the kind of people who can be depended upon to do a hard life's work. And God's call to His people is to "Fight the good fight of faith."

Yes, my friends, if the night is dark and long as Job found it, God gives songs. He gives songs of faith, songs of hope, songs of courage, songs of assurance, and songs of consolation and comfort. David wrote in Psalm 42:8, "The Lord will command His lovingkindness in the daytime, and in the night His song shall be with me."

And one day, there will be no more darkness. Night will change to day. There will burst upon our vision the light of the King's country and the King will come forth to meet us saying, "Come you blessed of my Father." With songs of everlasting joy, our sorrows will flee away and we shall walk with Him forever in the land of fadeless day, for there is no night there.

Abba, Father, I do indeed trust the course of my soul to Your hands. I ask only that as the times of trial and testing come into my life, You would help me to have a song of hope and faith in my heart, and a song of praise on my lips. Thank You. Amen.

November 30   The Place of Prayer

Scripture Reading: Acts 1:13-14

Key Verse: "These all continued with one accord in prayer and supplication . . . ." Acts 1:14

In the geography of the soul there are three places of power, the Mount of Prayer, the Desert of Meditation, and the Island of Vision, but the Mount of Prayer stands forth most gloriously. It has a recognized position on the continent of history. Tennyson wrote, "For what are men better than sheep or goats that nourish blind life within their brain? If knowing God, they lift not hands of prayer, both for themselves and those who call them friends? For so the whole round earth is every way, bound by gold chains about the feet of God. For we may search the World through, we still shall find that wide as spreads the ambient air, the common language of mankind in peril, want, or woe, is prayer."

The philosophy of prayer can be expressed in two thoughts: Divine contact, and Divine guidance. As for Divine contact, it is the secret of spiritual power. When the trolley pole is off the wire, the streetcar stops. As for Divine guidance, it is a moment-by-moment affair. Our Pilot guides us step by step through the shoals and currents of life. Continuing communication with God is how we receive this guidance.

Prayer is not something secondary, it is primary. It is not to be used or neglected according to our whims. We must turn to God in prayer if we are to have spiritual fruit in our lives. Then the power will come, sharing will be made easy, serving God will be joyous, the devil will retreat, God's kingdom will advance and the Lord will reign in our hearts.

Do we pray as Jacob prayed? As Paul and Silas in prison prayed? As Elijah prayed at Mount Carmel? As the Christian church did for Peter until the door of the prison opened? If our praying is to be transforming and transfiguring it must be the genuine outcome of a pure, devoted soul with faith and expectancy, holding on to God until the power falls.

Prayer should be joyous. The fifth Psalm says "Let all those rejoice who put their trust in You." Why do we ever pray otherwise? He is our creator, our liberator, our preserver, our friend and our King. He is our Lord, our Master, and our Father. We should rejoice in this blood-bought privilege of communing with such a friend and God.

A sea captain recounts the story of crossing off the Newfoundland coast. A certain passenger named George Mueller of Bristol asked the captain to pray with him, since he must be in Quebec by Saturday afternoon. "Impossible," said the captain, for the fog had been so thick for the last day that little progress could be made. "I have not broken an engagement for 57 years," said Mueller, "So if your ship can't take me, God will find other means to take me." The captain agreed to pray with the man thinking him a lunatic, but said, "Mr. Mueller, do you know how thick the fog is?" "No," he replied, "My eyes are not upon the fog, but upon the living God who controls every circumstance of life." He prayed a simple prayer and rose from his knees to see the lifting fog.

Oh beloved, that is the kind of prayer we need today. That is the kind of faith and life that will lift the fog of apathy, sin, selfishness, pleasure-madness, and coldness from sleeping hearts and lost loved ones today. Seek your Lord in prayer today, beloved.

Almighty God, cleanse me and forgive me of anything that is not pleasing to You, and dress me in the righteousness of Christ so that my prayers may not be hindered in any way. I love You Lord, amen.

December 1   Perspectives on Eternity

Scripture Reading: Ecclesiastes 3:1-15

Key Verse: "I have seen the God-given task with which the sons of men are to be occupied. He has made everything beautiful in its time. Also He has put eternity in their hearts . . . ."
Ecclesiastes 3:10-11.

The rationalist who rules out revelation is unable to give an answer for man's existence. If there is no God to glorify, and no hereafter to be concerned about, then no individual can find a sufficiently satisfying reason for wishing to live. Life here without faith, without God, is all odds against the one who makes the struggle. But, let the Bible speak and the picture is very different indeed. Yes, within the Scriptures we find that God did indeed have a purpose in putting man on this earth, and a plan for his destiny.

God made man for fellowship with Himself. We see in the story of the Prodigal Son the relationship between God and man. This little parable defines most of our theological terms. What is sin but the going away from our Father's house? What is it to be lost but to be in the far country, out of His circle? What, after all, is contrition but the homesickness of the soul? And repentance, but the return to the Father's house? And our salvation, like the return of the prodigal, is the joyous return to the Father's waiting welcome. Yes, man is made for fellowship with God, and there is no peace to be found without it.

Man is also to rule and reign over all the earth. In Genesis, God said, "Let them have dominion . . . over all the earth . . ." Here is man's commission. As Solomon said, "Fear God and keep His commandments, for this is man's all." This life is worth living if you know, as the catechism of yesterday taught, that "man's chief end is to glorify God and to enjoy Him forever."

But what of man's destiny? We have no proof of life after death save that of God's Word. There are certainly intimations which support, and confirm, the Book. There is intuition, an inborn belief that this life on this earth is not the end. There is the logical idea of completeness. No life is complete in this world, and just when we are best prepared to serve, death occurs or senility begins. If death were to end all, then the One who planned the universe had no eye at all to economy. And then there is affection; we love those who are gone from us not less but more as the years go by. Time intensifies our love. If they have ceased to exist, why are we not created to forget them?

The Scriptures have much to comfort us on the topic of man's destiny, however. The Bible teaches that when death comes, the body sleeps, the conscious self of the believer departs to be with Christ and when the Lord Jesus Christ comes again according to His promise, the dead in Christ will rise. Yes, add to the intimations of our destiny the clear teachings of the Word of God, and we have a complete system of truth and fact which to the believer is transcendently beautiful, positively alluring, and decisively convincing.

With our faith resting upon the revelation that God has given us, our knowledge is verified and established by experience. We can shout with John of old, "Beloved, now we are children of God; and it has not been revealed what we shall be, but we know that when He is revealed we shall be like Him, for we shall see Him as He is." The believer is a child of God awaiting an inheritance that fades not away, reserved in heaven.

Praise Your Holy Name, Lord, for You have not left me comfortless. Help me to see my life, my trials, and my future as You see them. Amen.

December 2   What Are You Living For?

Scripture: II Corinthians Chapter 5

Key Verse: "Therefore, we make it our aim . . . to be well pleasing to Him." II Corinthians 5:9

As a Christian, what is your ambition? What is the purpose of your life? What are you living for?

Life is God's gift to man. It is your trust and mine. It is a loan from God to Whom we shall render account for every deed and every idle word. How important that we live, live largely, live purposefully, live rightly.

The unconverted sees only one thing certain, and that is the grave; therefore no high ambition is produced. But to the Christian, God is certain, eternity is certain, the new birth is real. The grave is not the goal.

We were created by Him and for Him. We live and move and have our being in Him. For all these reasons we Christians have a new ambition, which is to be well pleasing to God.

Life is precious because of the service it may render to God in the advancement of His glory. You were not created as a piece of guesswork. There is a purpose in the creation of every human being. Is it merely the pursuit of happiness or is life an investment? Yes, an investment, and more!

Man was created to find joy in the Lord, but more. He was created to be Holy and thereby glorify God and enjoy Him forever. The double aim of life is duty first, and then joy as a consequence.

Yes indeed, life is an investment. It is not a gamble, not to be squandered, wasted, or ruined. It is to be invested rightly. There is only one time to decide what to do with your life. It is now, for you stand on the brink of eternity. Where will you spend it? I am weak at the thought of it. I tremble at the thought of its endlessness. Yet, you and I are destined to eternity with or without God. And that will be settled in this short span of time by a choice of life. This world is but the vestibule to eternity. It is but the porch of heaven or the gateway of hell.

How momentous then is life. How grand its possession. What responsibility in its every breath. What a crime to waste life. What a glory to consecrate it. And, may I pause for a moment to ask, what sort of life are you living? What then are you living for? What is your ambition?

Yes, there is a place for ambition in the Christian life. There are heights to be scaled, difficulties to be faced, and victories to be won. What therefore is your ambition? Scripture exhorts us to be well pleasing to God. Such an ambition does not spend itself in dreaming. It leads to persistent and determined effort, always going forward, onward, pressing toward the mark.

There are discouragements by the way, criticism and rebuffs, but there is a crown. Oh beloved, are you out for the crown? Are you running the race so as to receive it? Is your life pleasing to God? I urge you to run the race as a marathon, not a sprint, dear one. Prepare to run to the very finish line.

If we believe Jesus was right, we win just in proportion to the abandon with which we give ourselves to Him. Venture little, gain little. Stake all, gain all. Live to please God, and a life of deep joy, meaning and purpose will be yours. If your life is dull and uninteresting, give your all to God this hour and begin to really live!

Holy and Almighty God, I want to be Yours for eternity. I also want to spend my life wisely, filled with meaning and purpose. I look to You to guide me into this life of purpose You have planned for me since before my birth. I want my life to be well pleasing to You. Amen.

December 3   Be Happy

Scripture: Matthew Chapter 5

Key Verse: "Blessed are the merciful, for they shall obtain mercy . . . ." Matthew 5:3-12

Our key verse today is found in the famous passage called the "Beatitudes." In them, Christ shares the secret of happiness. While the Declaration of Independence asserts that certain rights are inalienable, among them life, liberty and the pursuit of happiness, it does not elaborate as to how to lay hold of them.

We crave happiness, but it is so elusive and seems to bypass most people. Jesus however looked upon men as possible heirs of life and children of God. Therefore, they were entitled to share in the joys of life. Yet each of the eight sayings of the Beatitudes run so counter to the current idea of happiness, that men find them hard to believe.

Some would explain them away by saying they are not for now, but are the laws in the coming Kingdom of God. But, since the Kingdom of God is within you, as well as its social and future consummation, its rules of happiness pertain to us now.

The first requisite for being blessed is to settle who is in authority in one's life. Jesus made much of this point when He said, "No man can serve two masters," and "if a house be divided against itself, that house cannot stand." We are to "seek first the Kingdom of God." Yes, we need to seek it in our lives, in our homes, and in our hearts.

So, step number one in the secret of happiness is to make sure God is in authority in your life. Make sure He is the ruler of your heart. Then, new sources of happiness begin to appear in our lives and the longer we look, love, and follow Jesus, the more real are these Beatitudes to our souls.

"Blessed are the poor in spirit, for theirs is the kingdom of heaven." Pride truly does lead to every other vice. It is nothing more than a spiritual cancer, in the end. Humility, conversely, is the foundation for all other virtues. The Word of God says "God resists the proud and gives grace to the humble."

Pride resists growth toward God, while humility is the foundational virtue because it possesses a grace of receptivity, which makes for growth. Pride closes the mind with self-patterns and with prejudice. Be humble, and you will be receptive to the things of God.

Pride poisons the mind and heart. The vanity of racial prejudice is an example of this. In contrast with this, the poor in spirit have the grace of humility. They are not ego-centric. Moreover, the poor in spirit are helped toward this happiness by a deep spirit of gratitude. Oh, how sweet to be truly grateful to God for all our blessings and for life itself.

The poor in spirit are not pushers in the rush for honor. They seek God's glory and give Him the honor for every achievement.

The poor in spirit keep their consciences sensitive by constant comparison with Christ. They are saved from smugness by the purity of their Master's sinlessness. In such contrite and humble hearts, the Eternal God can dwell. Theirs, most certainly, is the Kingdom.

Tomorrow we will continue examining these eight secrets to happiness as members of the Kingdom of God. Today, let us examine ourselves to see who is sitting in rulership of our lives, and ask ourselves if we are truly humble and grateful before God.

Dearest Father, Forgive me for the pride that raises its ugly head in my life. Root it out of my heart, Lord, and replace it with a correct picture of who I am in You. Thank You, Father, amen.

December 4   By-Standers or Stand-Byers?

Suggested Scripture: Nehemiah Chapter 4

Key Verse: "So we built the wall . . . for the people had a mind to work." Nehemiah 4:6

There are two sets of people, two attitudes, surrounding every question. And, so it was in the story of our text. In far off Persia, Nehemiah heard of the state of old Jerusalem. Enemies of God's people, the Jews, had broken down the walls, burned the gates, and destroyed the temple. Nehemiah wept, fasted, and prayed to God for help. God heard, and soon Nehemiah was on his way with letters from the king to ease his way.

There were enemies both within and without the city. There was Sanballat the Samaritan, and Tobiah the Ammonite who were openly scornful and threatening. Then, there were the disinterested or faint-hearted who were cowed as the taunts of the enemy were hurled their way. Isn't that the way it is today, as well? Many and varied are the enemies facing the church this day, but the grumblers and the spiteful within the church are no less dangerous than the more vocal enemies without.

Yes, Nehemiah had bystanders within and bystanders without, who hurled their epithets and jeers, who did not help, but hindered. But, Nehemiah also had "standbyers." He had a great host of faithful people. He had the assurance of God's great presence. Listen to Nehemiah's declaration, "Be not afraid of them; remember the Lord who is great and terrible."

Nehemiah also had the strength of right. A great man of old once said, "Thrice is he armed who hath his quarrel just." But, more even than this, Nehemiah had the power of prayer. Eight times it is recorded, "We made our prayer with God." And Nehemiah put feet to his prayer. He set a watch against the enemy, day and night. There was eternal vigilance against the enemy of their soul. Prayer, rather than slackening their energy, redoubled their efforts in the prosecution of the work. And, prayer gave them hope. They knew, "Our God shall fight for us."

There was perseverance, too, "So we labored in the work, and half of the men held the spears from daybreak until the stars appeared." Prayer was never intended, beloved, to foster idleness or diminish responsibility. There was a time to pray, and then there was a time to prepare to stand and fight.

Every builder was a soldier. With one hand they wrought in the work and with the other hand they held a weapon. Mutual co-operation went hand in hand with a joyous acceptance of their responsibility. And then there was Divine interposition. "God had brought all their plot to nothing." The adversaries of God's people were frustrated and defeated. Their threats of murder and merciless malice were detected and overruled by the hand of God. And this little band of faithful, prayerful, watchful, workful people wrought victory for the cause of God.

They, my friends, were stand-byers, not bystanders. And the lessons we see here are apropos for the work, warfare, and the cause of Christ and His church today. The fight will be hard and long. The demands may be stringent and require sacrifice. The task will look impossible, and the enemy will be watchful. But, God will be present and able. Trust therefore in the rightness of the cause of Christ. Trust also in God, for He shall prevail!

Dear Heavenly Father, I desire with all my heart to be faithful. I ask now for the strength to do the work You have prepared for me. I ask for the courage, the endurance, to run the race You have set out in the knowledge and assurance of Your ever-present help. Amen.

December 5   The World's Greatest Emergency

Scripture Reading: Matthew 9:35-38

Key Verses: "But when He saw the multitudes, He was moved with compassion for them, because they were weary and scattered, like sheep having no shepherd. Then He said to His disciples, 'The harvest truly is plentiful, but the laborers are few. Therefore pray the Lord of the harvest to send out laborers into His harvest." Matthew 9: 36-38

The world's greatest emergency was not that great catastrophe of War Number 1 in which we lost 60,000 of our finest boys and left a million more maimed and homeless. It was not the awful flu epidemic that took a greater toll of lives than war ever did. The world's greatest emergency was not the financial fiasco that struck this nation in 1930-32 and closed our banks and saw millions go bankrupt overnight.

The world's greatest emergency, beloved, is the fact that today, after 2,000 years of gospel preaching, 2,000 years of earnest praying, 2,000 years of education, culture, gospel music, and a care for others, there are still millions without God, like sheep without a shepherd. This is the world's greatest emergency. Everywhere, all about us, in every town, village, hamlet, city, multitudes are without God. The harvest is white and plenteous, but where are the laborers?

There are only two sides to the spiritual conflict, the Lord's side and the enemy's side. They are mixed up and intertwined. The wheat and the tares grow together until the end. They were in Moses' day, and he called for a separation. "Who is on the Lord's side?" Let us be separated not by distance, but by consecration to the Lord. Let the Body of Christ ring forth with a voice!

How will Jesus lead us back to His side? First, we must see the condition of the world as He sees it. We must see our own responsibility to God and all those around us.

Then let us pray for laborers in God's vineyard. Set aside everything

321

and pray. Too busy? It is the world's greatest emergency. You cannot be too busy for this. Pray for yourself. This is not selfish. Pray to see your fellow man through God's eyes. Pray for a heart-cleansing and a heart breaking. God will use you. Pray for each other. We need it. Pray that the Holy Spirit may get us back on the firing line. Pray for the unsaved; they won't pray for themselves. Pray until no man can say to God, "No man cared for my soul."

Then, we must go. This is Christ's command. It is His divine order. It is the order of Him who bought you by His own precious blood. Go weeping over the world's need, over the sins of God's people "He who continually goes forth weeping, bearing seed for sowing shall doubtless come again with rejoicing, bringing his sheaves with him." There will be no revival except by the weeping and prayers of God's people. Have you shed a tear? Look! Look upon the world, see it as God sees it, and it will break your heart.

Then, tell them about Jesus. Tell them about sin's redemption. Tell them how to be saved. You believe Him. You love Him. You can point a soul to Christ and do your part to meet the world's greatest emergency!

Almighty Father, I believe You. I see how it broke Your heart to see sheep without a shepherd. I ask that each person might consider Your loving invitation to come to You by hearing the gospel. I know it requires many workers to harvest all that would choose You, and I pray that You would send them out to Your harvest. Here am I, Lord, send me. Amen.

December 6   The Conquest of Faith

Scripture Reading: Hebrews 11:30-40

Key Verse: "By faith the walls of Jericho fell down . . . ." Hebrews 11:30

The story is so familiar that I need not relate it. The first step in the conquest of Canaan was the conquest of Jericho. It was a fortified stronghold and if they could not take Jericho they would fail in the conquest of Canaan.

But God gave them instructions even as He gives us instructions for the defeat of our "Jerichos." It was a strange procedure and contrary to all military and worldly-minded tactics. They were to march around the city walls once each day for six days and say nothing. On the seventh day they were to march around seven times, the trumpets were to be blown at a given signal and the people were to shout a great shout. These were God's commands and by faith they obeyed and by faith the walls of Jericho fell down flat.

It was a faith of preparation. It takes faith to prepare. There was much preparation before the victory came. It took six days to get ready for one day. It was a preparation of obedience. The reason of man could not interfere. Perhaps they had to endure the taunts of the enemy on the wall, but all these were part of a preparation by faith.

Theirs was a faith of initiation. They dared to do that which had never been done before. Adventure and daring were in their hearts. When faith loses its adventure and initiation, it loses its power. Theirs was a faith of starting something new. It had never been done before and God blessed the new way. Try it.

It was the faith of organization. Some people are afraid of organization. First, it finds a place of work for everybody. Second it perfects harmony, unity and victory. The difference between a mob and an army is organization.

It was a faith of co-operation. Every man found his place. Joshua, under God, was the leader. He issued hard orders, called upon the people for strenuous service, did seemingly foolish things, but there was full co-operation.

Then there was the faith of determination. They determined by faith first that they were right. Then their determination made them stick to their job in spite of all discouragements and difficulties until the finish.

Lastly, it was a faith of continuation unto consummation. This is a faith that finishes what it starts out to do. It required silence and obedience. It required self-control. What if just one soldier had responded to the taunts from the wall? It took continuation of faith to keep on going around that wall for six days, with their mouths shut, and in perfect order and battle array. It was not a question with them of what had happened or was going to happen but the question was whether or not they had marched around the walls as they were told.

In all of this, don't forget the objective of their faith. God was in the midst of that strange procession. In the center went the Ark of the Covenant denoting the very presence of God.

There are Jerichos all around us. But, oh thank God there is a secret to be experienced by faith, the joy of resting in God, going forward in faith, and possessing your Jericho.

Almighty God, This is my Jericho _____. I wait on You for instructions on how to conquer it. Then help me not to stand there, but to step out boldly, knowing that You are with me. In the name of Jesus Our Lord, amen.

December 7   This Great Assembly

Scripture Reading: I Kings 8:22-62

Key Verse: "May the Lord our God be with us, as He was with our fathers. May He not leave us nor forsake us, that He may incline our hearts to Himself, to walk in all His ways . . . ." I Kings 8:57

Our key verse today is a portion of that great ceremony of the dedication of Solomon's Temple. It was part of Solomon's appeal to his people in the light of the goodness and faithfulness of God throughout the history of His people. I am sure that no one in that great assembly questioned for a moment the truthfulness of the statement that the Lord God "was with our fathers."

Standing there, in that new temple with a united nation gathered before him, the cloud filling the house, and peace resting on all his land to the farthest border, the King looks back on the long road from Sinai and sums up the whole history in one sentence, "The Lord our God be with us, as He was with our fathers."

One name alone is worthy to be named. It is "the Lord" who has given rest to His people. We look on the past most wisely, when we see in it all the working of that one mighty hand. Communion with God explains much which is otherwise inexplicable.

Yes, God was a wonderful God in those far-off days of long ago. He was alive, near, and compelling. He directed individuals, controlled events, and made history. It was God who met Moses at the burning bush and sent him to Pharaoh to cry, "Let my people go!" It was God who divided that Red Sea and led His people through. And it was God who went before them in a pillar of cloud by day and fire by night. These are the stories that mothers told their wide-eyed children, and with which fathers inspired the patriotism of their sons. These are the stories that poets wove into song and warriors shouted in defiance to their foes. Surely, surely, Jehovah God was with their fathers.

But, here is the strangeness of it. There is no evidence that the fathers ever dreamed that they and their days and deeds were exceptional, or that God was with them in any miraculous manner. They came out of Egypt a frightened mob of fugitive slaves. They murmured against God, Moses, and the manna. They wanted to return to the land of their bondage. So far were they from realizing God's presence that they made a golden calf and worshipped it in God's place.

The fact is, in every age and with every people, it is easier to extol the past than to appreciate the present. The golden age is never <u>now</u>. The present is so noisy, and fussy, and fretful that it gets on our nerves. Its perspective is poor. It makes big things look little and little things big.

You must wait. Only through the softening vista of the years can you see "the good old days" of each successive generation.

It is always so. The product is not seen in the process. That is why you must wait until tomorrow before you can see today.

In the meantime, remember that God is the same, yesterday, today, and tomorrow. He still directs individuals, controls events, and makes history. He is yet alive, near, and compelling. He is truly still a wonderful God, and He is with us, as He was with our fathers.

Dear Father, I relish Your presence in my daily life! I know that at any moment of any hour, I can turn to You in prayer and You hear me. I can confide in You; I can confess my most foolish thoughts and my deepest longings to You. I can trust You. The great testimonies of the past only serve to encourage me to trust You more. Amen.

December 8   The First Lion Tamer

Scripture Reading: Daniel Chapter 1

Key Verse: "But Daniel purposed in his heart that he would not defile himself with the portion of the king's delicacies, nor with the wine which he drank; therefore he requested of the chief of the eunuchs that he might not defile himself." Daniel 1:8

When Daniel came down with the other three Hebrew lads, the pick of the young men of Jerusalem, to be educated at the court of Nebuchadnezzar, Daniel began his new life in Babylon by taking a stand for his God and his religion. The king changed his name, but he could not change his soul or make him forget the name of his God. Daniel's circumstances, unfavorable and pagan as they were, did not hinder the development of a great Christian character because Daniel grew not from the soil around him, but by being rooted in God Himself.

Daniel was tested immediately and in a matter most important, his very food and drink. What of this wine, which had been offered to heathen gods, and what of that meat, which was ceremonially unclean? What would Daniel do? And what would he advise his companions to do? Note well the obedient-disobedience of Daniel. He would be true to the higher law. As Peter said, "We ought to obey God rather than man."

An ordinary young man would have said, "Well, Jerusalem has fallen. I am a captive here, and here is to be my life. I can't afford to jeopardize my future by offending the king. So, while I'm in Babylon, I'll do what the Babylonians do." But, that was not what Daniel said. Instead, "Daniel made up his heart that he would not defile himself." What was the result of Daniel's stand? Not only did he prosper and grow strong on a plain diet, but he won the respect of the officers of the court and the king himself. And that is always true. Men may pretend to laugh at one who has standards and convictions, but in their hearts they respect such a person.

In the reign of Darius, by which time Daniel was an elderly man, he was about to be appointed to a position approximating that of a prime minister of all that vast empire. All good men will have critics, so the enemies of Daniel plotted for his downfall. They could find no fault in his political leadership, and his integrity and loyalty was beyond criticism. Only in regards to his religion and faith in God could they fault him.

Daniel's enemies tricked the king into signing a decree prohibiting prayer to anyone save the king. The king in his foolishness signed the decree. And Daniel prayed to his God as before. Without the least hesitation, Daniel effectually offered up his life in loyalty to his God.

Oh, how great is the influence of a godly man, and how great is his reward! And, hear me; those lions out of whose mouth Daniel was delivered are not extinct today. No, those lions prowl and roar today, "Your adversary the devil as a roaring lion, walks about seeking whom he may devour." We are still tested, as to our convictions. Will we stand? Will we be true?

The great inspiration of Daniel's life is that he shows us how to live a life of faithfulness. Daniel dared; Daniel stood; and Daniel, through God, overcame. When you do that, the same God who delivered Daniel and made him a blessing to the world, will do the same for you.

Dear Heavenly Father, I have made up my mind not to waver in my faithfulness to You. I want to follow You in faithful steps of obedience today and every day of my life. In Jesus' name, and for His sake, amen.

December 9   The Householder

Scripture Reading: Matthew 13:36-58

Key Verse: "Therefore every scribe instructed concerning the kingdom of heaven is like a householder who brings out of his treasure things new and old." Matthew 13:52

These parables of the kingdom are like little pieces of a picture. They do not each, individually, tell the whole story. Neither do they deal with the deepest facts concerning the kingdom of heaven. This very short parable follows a question and description, and must be considered in the context in which it is found.

"Have you understood all these things?" Jesus asked the disciples. And when they answered yes, He said, "Therefore every scribe instructed concerning the kingdom . . ." To understand the things Jesus taught is to be instructed in the kingdom of heaven. And, to be a scribe instructed concerning the kingdom of heaven is to have received His teaching, and understood it. The two sayings are mutually explanatory. The definition of the one is the other.

When the disciples declared that they did indeed understand His teaching, Jesus proceeded to declare their responsibility. He described their position in these words, "a scribe instructed concerning the kingdom of heaven." The word scribe is significant, for it is a specific office. The class of scribes began in Ezra's day to be readers and expounders of the law of God. Ezra had been a fine example of a true scribe. He stood in the midst of the people and read the words of the law, indicating the meaning of them by comment, annotation, exposition, and elocutionary perfection.

Now in Jesus' day, scribes were still the professed expounders of the law but they had degraded the office by including oral tradition and by interpretation by the strictest letter of the law. In Jesus' day, therefore, the scribes were in constant antagonism to Him who ruthlessly swept aside all their traditions and yet lived within the Law.

Actually, Jesus was saying to His disciples, I want you to take this office of scribe which has been so abused and I want you to fulfill it.

They were to become in their age the interpreters of the Law of God. They were to be the new scribes, the interpreters of the kingdom, those through whom the age will know the facts concerning the government of God. Each one would "bring out of his treasure things new and old."

A householder is one in authority, the master of the house, and the picture here is of the householder lavishly scattering out of his wealth the things which are necessary for the supply and government of the household. This is a position of profound dignity and responsibility, and it is the position of Christ's disciples until this day. It is our task today and until His return.

We need to testify of the God of our fathers, His kingship, His power, His holiness, glory, and grace. All of these have been revealed in the person of His Son. Let us bring out the treasure of the cross, and give it to this age. Let us testify of the God of Abraham, Isaac, and Jacob, and give this treasure to our age. This it the work of the people of the Kingdom of God.

Think of the profound dignity of our task. Jesus sweeps aside all the thrones, kings, and governments of men and says, for the purposes of God's great and only kingdom throughout this age, the ruling authority is to be vested in the disciples who are instructed concerning the Kingdom of Heaven. We, beloved, are to represent Him in this world. Do you?

Dear Father, I am inadequate for this task, alone, yet I am honored to be Christ's ambassador in this world. Empower me to glorify You. In Jesus' name, amen.

December 10   What is Man?

Scripture Reading: Psalm 8

Key Verse: "When I consider Your heavens, the work of Your fingers, the moon and the stars, which You have ordained, what is man that You are mindful of him . . .?" Psalm 8:3-4a

If God is a mystery, then man is a marvel. What is man? Well, science and philosophy will help to examine the question, but the final answer is found only in revelation, to be accepted by faith. For, while the subject of anthropology is both theological and scientific, there is so much in man that cannot be scientifically explained that we are thrown back upon God's revelation in His Word for any knowledge that we may hope to possess. And, revelation must be taken by faith. Unless we believe, we shall not see.

So, what is man? Well, first we must divide the question. What is man physically? That is not hard to answer. Man is derived from the earth, and to the earth he must eventually return. Man is composed of a definite mixture, proportionately measured, of oxygen, nitrogen, carbon, sodium, sulfur, silicon, iron, potassium, hydrogen, phosphorus, iodine, and more.

There is enough of man for seven bars of soap, lime enough to whitewash a chicken coop, phosphorus enough to cover the heads of 1000 matches, iron enough for a ten pennyweight nail, and starch enough for a few collars. That is what man is physically. And, these observations are in line with God's Word, which reads, "God made man of the dust of the ground."

But, yet that is not all. For, organically the problem is more complex. The human anatomy is fearfully and wonderfully made. It is an impressive fact that there is a perceptible difference in each member of the human race, yet there is a similarity, both of structure and function. The framework of the body, the joints as hinges, the ropes of muscle and tendon, the bellows we call lungs, the main pump of our heart, the camera that records the picture of our world through our eyes, and the channels through which our blood flows, are all controlled by a telegraphic system of nerves from the superintendent's office in our brain from which all the orders are issued. In this respect, certainly, all individuals of the human race are alike.

We are also similar in many respects, physically, to the other animals of God's creation. Yet, while we are built along the same general line as other animals that live on the earth, man is actually a unique creature.

Man differs from other animals in a thousand points. Man alone makes use of writing, and possesses articulate speech. Only man has a culture, and civilizations. Man is the only harness maker that God created. And, above all, man is the only animal that participates in religious worship, because man alone has God-consciousness. These and a myriad of other differences put man in a class by himself.

Man's physical being does not explain our dealings with God; our prayer, our faith and our fellowship. The mere existence of our bodies does not explain our art, our regrets, or our dreams.

For man is more than body. Man was created in the image of God. And as this image, let us be continually looking to Him as the pattern for our lives. Indeed, "What is man that you are mindful of him?"

Dear Lord, I am overcome at the awesomeness of Your creation. I am privileged just to be a part of Your plan, thankful to have been formed by Your hand. Praise Your name, for You have not forgotten the smallest sparrow, and You are mindful even of me. I am made in Your image, and I truly desire to mold my life and my character after You. Amen.

December 11   The Mind of Man

Scripture Reading: Psalm 139

Key Verse: "Search me, O God, and know my heart; try me, and know my anxieties; and see if there is any wicked way in me, and lead me in the way everlasting." Psalm 139:23-24.

We have seen that physically man is but dust, and organically man is classified in the animal kingdom. Yet, we know there is more. This leads to the question, what is man mentally? The complexity of our problem increases as we ask this question, because no one seems to know exactly what our mind is. It seems to function through the brain, and yet it is not "brain." It is associated with the body, and yet it is not the body. A great mind may exist in a weak body, and a weak mind in a strong body.

Paul cried, "May your whole spirit, soul, and body be preserved blameless at the coming of our Lord Jesus Christ." Our bodies are the physical house we live in. The soul lives in the body and after the death of the body, lives on. The soul is the seat of affections, desires, emotions, and of the will. The spirit is the inbreathed life of God. God tells us that man was created in the image of God, and God is a spiritual trinity.

The likeness of man to God is in shown in the fact that it is the spirit of man, like the Spirit of God, which knows; "For what man knows the things of a man except the spirit of the man which is in him?" 1 Corinthians 2:11. Also the soul of man, like the soul of God, experiences emotions, "Now the just shall live by faith; but if anyone draws back, My soul has no pleasure in him." Hebrews 10:38.

Man also has mental experiences that can hardly be accounted for by mere physical conditions. We thirst for truth for its own sake. We love virtue when it stands alone. We delight in the fellowship of kindred souls. We put the highest value on things that are intellectual, ethical, and spiritual. These can only be explained in the light of the soul and spirit of man. Any being that has self-consciousness and self-determination is a person. Man is such a being; none other among the visible creation is.

And so we finally arrive at the crux of the matter; what is man spiritually? Man exists in the image and likeness of God. That image, marred by sin, is not lost. It is defaced, but because the image remains man can never free himself from the consciousness of God, nor be at rest apart from God. Because that image is damaged by the sinful state, natural man cannot know nor understand God. In regeneration through faith in Christ, the Divine image is renewed in man.

Since the day of Adam's fall, this world has seen but one perfect image of God, but they who by faith accept the Son, who is that image of the Father, are by degrees transformed into the same image; "But we all, beholding as in a mirror the glory of the Lord, are being transformed into the same image from glory to glory, just as by the Spirit of the Lord." II Corinthians 3:18.

And so this is the final answer to the question, "What is man?" In his chemistry, man is a brother to the insensible rock. In his organic structure, he is an animal homologous with the lower creatures of the earth. But, in his mentality, he is a person infinitely removed from the highest brute; and in his spiritual constitution he is the image of God, visited with the knowledge of God and capable of communion with Him. What a privilege. What a joy. What a responsibility.

Please guide me through this day, allowing me to grow more transparent, revealing the You in me to others. For Your glory, amen.

December 12   That the World May Believe

Scripture Reading: John Chapter 17

Key Verse: "I do not pray for these alone, but also for those who will believe in Me through their word; that they all may be one, as You, Father, are in Me, and I in You; that they also may be one in Us, that the world may believe that You sent Me." John 17:20-21.

Here is the holy of holies in Christ's life and teaching. Under the very shadow of the cross, He holds communion with His Father audibly in the presence of our representatives, the first disciples. Three times Jesus says, "I pray," and we see His expressed desires concerning Himself, the men about Him and then for you and me and all who will believe on Him.

First, He prays that as God glorifies Him, He would be able to glorify the Father, and that eternal life would be given through Him. His deep passions were the glory of God and the saving of men. This glory that would bring about the salvation of man was the glory of the cross. Jesus desired the cross because by way of the cross alone would He put life at the disposal of humanity, according to the purpose of the Father.

"And now, O Father, glorify Me together with Yourself, with the glory which I had with You before the world was," Jesus is here expressing His desire to return to that of which He emptied Himself when He became a servant and was made in the likeness of men. The desire for return to this glory was to be fulfilled through the way of the cross.

Next, Jesus begins to pray for the men about Him. First, He refers to the work He had already done with them, "I have manifested Your name to the men whom You have given me." The great, glorious fact to see is that by His signs, Christ proved His deity and literally manifested that name. Jesus prays, "Keep them through Your name" that they may be one even as We are One; keep them from evil, and sanctify them in the truth.

And so also in the Master's prayer, we hear these arresting words,

335

"I do not pray for the world, but for those whom You have given me." Contrast that with, "That the world may believe . . . that the world may know." The world was on His heart, but He was first praying for these who would reach the world for Him. And if these instruments, multiplied down through the ages, are to bring relief and knowledge to the world concerning God, then ". . . Keep through Your name those whom You have given me, that they may be one as We are." This is not oneness of sentiment, or intellectual opinion. No, this is a living oneness; one in life, one in light, and one in love.

Next we read of ourselves in Christ's prayer, "I do not pray for these alone, but also for those who will believe in Me through their word; that they all may be one . . ." We are to be in vital relationship with other believers, because of having vital relationship with the Father and the Son. The purpose of this unity is that "The world may know."

Finally, we have the last "I desire" Jesus prays. This is my will, my determination. This is my decision, "That they also, whom You gave Me may be with Me where I am, that they may behold my glory . . . ."

The belief of the world has been the result of the answering of these desires of Jesus. Our faith in Him is the direct result of His willingness, His desire, His will. But, let us examine our own hearts. Am I one with other believers in the way Jesus desired? Is our unity and love for each other such a testimony that the world may be won by it?

Dear Father, Please strengthen the bonds in my own local body. Help us to truly be such an example, that the world may know. Amen.

December 13

His Son

Scripture Reading: Hebrews Chapter 1

Key Verse: "God . . . has in these last days spoken to us by His Son, whom He has appointed heir of all things, through whom also He made the worlds." Hebrews 1:1-2

This glorious chapter in Hebrews proclaims for us that which is no longer popular to teach, that Christ is separate from and superior to all others. It declares the seven-fold glory of the Son in unmistakable and particular terms.

The first thing we see in this opening sentence is the assumption that God is, and that God makes Himself known to man, "He speaks." Remember that He is recorded as having spoken first directly, and then through angels, as no prophet or priest is found in Genesis. Then God spoke through leaders such as Moses and Joshua. Next came the prophets, and finally His Son, the essence and embodiment of God's Word.

This Son is the first heir of all things, we see in our text. Secondly, it is through Him that God fashioned the world, and the ages of the world. In Himself, Jesus is the radiant splendor of the Divine glory. Next, He is the very image of Deity. Christ is spoken of as upholding all things by "the Word of His Power." Sixth, the Son is revealed also in His redeeming activity, making purification of sin. Finally, His administrative position is declared; He sat down at the right hand of the Father.

There are seven Old Testament passages given to portray the superiority of the Son to the angels, and His worthiness of worship. He is out of comparison with all others. This is the Christ; this is the One. This is the Son; God has spoken.

So, here is God's divine seal to the Scriptures. The Scriptures are the Word of God. The Old Testament reveals time past, when He spoke through the prophets to the fathers.

But, in the New Testament is the record of His speech through His Son. II Peter 1:21 says "Holy men of God spoke as they were moved by the Holy Spirit." The prophets were simply the organ of prophecy. Christ, the Word, was the originator and object of the prophecy. They were a voice, He was the Word. In Him is the final revelation.

His Word is ultimate and final. No matter what practitioners of other religions say, God has spoken and there is no other word from Him but that found in His Son. Do not be deceived.

We cannot fail to see that it is Christ alone who is worthy of our praise, who is worthy of our worship, and who is worthy of our adoration. He is the brightness of God's glory.

He is the magnificent One who is "upholding all things by the word of His power." Not only does He bring sustaining succor to the material universe, but also to the moral order of the universe. Oh what joy is ours when we understand this concept! Things are not going to pieces, for He is upholding all things. What we call "History," is really the providence of God.

Christ stands, the separated, sanctified, solitary Son of God. He purged our sins by Himself. He did it alone because He alone could do it. Of all the people there were none with Him because of all the people there were none like Him. Our faith is in Christ and Christ alone.

Dearest Lord, Thank You for providing the atonement for my sins, for advocating for me before the Father, and for expectantly waiting for the day in which Your enemies will be made Your footstool. Truly, You alone are worthy of my praise. Worthy is the Lamb that was slain! Amen, and amen.

December 14   The Angelus and the
                                 Businessman

Scripture: I Timothy Chapter 6

Key Verse: "Now godliness with contentment is great gain." I Timothy 6:6

In times recently gone by, the bells of the Angelus would sound morning, noon and evening to call the hearers to prayer. There was even a lovely, popular painting titled "Angelus" which caught this moment on canvas. It was not famous for its coloring or for its commemoration of some world renowned event. It was simple in creation and subdued in tone, nevertheless it commanded the attention of art lovers all over the world.

The Angelus presents a simple peasant standing in a field with his wife at his side. She, with a blue apron over her skirt, cap upon her head, is standing with clasped hands, looking up with exalted expression of devotion. He, removing his hat, holding it in his hand, is bowing his head in an attitude of reverence. It is early evening and the setting sun is lighting up the clouds of the west with rainbow coloring.

Their days' work is about ended, a digging fork stuck in the ground. There is a basket of potatoes and nearby rests a wheelbarrow. The light of the setting sun falls upon the woman's clasped hands and the man's bowed head as they pause in their work to worship.

Why does Millet's Angelus cast us into a worshipful mood? The answer is not far to seek. In the background of the picture rises a church spire. Like a human finger it points upward toward God.

What a picture that is of the instinctive devotion of the human. Worship is the movement of the soul toward God, and both the peasant of the French field and the sophisticated business man need to keep their ears attuned to catch the sound of the summoning Angelus calling them from potato digging or desk digging to the thoughts of God and heaven and holiness.

The Psalmist declared that a day in God's courts is better than a thousand days anywhere else. We too will confess our best days have been spent in common with worshipping thousands bowed in prayer in thousands of churches where there has been for us a "movement of the soul toward God."

There is a beautiful story about Ole Bull and Erickson, the great inventor of the Monitor which turned the tide of Victory for the Northern forces in the civil war. Erickson, giving himself to his inventions, lost his taste and ear for music. Ole Bull went to see him one day at his shop hoping to win his interest once again to music. He asked Erickson's advice about a certain piece of wood that he wanted to put into the violin.

When Erickson had finished examining the wood of the violin, Ole tried it out to show Erickson the sound. Then, putting his very soul into it he kept on playing right there in Erickson's shop until finally Erickson lifted his eyes, filled with tears and running over like a mountain brook. He said to Ole Bull, "I knew that something had gone out of my life, but I never knew before what it was."

Oh, dear business man or woman, too busy for the Angelus, that something that has gone out of your life is the sense of God and your need of Him. It will come back, if you will come back to God. Give Him the rightful place in your life, the rightful part of your time, the rightful part of your love, the rightful part of your talents.

Awesome Father who knows me well, thank You for reminding me that too busy for You is too busy. Help me to hear the Angelus and remember to worship You, no matter how busy my day might be. Amen.

December 15 Gifts to the Giver

Scripture Reading: Matthew 25:14-30

Key Verse: "For everyone to whom much is given, from him much will be required." Luke 12:48 "For what profit is it to a man if he gains the whole world and loses his own soul?" Matthew 16:26

Many years ago in the hill county of Ephraim there lived a young man by the name of Micah, with his mother. One day she found that her earthly wealth, 1100 pieces of silver, had been stolen. In her son's presence she uttered a curse upon the thief. Micah was so frightened he confessed he had taken it. Mother was so delighted at the return of the silver that she secured for him a molten and graven image. But one day the Danites came while he was away and stole his god. When Micah arrived home and found it gone, he at once followed after them saying, "You have taken away my gods and what is there left to me?"

Micah's experience is not entirely unique. In the days of the great depression in 1929, hundreds of men and women who had made possessions their gods began to cry, "You have taken away my gods, what is there left to me?" Some committed suicide; others became mentally unbalanced, suffered moral collapse, or became physical wrecks. Why? Surely our life is more than the sum total of our possessions however valuable they may be. Jesus spoke the truth when He said, "One's life does not consist in the abundance of the things he possesses." It is ours to find the life that is still rich when everything that we possess has been taken away.

Now it is true that how we look upon and what we do with our possessions reveal our heart. In Edwin Markham's Parable of the Builder, is a story of a certain rich man who had it in his heart to do good. "One day he walked over his great estate and came upon a little house in the hollow where lived a carpenter with a large family.

The rich man sent for the carpenter and put before him plans for a beautiful home, and said 'I want you to build a lovely house like this over on that hill. Employ only the best workmen. Use only the best materials for I want it to be a good house.'

Then the rich man went away on a long journey leaving it all to the builder. After the rich man left, the carpenter said to him, 'This is my chance.' So he used poor materials and gave poor workmanship that he might have more money for himself. At length the rich man returned and the carpenter brought him the keys and said, 'That is a fine house I built for you over on that sunny hill.'

'Good,' said the rich man, 'I am glad it is a good house. I have intended all along to give it to you when it was finished. The house is yours.' The builder was heart-broken for he had cheated only himself when he thought he was defrauding another."

Well, every person is building a house for himself in which he is living for eternity. The materials that go into it are of his own choosing. It may be said that what a man receives goes into his character, but what he gives goes into his soul.

The exercise of stewardship is the revelation of the heart. The methods one uses reveal his principles. The things one enjoys reveal his pleasures. The things for which one sacrifices reveal the objects of his devotion.

Everyone has a personal schedule of values. Have you examined yours recently?

Dear Lord, thank You for the abundant blessings You have given me. I want to be a good steward for all of these possessions. Help me to remember that they all belong to You and I am only managing them. Amen.

December 16   Gifts to the Giver II

Scripture Reading: Matthew 25:14-30

Key Verses: "For everyone to whom much is given, from him much will be required." Luke 12:48 "For what profit is it to a man if he gains the whole world and loses his own soul?" Matthew 16:26

In the little valley of Northfield Massachusetts, there lived two young men. The one was born in luxury; the other was the thirteenth child of poor parents. The rich boy was left an estate of 26 million. Interested only in himself, he spent a fabulous sum on a replica of a French Castle, with furniture, double-spiral stairways, paintings, and even basement dungeons as a surprise for his bride. She refused to live in it and it stands unfinished, an evidence of a rich man's folly.

The poor boy decided to give God a chance to use his talents as no other man ever had. When he died he left as his monument, the Northfield Schools and Moody Bible Institute, valued at nearly thirty million dollars. He was Dwight L Moody. The other man's name? Well, you have never heard it and what is more, you never will. For, you see, it is not so much what we have, but what we do with what we have.

Our text says, "For everyone to whom much is given, from him much will be required." All men are not equal in physical stamina, in intellectual acumen, in material possessions or in spiritual sensitiveness. We did not cause or create these advantages. We did not earn them, but we received them as gifts of God. We cannot be blamed if we do not have them, neither can we take credit for possessing them. Jesus made it clear, "Everyone to whom much is *given.*"

These advantages can get us into trouble, for it is not our weaknesses that are the places of peril. We stand guard over them. The place where life breaks is not where we are weak, but where we are strong. It is too easy to fall into arrogance and pride, feeling we need no help from the Father because of our various talents.

How then, can we live with these advantages and use the privileges with which God has endowed His children? There are just two attitudes which you may take toward them. It is possible to think of these advantages in terms of ownership and connive how to make them bring you personal glory and thereby waste them upon ourselves.

But there is another attitude which you may take to these gifts with which God brought you into the world. It is the attitude of stewardship. The steward of God's grace does not waste His gifts. He uses them to meet the needs of the world. He does not spend them upon himself. He serves those in want. It was by that principle that Jesus lived. He became the servant of all. And there you have the greatness of Jesus. He never lost His compassion. He cared what happened to the sheep that were lost and the sparrow that fell.

Dear Friend, what are you doing with the gifts the Father has entrusted to you? Are you using the wisdom He gave you to lighten the burden of the world? Are you using your great capacity for friendship for selfish end or to increase the spirit of good will among men? Won't you go to bended knee today and consecrate all you have to Him?

Lord, My Father, I release my hold on all that I have, knowing it is Yours in the first place. You have freely given to me, may I always freely, generously and lovingly give to others. Amen.

December 17   His Name is Wonderful

Scripture: Isaiah 9:6-7

Key verse: "For unto us a child is born, unto us a Son is given; and the government will be upon His shoulder. And His name will be called Wonderful, Counselor, Mighty God, Everlasting Father, Prince of Peace." Isaiah 9:6

For those of us who know the power of His saving grace, His coming into the world is altogether wonderful.

As we look back upon His life and service we would say He was wonderful even in His incarnation. A child, conceived by the Holy Spirit, and born of the Virgin Mary became flesh and dwelt among us. It is wonderful beyond our comprehension.

Wonderful are the events surrounding His birth. Think of these facts: The King of Glory, maker of Heaven and Earth and all mankind was willing to come to earth, taking upon Himself human form, coming only to save a world lost in sin and shame. Yet for this King of Glory, there was no room in the inn. Oh how wonderful that He was willing.

He was wonderful in His life. See Him, subject to His parents, sinless in His life, conquering all temptations, honored of God at His baptism, and at all times a friend of sinners who spent His time with the poor and the needy.

And, He was wonderful in His miracles. Look at Him stilling the tempest, feeding the multitudes, cleansing the lepers, opening the eyes of the blind, healing all manner of diseases, casting out demons and raising the dead.

And, He was wonderful in His death. Think of it. He, the King of Glory, going the way of the cross; betrayed, rejected, despised, beaten, stripped, mocked, and crucified by those to whom He had come to be their Savior. No wonder the centurion cried "Truly this man was the Son of God." No wonder the wise men from the east said He is "The King of the Jews." Angels said "A Savior who is Christ the Lord." But the story did not end here. On the third day, early in the morning, while it was still dark, a stone was rolled away and Jesus came forth as victor over sin and death. He arose because death could not hold Him. Wonderful? Oh yes beloved! But there is still more. Suddenly on the hillside of Galilee He said goodbye to His little flock hurling into their hearts the Great Commission, "Go into all the world." How glorious.

The most wonderful thing about Him is that we will see Him as He is. This Savior is not only the Babe of Bethlehem, the Boy of Nazareth, the Healer of the Sick, the Sin-Bearer of Calvary, the Resurrected Lord of Glory. But, He is the Earth's Coming King. And when He comes the Scriptures say that every knee shall bow and every tongue confess to the glory of the Father. Then, they will call Him "Wonderful."

We may take part in this Christmas-tide, yet fail to catch the spirit of Christmas. We may participate in the Christmas of the eye and of the ear, the decorations, the music, and the gifts. But the Christmas we need to know and enjoy is the Christmas of the heart. In Ephesians 3:17 Paul prays, "That Christ may dwell in your hearts through faith." A home is a permanent abode. There is an inner and personal awareness of the presence of Jesus Christ. Is this not the greatest prayer we could make today? Is this not the greatest Christmas wish? This "Christmas of the Heart" is the only kind of Christmas worthy of His wonder. With Him in your heart you will really have a merry, merry Christmas and you too will call Him "Wonderful."

Dearest Father, thank You for reminding me today of the wonder that fills this season, the wonder that is Christ. I want my Christmas to be a "Heart Christmas" this year. Amen.

December 18   The Incomparable Christ

Scripture: Luke Chapter 2

Key Verse: "For there is born to you this day in the city of David a Savior who is Christ the Lord. And this will be the sign to you; You will find a Babe wrapped in swaddling cloths, lying in a manger." Luke 2:11-12

Our God, who made the worlds and all that is in them, looked down upon His creation and knowing its greatest need, sent the angel with the only message that would meet the need of the hour.

The angelic messenger did not say "Unto you is born a great general." There were many generals in that day, perhaps too many for the peace of the world. To have added another to the list would only have foretold more bloodshed, misery, and woe.

Nor did the angel announce the birth of a great educator. If education could have saved the world a utopia would have been ushered in long before. Socrates, Plato, Aristotle and the rest had been great teachers in their day.

The message brought that first Christmas morning was not "Unto you is born a great statesman." Rome specialized in that sphere. Somehow, happiness, righteousness and peace cannot be legislated into the human life. They cannot be brought about by outward circumstances, but must be produced by an inward condition of the heart.

What if the angel had announced the birth of a noted philosopher? There were many thinkers in those days who exhorted the people to living but exhortation was not enough. What good was knowledge without ability? Of what avail is it to stand calmly on the shore and deliver a lecture on swimming to a drowning man? What he needs is not a lecturer, but a life-saver. What the world needed was not a philosophy of life, but life.

God's message to earth was: There is born to you this day in the city of David, a Savior, who is Christ the Lord. Earth's ills are fundamentally spiritual. Great generals may remake the map of the world, but they cannot change the human heart. Educators may develop the mind but they cannot regenerate the spirit. Statesmen may, by legislation, govern to a certain degree mans acts, but they cannot change his motives. Philosophy may paint a beautiful picture of idealism but it cannot give the power to perform. It was only a Savior that could meet the need of the world yesterday, and our needs are the same today.

Thank God for the message of Christmas. "There is born to you . . . a Savior which is Christ the Lord." He put on humanity that we might put on divinity. He became a son of man that we might become sons of God. He came from Heaven where the rivers never freeze, the winds never blow, frosts never chill the air, flowers never fade, no one is ever sick and no one ever dies, to a world of sorrow, sin, sickness and death, all for us.

In infancy He startled a king. In boyhood, He puzzled the rabbis. In manhood, He ruled the course of nature. He walked upon the billows and hushed the sea to sleep. He healed the multitudes without medicine and made no charge for His services. Great men have come and gone, but He lives on and on. Herod could not kill Him. Satan could not seduce Him. Death could not destroy Him, and the grave could not hold Him.

This incomprehensible Christ, is the reason that our hearts are full to bursting this wonderful Christmas season.

Almighty Father, thank You for loving us so much You gave us the greatest gift imaginable, our Blessed Savior. What a truly incomparable, incomprehensible gift! Amen.

December 19 Christmas In Norway

Scripture: Revelation Chapter 7

Key Verse: ". . . Behold a great multitude which no one could number, of all nations, tribes, peoples, and tongues, standing before the throne and before the Lamb." Revelation 7: 9

Imagine the day promised in the book of Revelation, where a multitude of believers from every people group in the world offer praise to God. Even now, here on earth, our brothers and sisters in Christ are praising Him in their own languages and with their own customs. We are like flowers in God's garden, each blooming in a different color, in a different season and a different way, yet all turning our faces to the shining "Son."

At this time of year, it should be interesting to tell you some Christmas customs of a far-away land. In Norway, with its long, cold winter of little sunlight, Christmas brings joy and gladness to people and animals alike.

Mother, Sister, and Grandma are busy for weeks preparing for the Christmas feast. Father and brothers go to the forest and cut down a tall Christmas tree. All the children are kept busy tying corn and oats into bundles. The day before Christmas the bundles of oats and corn are tied to trees and fences or put on housetops or barns. This is the bird's Christmas.

The children carry to the farmyard fowls dishes of wheat or rice mixed with milk. They give the horses and cows all they can eat, and even the dog is freed from his chain and given a large bone covered in meat. Yes, Christmas is a happy time for animals as well as people in Norway.

On Christmas morning the sleigh with its warm robes is brought to the door and the whole family rides to church. When they return, the guests who are to spend Christmas with them follow in their sleighs. At noon all gather around the big table loaded with bounties, soups, meats, vegetables, round cakes of hard rye bread, puddings and all kinds of cake. The children like best the iced cookies cut into shapes depicting dogs, cats, Christmas trees, and people.

What laughter and joy as they open their packages for all to see. Then there are games and songs until the short day is ended. The guests get into their warm coats and lap robes and away they go over the glistening white snow to their own homes.

Father says, "It has been a blessed day. Let us thank the good Lord for His Son who came into the world to save it." They go to their beds in that distant land of the midnight sun, thankful that Jesus came to earth.

This season, as we are busy with our own customs and Christmas rituals, let us remember that the family of God is very wide. For twenty-four hours there will be joy and merrymaking all over the world to celebrate the Lord who was born in a manger. As one part of the world sleeps, another will wake and take up the joyful sound. As one group of sleepy children lay their heads upon soft pillows, another group will awaken to the sound of carts and oxen, or buses and late-model cars, or fathers on fishing boats, all calling forth wishes for a happy celebration of the Savior's birth in languages as diverse as the earth itself. Happy Birthday, Dear Savior, Happy Birthday!

Lord Jesus, may I always remember that You are the reason the whole world celebrates this season. May those who don't know You, find you this year so that we might see them at Your throne one day in Heaven. Amen.

December 20   The Mighty Savior's Name

Scripture: Luke Chapter 1

Key Verse: "And behold, you will conceive in your womb and bring forth a Son, and shall call His name JESUS." Luke1:31

The Hebrews devised names for their children as a memorial to some circumstance connected with the family or some hope entertained by the parents for the child when the child should grow up. Here in America, we used to follow that custom when we were more Godly. We named our daughters Charity, but they were not always charitable. We named them Peace and then they were sometime keen to fight. And so we allowed the custom to go.

The name of Jesus was not a new name then or now. In the Old Testament to find the equivalent of Jesus we turn to the book of Numbers and read, "And Moses called 'Oshea' the Son of Nun." That is the root of Joshua, which means "Jehovah is salvation". Joshua in the Old Testament and Jesus in the New Testament are one and the same name.

Joshua was the name of a great national leader, the one who brought the people out of the desert, back into the quietness of green pastures. He was that mighty man who had led them back to their lost inheritance. The significance now begins to be apparent. Call His name Jesus for He has come to lead us back to our lost inheritance. He has come to bring us out of the barrenness of the wilderness into the green pastures and on beside the still waters. He has come where we are, to do for us that which we cannot do for ourselves. He is the deliverer. He is the Savior.

Think how enduring this very significant name has been. When Pilate stood up that day and washed his cowardly hands he thought he was washing Jesus off the pages of history, but one hundred years from then nobody ever thought of Pilate except as he appeared in the presence of Jesus. Whatever the flood, whatever the famine, whatever the storm or revolution, He goes on in power. His name lives on in spite of the Hitler's, the Stalin's, Khrushchev's, Marx, and all the rest. And Jesus and His name will prevail against future figures in history who rail against God and His people. Yes, count on it, there will always be such figures in the history of man. The name of Jesus will last, they will not.

Do not be afraid. Do not run around propping up His church. It is neither dead nor dying, for He is Lord and leader of it and He is alive. The only reason we fear the Stalin's and the Khrushchev's is that we forget Jesus. "Do not be afraid" He has said. "I am alive forevermore and I have the keys of Hades and of death." Also, He proclaims in Matthew, "I will build my church and the gates of Hades shall not prevail against it."

Think how gracious is the name of Jesus. It is the first name we teach our children while they are still in our arms. It is the name that weaves like a scarlet thread in all our prayers and praise. How divine is the name of the Babe announced by the heavenly host. So divine that upon that authority we sanctify the couple joined in marriage, dedicate the baby, and commit our dead to His care. All rites are given under the authority of that name.

Jesus is the one given and named by God Himself. Fold Him into your life and all the faith, courage, joy and authority of His name will fold into your life as well. It is the very first "Merry Christmas" ever conferred.

Father, in this Christmas season, help me to remember the Name above all names and the One that name represents. Time is short, circumstances might be frazzling, but let me always remember the focus is Jesus. Amen.

December 21   What if There were No Christ in Christmas?

Scripture: I Corinthians Chapter 15

Key Verse: "And if Christ is not risen, your faith is futile." I Corinthians 15:17

Whatever their reasons, there are men today who propose a revolution against Jesus in thought and life, in word and action. When I ponder this thought, I wonder where would we go in our hour of deepest need if there were no Christ, if Christ had never come to earth? As our bodies need food, our intellects crave truth. But where shall we find it, if the truth were taken away? When men were starving in World War II, they sought a substitute for wheat in the roots of the trees and field. But what could you substitute for Christianity? It cannot be found in religions with dead leaders, for only a Living God can meet our needs.

No, you know as do I that the living Christ has the only rational explanation to the problems of life. He gives the only anecdote for human selfishness and greed. He gives the only true and blessed philosophy of life. He gives the only true motive for service and heroism. If there had been no Christ, there would be no hope, for immortal hope perishes with Him.

If it should be as these men wish, and the light that was given was withdrawn, why then henceforth for love there would be hatred, for peace there would be war, for hope there would be hopelessness and for liberty there would be license.

The brilliant author Henry Rogers once wrote a book called *The Eclipse of Faith*. In it, he imagines that some powerful hand has wiped the influence of Christ out of civilization, as a hand wipes chalk from off the classroom board. First he discovers in his library that every vestige of Christ's life and words has wholly disappeared. The law books are emptied of laws safeguarding children and labor, the art history books showed only emptied frames where masterpieces had been depicted, and the greatest poems of Dante, Milton, Wordsworth and Browning were just empty leaves of paper. As Rogers continued his imaginary journey of discovery, he discovered to his horror that the great cathedrals were nothing but great gaping holes; schools, hospitals and beautiful philanthropies were all perished as if shaken down by some cosmic earthquake. No, Rogers concluded, he would not want to inhabit an earth where the influence of Christ was not known. There, death would be only a leap into the dark.

When Jesus' feet stood on our earth, His message concerned life immortal. What others talked about and questioned, He answered authoritatively. With a personal knowledge of that which lay beyond man's horizon, He plucked fear out of men's souls. He taught men that dying was a home going, and that heaven was the Father's house. The sweetest music that ever fell on the ears of humanity was the words, "In my Father's house are many mansions, and I go to prepare a place for you."

It is His coming into this world as a babe, in the glorious quest for salvation for man, that we honor this Christmastide. It seems to me that we should be greatly concerned that our devotion for Him and our gratitude to Him increase. As we plan our Yuletide festival this year, let us make Christ the very center of it, as is proper and fitting. It is His birthday we celebrate, so let us join the celestial choir and the great Christian host throughout the world in acceptable worship to Him, whose name is Jesus.

Dearest Father, Your love has infinite reach. Thank You, Lord, for reaching out to me. Amen.

December 22

When the Angels Have Gone

Scripture: Luke Chapter 2

Key Verse: "So it was, when the angels had gone away from them into heaven, that the shepherds said to one another, 'Let us now go to Bethlehem and see this thing that has come to pass, which the Lord has made known to us.'" Luke 2:15

Let us reverently enter God's house to attend the world's first Christmas service. The lovely stars, the forget-me-nots of heaven, are shining quietly down and half the troubled world is in slumber. It is also the night of human history. Men's faith has gone down like the setting of the sun. The religion of the Jews, the purest religion of the world, has become a weight too grievous to be borne. But, the infinite bells of God's eternal purpose are chiming, and the time has come for the first Christmas service.

The congregation is assembled from two worlds and the Judean hills have become a temple. "And behold the angel of the Lord stood before them, and the glory of the Lord shone round about them and they were greatly afraid." The sermon, of course we are anxious to hear that, for this preacher is from a land where uncertainty gives way to certainty and this preacher has been trained in the Seminary of Eternity. He has learned his theology about the steps of the throne. Certainly his sermon will be worth hearing!

"Do not be afraid, for behold I bring you good glad tidings of great joy." That is the message, and this good news is for everyone. The report of Waterloo, you know, sent the bells of all England ringing, but it draped France in black and broke Napoleon's heart. Praise God, the gospel this angel brings is good news for everybody, rich and poor, learned and ignorant. But, what is this good news? "There is born to you this day in the city of David a Savior, who is Christ the Lord." A Savior! Yes, beloved, He was and still is the supreme need of the world, "for all have sinned and fall short of the glory of God." So, here alone is the One who can save us from our sins, our Savior, Christ, and Lord.

And when the angels were gone, what effect did the sermon have on its hearers that night? "Let us go," the Shepherds said. Let us put the Gospel to the test! And, when they did test this message, they found the Savior.

I well remember the first Christmas tree that I ever attended. The tree was a giant from the forest laden with presents that seemed to me absolutely wonderful. Santa Claus was showering presents to everyone around, and my present was among the others. Yet, I don't remember what it was. For, there was one young fellow there, mentally handicapped, looking at the tree with eager eyes and standing, waiting. At last, Old Santa took down a big box, the largest on the tree and called his name. A look of radiance came over his face as he held out eager hands for the prize. With nervous hands, he opened the box, and then his expectations gave place to despair. For the box was empty, absolutely empty. Some young, foolish fellow had mistaken a tragedy for a joke and had given him an empty box.

We are all hanging presents upon the world's greatest Christmas tree, and the presents we hang are our own lives. Some of us are hanging tragically empty lives. But our privilege is to hang lives so full of Christ that those who come near us will find Him in them. Doing this, our gift to the world will be in our finite way the gift that Christ made, the gift of Himself.

Dear Lord, the thought of Your gift to me is awe-inspiring. Please help me to live a life that reflects Your love to those around me. Thank You, Father. Amen.

December 23   Who Can Stand Christmas?

Scripture: Malachi 3:1-4

Key Verse: ". . . The Lord, whom you seek, will suddenly come to His temple, even the messenger of the covenant, in whom ye delight. Behold He is coming, says the Lord of hosts. But who can endure the day of His coming? And who can stand when He appears? For He is like a refiner's fire and like launderers' soap." Malachi 3:1-2

A delightful Saturday Evening Post illustration pictures a salesgirl in the toy department of one of our great stores. The date on the calendar is December 24th, and the hands on the clock point to five minutes past five. The poor girl has slumped upon a pile of toys behind the counter, dress askew, hair disheveled and arms limp at her sides. She has slipped off her shoes and her eyes have rolled back as if she were to breathe her last. She has just made it through another great American Christmas! And, we all know just how she feels. There are moments when we glimpse that marvelous childhood Christmas again, but the mad crush catches up with us and we find ourselves asking, "Can I stand another year of it?"

There is, however, a far deeper sense to the question, "who can stand Christmas?" Quite apart from the customs that have grown up around the celebration of Christ's birth, the question must be asked about that event itself. Who can stand before the birth of Jesus Christ? This is the question Malachi is asking in our text, posing it to warn a people who thought themselves quite ready for Christmas. But the answer to their prayers was dreadfully more than they had asked. They sought the Lord as an end to troubles; they wanted a Messianic panacea for peace and prosperity. But the coming One was the Lord indeed, and as the Lord they must meet Him.

He comes not to play favorites on their terms, serve their dreams and establish their kingdom. He comes to bring peace through judgment, to deal not only with the sins of their enemies, but with their sins. Could they abide His coming? The One whose coming is the subject of prophecy. The Word, Who was in the beginning with God, by Whom all things were made and Who is very God, this is He who became flesh and dwelt among us. Only because He veiled His majestic glory behind the curtain of His flesh could men even look upon Him.

Even so, think how those times came when His majesty and might flashed forth in overpowering manifestations. Think of how those moneychangers fell back under the lash of His scourge as He cleansed the temple. Think of the moment of His arrest in the garden when he said, "I am He" and those who would seize Him fell to the ground. Or think of the centurion who stood beneath his cross as the earth quaked and the lightning flashed and the thunder rolled in tribute to His deity. Think of that hardened soldier crying out, "Truly this man was the Son of God!"

Yes, Christmas declares to us the unveiling of the invisible God. Ponder that today, beloved. And tomorrow, let us consider the implications of God, with us.

Dear God, the reality of the incarnation is overwhelming. Please help me this year to prepare to celebrate Christ's birth with all its implications for my life and for the world. Guard my heart against the crowding out of Your Son by the urgent everyday things of the season. Protect my mind, keep my thoughts clear, as I seek You. Amen.

December 24   Standing Before Christmas

Scripture: Malachi 3:4-7

Key Verse: "He will sit as a refiner and a purifier of silver; He will purify the sons of Levi, and purge them as gold and silver, that they may offer to the Lord an offering in righteousness." Malachi 3:3

Christ came not that we might glimpse the glory of God for a few years, but He came that God might dwell forever among men and that dwelling among us; His righteous law might exercise its sway over our lives. The Coming of Christ is in the most vital sense the coming of God's Kingdom.

The Kingdom of God does not await the second coming of Christ and the final, full manifestation of His sovereignty, for the prophet is here speaking of His first advent. Christ's birth began that kingdom in which men of every tongue bow and confess that He is Lord. And if we cannot bear His coming, how can we bear the coming of His Kingdom?

Thus, we can see that the coming of Christ is the coming of the King of righteousness, not some abstract far-away concept, but, like the refiner's fire or the fuller's soap, a most concrete and personal design.

Malachi had just reminded the people of their transgression against the law of God, and when he hears them express a desire for Messiah's coming, he cannot but remind them that the One in whom they profess delight will, when He comes, deal harshly with their sin.

The refiner puts his metals into the fire to burn out the impurities. The fuller soaks his soiled cloth in soap and water and then tramples it up and down to remove the dirt from the very fibers. And it is the essence of the Kingdom of God to deal with sin. Christ came not only as the Prince of Peace, He also came as the King of Righteousness and He must perform His work of righteousness in order that His work of peace might appear.

In His first coming, Christ was Himself consumed by that refiner's fire. He became our sin bearer and bore the wrath of judgment for us.

In His Second Coming, that work of judgment will be completed. Then the dread that is expressed in these words of Malachi will be upon the lips of all those who have turned from His righteousness.

Who is sufficient for these things? Who can stand such an appearance as this? The coming of God Himself to establish His rule of perfect righteousness over the life and thoughts of men?

We say we want and we need the celebration of Christ's birth. The Christmas spirit, we say, will warm the earth with kindness and love to one another. Oh, yes, let us have Christmas, for God forbid that we should ever be indifferent to the coming of His Son. But, welcome His coming for what it is. Worship Him who was born Wonderful, Counselor, the Mighty God, the Everlasting Father, and the Prince of Peace.

One day He will come again in power, but our King has already come and is sovereign of all our lives. Submit to His refining, cleansing work. Fill your minds and hearts with His Word that in you may appear the fruit of the Spirit, which is love, joy, peace, patience, gentleness, goodness, meekness and self-control.

So may we welcome the news of His coming and sing with new meaning, "Hail the heaven-born Prince of Peace!"

Dearest Father, the baby dear in the manger was come as a conquering King to reign in the hearts of men. Please help me to give Him his rightful place in mine. In His Holy Name, amen.

Scripture: Matthew 1:18-25

Key Verse: "For there is born to you this day in the city of David a Savior, who is Christ the Lord." Luke 2:11

Deep in the heart of humanity has been planted the desire to know God. Like Job of old, man is constantly crying out "Oh, that I know where I might find Him."

Phillip later voices our cry when he says: "Show us the Father and it is sufficient for us." Christmas then, is God's entrance into human history through the little babe at Bethlehem.

Joseph saw more than a babe. He saw Emmanuel. Mary saw more than her first-born, she saw the Son of God. Elizabeth, the mother of John called him My Lord. Zacharias called Him "The Most High." The angels declared Him to the shepherds as a Savior which is Christ the Lord. The wise men called Him the King of the Jews. Simeon called Him a light to lighten the Gentiles. Anna referred to Him in terms of the Redemption of His people.

Yes, Christmas is the birth of a baby boy to a virgin. He had no earthly father, but He had an earthly mother. Heaven and earth then became united in that little one. Christmas is a revelation.

Christmas is the birth of saving love. Jesus said, "I did not come to judge the world but to save the world." Again, He said, "I did not come to call the righteous, but sinners, to repentance."

On July 31st 1838 William Knibb gathered together 10,000 slaves on the Island of Jamaica for a praise meeting. Their thanksgiving was for the putting into effect the Emancipation Act. They were now to be free.

In order to symbolize it in such a way that all could understand, they brought in an immense coffin and they filled that coffin with whips and branding irons, handcuffs and fetters, slave garments and all the memorials belonging to that horrible system of slavery.

Now, at the first stroke of midnight the Missionary Knibb shouted

"The monster is dying." And at the twelfth stroke, he shouted "The monster is dead. Let's bury him." And they screwed the coffin lid down and lowered the twelve foot casket into the ground and covered up all those unspeakable things that made human life so bitterly painful in bondage.

And that night the beating of every pulse was quickened in every throat as those 10,000 liberated slaves shouted and sang for the joy of freedom.

Christmas is the birth of freedom. Jesus has obtained for all believers the release from sin and He has buried the galling and slaving iniquity of man in His own grave. Should anyone wonder at our joy?

Should we temper our elation that God has given the greatest gift of all time? Should we not sing and feast and decorate and celebrate? Should we not lift our voices with laughter and praise and hug our families or even the stranger? Should we not share everything God's given us? Including the reason for our happiness? Should we not open wide our doors, our purse-strings, and our hearts?

Yes, a resounding yes! For, we are free!

The old is dead and buried and done with. Christmas has brought "good tidings of great joy which will be to all people. For there is born to you this day in the city of David, a Savior, which is Christ the Lord."

Dearest Father, praise your Holy name for sending us the emancipator. May all the joy and glory that surrounds this season be directed toward You, our loving God. Amen.

December 26

What's in a Name?

Scripture Reading: Philippians Chapter 2

Key Verse: "Therefore God also has highly exalted Him and given Him the name which is above every name, that at the name of Jesus every knee should bow, of those in heaven and of those on earth, and of those under the earth, and that every tongue should confess that Jesus Christ is Lord . . . ." Philippians 2:9-11

He was the Son of God from all eternity, but when He became the Son of Man, the second Adam, God gave Him a human name and He has that name yet today. He is the Good Shepherd, the Prince of Peace. He is called Wonderful, Counselor, and Mighty God. In Philippians, we read that because He made Himself of no reputation, God highly exalted Him. God has given Him a name that is above every name, a name that will cause all to bow.

There is Salvation in the name of Jesus. Acts 4 tells us, "Nor is there salvation in any other, for there is no other name under heaven given among men by which we must be saved." It is only in Jesus that we are secure, beloved. It is only in that precious name of Jesus that we are bought and paid for. It is only His death on the cross that brings hope and life eternal.

There is also comfort in the name of Jesus. "For as the sufferings of Christ abound in us, so our consolation also abounds through Christ." There is nothing this world has to offer that will grant you peace or true joy. Those eternal things are only found in Jesus. Jesus is the only One who has lasting peace, the joy of true contentment, and comfort that transcends the circumstances.

Perhaps most awesome, indeed, is that we have access through the name of Jesus to God Himself. "There is one God and one Mediator between God and men, the Man Christ Jesus, who gave Himself a ransom for all," we are told in First Timothy. Also, Jesus Himself told us, "No man comes to the Father but by Me." And, we don't just have access in our own filthy rags. No, Jesus has covered us with the glorious garment of His righteousness. When we approach the throne of God in Jesus' name, we come with the privileges of that name, "If you ask anything in My name, I will do it." Oh, what a fearsome privilege; what an immense responsibility.

There is also victory in the name of Jesus. "Yet in all these things we are more than conquerors through Him who loved us," Romans assures us. "The sting of death is sin, and the strength of sin is the law. But thanks be to God, who gives us the victory through our Lord Jesus Christ.' There is deliverance in His name, as well, beloved. It does not matter how deeply enslaved in sin one is. It does not signify how many years one has served the wrong master. The snare of sin is strong, surpassing strength of man to escape. It is only the blood of Jesus that has the power to deliver us. As Thessalonians proclaims, "They themselves declare . . . you turned to God from idols to serve the living and true God, and to wait for His Son from heaven, even Jesus who delivers us from the wrath to come."

Oh, how beautiful is the name, Jesus! How deserving of praise! Don't be ashamed of the name of Jesus, beloved, but wear the name Christ-follower, or Christian, as the wonderful gift it is. "For I am not ashamed of the gospel of Christ, for it is the power of God to salvation for everyone who believes."

Dear Jesus, my Lord and Savior, I love You and I praise Your name. My knee is bent to You today, and I am humbled before You. Your mighty name stands before us, and the power, victory, comfort, and deliverance contained in Your name amaze me. My heart swells with the honor of being Your follower, and friend. Thank You, amen.

December 27   Our Father

Scripture Reading: Luke Chapter 11

Key Verse: "Our Father in heaven, hallowed be Your name. Your kingdom come. Your will be done on earth as it is in heaven." Luke 11:2

It was through His own prayer life that Jesus brought His disciples to the realization of their inadequacy in prayer. So they came to Jesus wistfully and hopefully with this wise request, "Lord, teach us to pray." Does such holy ambition beat within our hearts today? I hope so. For Jesus did not turn away from them, and He will not turn away from the same request today, if it is offered in the same spirit.

Jesus shows us, however, that prayer begins with the recognition of the relationship God has with us. "Our Father," Jesus says. The word "Father" indicates authority, and spells out a sovereignty of love. The word "Father" also implies holiness because of the clause, "which art in heaven." His authority and holiness are the alpha and omega of His love. His authority is not separate from His love. His sovereignty is not separate from His love.

It is not just Jesus' Father we speak to in prayer, it is "Our" Father. The whole church is in the word "our." In that one word racial, economic, and social barriers are knocked down. Brotherhood starts at the place of prayer. So the first two words of the Lord's Prayer bring us under the sovereignty of God, expose us to the fires of His holiness, and hold us in His love. At the same time, these words "Our Father" bind us as family with every born-again child of man. All this is in just two words.

Now since God is our Father we are to take the position of sons. John declares, "For as many as received Him, to them He gave the right to become the children of God." Therefore, hear this joyful shout across the far spaces of the years, "Behold what manner of love the Father has bestowed on us that we should be called the children of God." We are made family through Jesus. We are made family by faith. And we are to come to our heavenly Father to pray as His children.

How should the recognition of our relationship to God affect our prayers? Well, we will come with hope and familiar confidence for, "Your Heavenly Father knows what things you have need of." Does a father love to have his children about him? Yes. Does a child shrink from telling his wishes to his Father? No.

Recognizing the fatherhood of God draws our hearts and our hopes to our Father's home. It delivers us from worship of the visible. It is not the external, but the Eternal we must worship. It proves that God is not only imminent but personal, a God who loves and cares about me and knows all about me. Even my hairs are numbered. He understands me.

It is true that if I believe that I am God's child, it will make me reverence Him. "The fear of the Lord is the beginning of wisdom," Proverbs tells us. But it will be a fear of love and reverence, out of recognition of His purity, holiness and perfect love.

Oh beloved, as we think of our relationship with God, let us think how noble our destiny is. God has called me. He made me. I am a child of God, and as His child my life becomes a great thing. And so I pray, not to get something I might better not have, but to know and do the will of Him who saves and keeps me, to fulfill His purposes for me, and to say with Jesus, "My food is to do the will of Him who sent me."

Dearest Father, You are praiseworthy. Please accomplish Your will in my heart and in my home. Glorify Yourself and mold us into a fitting bride. Amen.

Scripture Reading: John 6:22-40

Key verse: "For I have come down from heaven, not to do My own will, but the will of Him who sent Me." John 6:38 and "That I may know Him and the power of His resurrection, and the fellowship of His sufferings, being conformed to His death." Philippians 3:10

The supreme passion of the Christian heart is to know Christ personally, intimately and experientially in the power of His resurrection. We yearn to know Him in that deepest and closest of all ways, in the oneness of a sympathetic heart to heart fellowship.

Paul is now an old missionary, near the end of his earthly journey, worn out, and facing martyrdom, yet still talking about gaining Christ. What did he mean? He did gain Christ back many years before at the Damascus road, so why was he still seeking to "gain" Christ?

In Scotland, coal miners call their mining, "coal winnowing." The mine owner goes down to his mine and takes that which is already his and brings it up for service in the actual every day needs of life. So Paul wanted thus to bring Christ into his practical day-to-day life.

Two men, returning from a walk one day drew near to the open door of the house. One stopped and with his cane, pointed to the open threshold and looking at his friend said, "Can you step over that threshold?" "Of course," was the impatient reply. "But will you?" said the man.

You are that close to being a fully surrendered Christian. The door to that kingdom is labeled "obedience." When Mary, the mother of Christ, was told by the angel that she was chosen to give birth to the Son of the Most High God, she cried, "Let it be to me according to your word." She had crossed that threshold and therein is the secret to the understanding of her character. Her life's philosophy was summed up in those words. She was submissive to the Divine will for her life and she discovered that the key to the victorious God-life was obedience, obeying God.

Oh beloved, how I wish we would get in the will of God. Are you in His will? What has He whispered to your heart? Perhaps God's will is that you enter His service as a full-time worker, a consecrated layman, or to serve in your church through its organization. Perhaps He is calling you to prayer or His word. So many stand on the wrong side of the door arguing with their conscience, professing to be puzzled about some religious truth, while the fact is that all the time there is one truth which they are evading, the truth that they ought to obey God. Trust Him, and cross that threshold of obedience.

Perhaps you are asking with an honest heart, "How may I be and keep in the will of God?"

Abide in Christ in our thought life, thinking on what things that are true, honorable, just, pure, lovely and gracious. Converse with Him in prayer and we must watch against sin. The only thing that will hide God's face from us is unconfessed sin. Make much of the companionship of Christians. Be busy for Him. Make much of His Book as His Son was His first gift and His Word was the second.

Lastly, if we would be in His will, we must pay the price to know Him. Invest love and time in the relationship. It is all spoken of in His Word. It all comes down to whether we will cross the threshold of obedience.

Dearest Father, I sit before You, asking that You direct my paths. Help me to be hear You clearly in my heart and in Your Holy Word. I want to know You in a deep and close way, and I want to follow You and live Your will for my life. I surrender, Lord. Amen.

Scripture Reading: 1 John Chapter 2

Key Verse: "Now by this we know that we know Him, if we keep His commandments." I John 2:3

Our government has a bureau of standards in Washington where standard weights and measures are kept as a basis for all the nation's transactions. All scales and yardsticks must be tested and measured by these particular standards. It is not a matter of one merchant's opinion against another's. It is a matter of a standard of authority. As Christians, what are our standard measurements for a life of faith? The Biblical standards are true and sufficient. The standard of our authority is, "Thus saith the Lord."

God's measurement standards are very simple. First, "Now by this we know that we know Him, if we keep His commandments." Knowing God and knowing about Him are vastly different things. The proof of a man's faith is not his language, but his life. This is far more than a ritualistic or legalistic keeping of certain ordinances. It means purity and righteousness of life. It is far more than the observance of a set of rules. It is the recognition of righteousness as the law of life.

So the first measurement of a true Christian faith is a positive test, not negative. It concludes that the proof of knowing God is not that we omit what is evil, but rather that we do what is good and pleasing before the Lord.

Then the test is extended. It says, "He who says he abides in Him ought himself also to walk just as He walked." The direction in which a person travels certainly is some indication of the genuineness of his faith, for it determines the company he keeps and the destination he hopes to reach. When one walks with Christ there will be both an effect and an assurance. The effect will be that we will be pleasing to God, and the assurance will be that we will be kept by God. The security of our life will be in the certainty of His Word.

Then, we find the second standard, "He that says he is in the light and hates his brother is in darkness until now. He who loves his brother abides in the light, and there is no cause for stumbling in him." Jesus also advanced love as a test of life, saying, "By this shall all men know that you are my disciples if you have love one to another." Prior to this, men judged fidelity to God by the keeping of the law. Jesus here introduces a new test, and a conclusive proof—love.

Lastly, note that the test of each measurement is centralized in Jesus Christ. When the Bible speaks of keeping the commandments, they are Christ's. When the Bible speaks of walking, it is to walk as He walked. And when the Bible speaks of loving our brother, it is a brotherhood founded on Christ.

Do not look around at others, seeking to judge their lives. That is not what God has given us these standards for. Rather, measure your own lives against God's measuring stick, beloved. Are you searching the Word of God, and obeying what you find there? And can you honestly say that you have love for the brethren? The true object of the church is to reflect the glory of its founder. A life centered in Him can do nothing less.

Dear Lord, thank You for the reminder that the state of my faith is not how I feel, or what I abstain from. And thank You that when I fail to walk worthily, or when I disobey, I know Your forgiveness is as nearby as a prayer. Praise You for having a standard as high as the mountains, and a well of grace as deep as the sea. Amen.

December 30   Getting the Best of Myself

Scripture Reading: Luke Chapter 21
Key Verse: "By your patience possess your souls." Luke 21:19

Once in a dream, a man was thwarted and hunted by a mysterious figure. As soon as he gained a fortune, the veiled figure snatched it away. When about to find joy and peace, the veiled figure attacked his mind with fear and anxiety. When the man was hungry and about to eat, the figure snatched the food from in front of him.

Enraged, the unhappy man cried out in his dream, "Who are you?" and stretched out his hand to seize the veil. Ripping the veil from the face of his tormentor and foe, the face that he saw was that of his own.

Man is truly his own worst enemy. It is not the stars of the zodiac that are at fault, but men make their own ruin so frequently. There is no city, no kingdom as rich as the kingdom of your own soul. And he who takes that city and rules it in the interest of reason and faith is truly a notable conqueror.

So it is written by one of the greatest kings in history, "He that rules his own spirit is greater than he that takes a city." For, the chief foe and adversary of life is our own sinful self. We are reluctant to admit this, but it is true.

A minister visiting a penitentiary was going from one inmate to another. As he went, he asked, kindly, why they were there, and who was to blame. Nearly all of the prisoners tried to give the impression that they were innocent of wrong doing, and were the victims of injustice, or circumstance.

But, in talking with one man, he asked the cause of his trouble and was told, "Oh, no trouble, sir, but myself." Yes, so it is. The deepest and most dangerous troubles which afflict man's life come from within, not from without.

Outside dangers and temptations have no power over us until they receive the cooperation and help of our own flesh. Others can advise you, warn you, counsel you, and pray for you, but in the battle you are the sole commander. You get to decide.

But, in the battle of the soul, we do not fight alone. We have the presence and the help of the Captain of our Salvation. If He be for you, who can be against you?

Thank God that within every life there is the capacity for greatness. We were made in His image, dear ones, and beneath the rubbish of sin and the defilement of life, lays our soul.

That soul is yours by virtue of your creation in the Divine Image. That soul, for the redemption of which Christ shed His precious blood on Calvary's tree, is worth more than all the world.

Now, in the battle of life, we must expect hardships and pain and denial and suffering to come into our lives. In the chapter of our text we see that Christ warns about some trials and hardships yet to come. But, no matter the circumstances, the desire of God for every one of us is that we turn over to Christ our every thought. By yielding our lives into His control, He wins the victory.

Dear Lord, You know the circumstances of my soul, my life. Truly, the desire of my heart is to glorify You in all I do and say, in any and every circumstance I may encounter. I understand that having put on the armor You have provided, it is yet I that must stand. Nonetheless, I ask You for the strength to stand, the strength to choose correctly, and the strength to be a good testimony for You. Amen.

December 31   The Backward Look

Scripture: Deuteronomy Chapter 8

Key Verse: "And you shall remember that the Lord your God led you all these forty years in the wilderness, to humble you and test you, to know what was in your heart." Deut. 8:2

The days of our lives generally slip along smoothly and quickly. But days like this last day of the year are like a knot in a sailor's rope. As that knot marks off how fast the rope is being run off from the reel, so marking these special days helps us to keep account of the time as it swiftly passes.

In our text, the people Israel, too, were at a knot in the rope. There was a change imminent, a change of leaders and a change of circumstances. Moses' work was accomplished, and Israel faced a new land of greater opportunity. Moses thus delivers his final charges to the people, reviewing the way they had come and the years of his leadership over them. But, Moses knew that their history was not finished. He knew that the greatest achievements lay ahead if they were true to God. So to encourage them to greater consecration, Moses charges them to remember the way the Lord their God had led them in the past.

Now, it is good to forget certain things, as Paul has said, but it also behooves us to remember certain things. The word "remember" here implies to mark well, to emphasize, to especially note. It is the picture of a chart along which the way of a pilgrimage has been marked out and the pilgrims are charged to look back over the way to see certain facts of their journeyings, certain crises along the way. As a result, they were to lift their faces to the untried and unplodded paths of the future with courage, discretion, and intelligence.

Moses emphasized three particular areas in Israel's past history, and we can examine them in our lives as well. Firstly, Israel needed to remember that their journey began by God's deliverance from bondage. Our history, like Israel's, is founded in redemption. We too are a ransomed people, are we not? All we are individually is due to God's emancipation. Oh, beloved, look back upon this year and remember! God hath redeemed us!

The second point that Moses made to Israel was that their history was characterized in its continuity by the perpetual and persistent guidance of God. He had always led them. Whether you have been called to walk through an unknown wilderness this past year, or through the Valley of the Shadow, or whether you are walking on the mountaintops, God has not forsaken you. You traveled not alone this year. God led you, and He led you this way for a purpose.

Lastly, Moses bid Israel to remember the resources of God. Has God ever left you without that which has been necessary? I venture to affirm today that though some passage can be very dark, and the need may seem great, yet God in His time has met every need.

God does not want us to look back merely to see the past. By remembering our past, we remember the faithfulness of the guidance and provision of our dear Father. Therefore, we can face the unknown future; face the perils, sorrows, battles, losses and victories of life saying, "Lead me on, Lord." For we have seen that He is faithful indeed.

Father, thank You for the mercies You have extended to me this past year. I thank You for Your constant presence, Your guidance and Your supply of my needs. I thank You, Lord, even for the hard lessons. As I look forward to this New Year, I ask that You would use me to bring glory to Your Name. Lead me on, Lord. Amen.

June, 2011

We are thrilled that Classic Christianity, A Year of Timeless Devotions has found its way to your hands. As an introduction to the character and reputation of our grandfather, the Rev. L.A. Meade, we wanted to acquaint you in a more complete way than the author introductions provided in the manuscript. We felt perhaps the most objective, thorough introduction we could provide would be to allow you to read the opinions of pastors from many denominations and communities who had worked alongside our grandfather. So, following you will find copies of letters, clippings, and pictures to substantiate the character and reputation of the Rev. L.A. Meade, our Papa. These are just a few samples of the many, many letters we hold from pastors from across the continent, Los Angeles to Leesburg, Detroit through Kansas to Daytona Beach.

We would urge you to notice the broad range of denominations and locations represented by the letters and clippings. The Rev. Meade preached in little towns, and in large cities, from 1914 to 1971, appealing to the Scriptural truths that bring Christians together at the feet of their Lord. Those truths still have the same power, the same potential to appeal to a broad spectrum of Christians with life-changing results.

It is our deepest hope and constant prayer that this book of heartfelt words of praise, worship, and teaching will be a blessing to you and many others.

God Bless You,

Patricia A. Ediger
Cara L. Shelton

Lawrence Adelbert Meade
1892-1971

Michigan

BY FRANK L. SULLIVAN

I am in this great and good State for a few weeks by the special invitation of several pastors. Several of these pastors I met at Indianapolis last June. They were among the twenty-five from all over the

REV. L. A. MEADE.

country who invited me to visit them and canvass their churches for THE WATCH-MAN-EXAMINER. On my way from Ohio, where I spent profitably and pleasantly the month of July, I had two hours to wait between trains at Hillsdale. So I had a delightful visit with Pastor H. M. Ford. He showed me the college buildings, pointing out their recent improvements. We met Dr. J. W. Mauck, president for the past twenty years. He showed me the picture of the new president from Franklin College, soon expected on the ground to take up his work. Dr. Ford has just resigned after a successful and satisfactory pastorate of three years. The resignation takes effect October 1, and was accepted reluctantly. He will leave the church in excellent condition, with more than 400 members, nearly 200 having been added during his pastorate, many of them by baptism.

I had a cordial welcome to the comfortable parsonage of the South church, Lansing, through a letter in the mail box, enclosing the key to the premises. Pastor Heaton, in his absence for the month, extended to me the hospitality of the house and bade me feel at home. This I had no difficulty in doing for several days, having learned long ago with an ancient traveling preacher "in whatsoever state I am there

to be content." After a respectful hearing the next morning at the South church I was speeded ten miles away to Grand Ledge by Pastor Meade. There a full house greeted me, seeming to take a personal interest in "The Milk-Tree" message, judging by the fervent amens from the young, enthusiastic pastor on the front seat, and the rapt attention of the well behaved young people on the back seats. These people know how to sing, and their pastor knows how to conduct a praise service, and young Mr. Lord, nephew of Dr. Lord, of New York city, knows how to preside at the piano. Grand Ledge has a population of 3,500 and is the center of a fine farming section. Our church of 270 members has a well located house, and a good parsonage on the adjoining lot. The buildings are in good repair, $1,200 of improvements having been made during the first year of the present pastorate. The house seats 270, and has been crowded many times. The church is well organized and is run without fairs, festivals or pay suppers. Its Bible school enrols 300, averaging last year an attendance of 218. There are flourishing Young People's Unions, both senior and junior. The missionary contributions during the first year of this pastorate were $250; the second year $3,000; last year $2,500. It is expected that they will be $2,500 this year. A missionary family in India is supported by this church. The family is known to the pastor personally and doctrinally. Several native children on that field are supported by the children of this church and school. A woman from that mission recently spoke here. The personal touch counts much with this people, as with most people.

Rev. L. A. Meade is well on his fourth year here. He is a graduate of McMaster, Toronto, Canada. After doing evangelistic work for three years he entered upon this, his first pastorate. Evangelism is still his forte. He has carried on six evangelistic campaigns here and elsewhere during this pastorate. He has had no trouble to gather congregations in a town not distinguished for church attendance. He preaches the Word as he understands it. He is giving a series of sermons on "The Bible." This year he is indoctrinating and edifying the new members. He also has a training class for children. Pastor Meade belongs to a family of religious workers. His father, though seventy years old, is pastor at Websterville, Pennsylvania. His oldest brother is pastor of the Immanuel church, Detroit. Another brother is a Young Men's Christian Association secretary. His sister is the wife of the pastor of the First church, Johnstown, Pennsylvania. All are Baptists.

Illinois

379

HERE IS THE MEADE FAMILY—FIVE SONS AND FATHER—ALL ORDAINED PREACHERS. FOUR OF THE PARTY WILL CONDUCT THE MEADE REVIVAL IN LEESBURG, BEGINNING SUNDAY, OCTOBER 17TH. IT IS POSSIBLE THAT THE FATHER AND ALL FIVE SONS WILL BE HERE AT ONE TIME DURING THE CAMPAIGN.

WE APPRECIATE YOUR LOVE AND CO-OPERATION. MAY GOD ABUNDANTLY BLESS YOU.
THE MEADE FAMILY.

To the Christian Ministers of Palatka, Florida.

Brethren:-

For more than six weeks, we have had the Meade Brothers Evangelistic party with us.

They are entirely satisfactory to us. Their methods are wise, sane and Biblical and utterly without extravagance of any kind. They are a remarkable group of Christian men and women. There is not an objectionable feature in their program.

They are most loyal to local pastors and to our churches and are now urging the converts to unite with our churches.

We have had the Rev. W. A. Sunday, Dr. Biederwolf and others in evangelistic campaigns in our City but none of them were as successful as are the Meade Brothers.

In His cause,

I am fraternally,

D. H. Rutter

Pres. Ministerial Association.

382

J. RAY ARNOLD LUMBER COMPANY

MANUFACTURERS OF

FLORIDA DENSE LONG LEAF PINE AND GULF CYPRESS

MILLS
GROVELAND, FLORIDA
LAUREL, FLORIDA

HOME OFFICE:

MEMBERS:
GEORGIA-FLORIDA SAW MILL ASSN.
SOUTHERN CYPRESS MFGRS ASSN.
FLORIDA LUMBER & MILLWORK ASSN.

GROVELAND, FLORIDA   May 3, 1926.

Evangelist Lawrence A. Meade,

     Groveland, Florida.

Dear Mr. Meade:-

        As the father of a large family, as a citizen and as an employer of hundreds, who have been blessed by the power of your Gospel messages, I wish to avail myself of this earliest opportunity to give written expression to my appreciation of the work which you have just concluded in our community.

        To have led to Christ almost the entire student body of our Senior High School, not to mention the many older, as well as those more youthful, is an outstanding tribute to the versatility of your efforts, not to mention the liberal monetary contributions made.

        With all respect to any who have preceded you here and despite the fact that we have been favored in the past by many Christian workers of no mean ability, I am sure that I voice the sentiment of this entire community in stating that there has never been in our midst an Ambassador of the King who brought such powerful and effective Gospel messages; and it is very gratifying to hear on all sides from men of various denominations and in all walks of life

CYPRESS
THE WOOD
ETERNAL

Evangelist Lawrence A. Meade - - #2.

unreserved expressions in like favor.

In conclusion, and in addition, permit me to inform you that a group of business men, drawn from several denominations here, interested in the moral and the spiritual, as well as material, propose, subjected to plans yet to be developed, to underwrite your efforts in the amount of a substantial sum, to be used in obtaining more effectual ways and means for the promotion of and furtherance of your opportunities to serve the Master.

Praying that God may keep that which thou hath committed unto Him and that the development of your priceless Talents in His cause may continue and ever be exercised with increasing power and success, I am

Yours sincerely,

JRA:S.

SECRETARY OF MISSIONARY EDUCATION
WILLIAM A. HILL
276 FIFTH AVENUE
NEW YORK CITY

FIELD SECRETARY
FLOYD L. CAR
276 FIFTH AVENUE
NEW YORK CITY

ROYAL AMBASSADORS
A World Outlook Organization for Baptist Boys
UNDER AUSPICES OF THE
DEPARTMENT OF MISSIONARY EDUCATION
OF THE
BAPTIST BOARD OF EDUCATION
Monmouth, Oregon
3/25/30

To Any Interested In Saving Souls:

As a pastor and Christian worker I most heartily commend my Brother, Evangelist L. A. Meade, to any church or group of churches for evangelistic services.

My church and the local Evangelical Church of Monmouth, Oregon, united in a meeting with Brother Meade and the blessings and results in souls were far beyond our faith and expectations.

His wholesome, optimistic personality; his plain but powerful and saving Gospel; his pertinent, pithy address and his ability to organize a campaign and inspire cooperation, together with his selfless devotion to his work, combine to make him a most acceptable evangelist in any size church or community.

We have not had a single unpleasant reaction from his meeting.

L. L. Daily

L. L. Daily
Pastor Community Baptist Church
Monmouth, Oregon.

FIRST PRESBYTERIAN CHURCH
DALLAS, OREGON
JAMES AIKIN SMITH, Pastor

March 23/30

To whom it may Concern

The Meade Evangelistic Party has just closed a great
Union Campaign here in Dallas,with Eight Churches co-operating.

We have found the party a most congenial company to
work with.The Preaching of Rev.L.A Meade is forceful,sane,
Scriptural, without any of the ranting or scolding that so
often characterizes Evangelists. His morning messages for
the development of the Christian life are of a very helpful
character.   His sermons all center around the one great idea
of leading folks to Jesus as Savior and Lord.
        He is not only a good,strong Preacher of the Word,but
is untiring in his personal work.He is very happy in his manner of approach to business men in particular. He wins by
being winsome .

The Children's work is splendidly carried on by Bro. Harold
Meade .ably assisted by Mrs .L.A Meade .They quickly win the
love of the Kiddies and put on Programs of song and varied ex
ercises that attract favoral attention.

Brother Harold is a master at the Piano,and very apt in
securing special music and in getting the best out of a large
Chorus Choir (We had 100 in the Choir here)

As Pastors of the co-operating Churches we heartily commend them to any place that wants a real spiritual uplift.
They leave us with the best wishes of all .They have done a
good work in Dallas,A Number were led to Christ and the members
of the varied Churches were greatly helped .

Fraternally

Jas. A. Smith ___ Pres-Ministerial Assn- ___
J. M. Farrell ___ Sec ___ Pastor M. E. Church
R.E. Reschke ___ Salt Creek Baptist Church ___
G. M. Boelyer ___ Pastor Mennonite Church
D.L. Penhollow ___ First Christian Church
Jacob Stocker ___ First Evangelical Church
F.F. Wall ___ Mennonite Brethren Church.
J. H. Reising ___ Mennonite Brethren Halbur St.
D.H. Bollman ___ Chairman Executive Committee

A Sunday afternoon crowd at Dallas, Oregon.

Harold, Walter, Lawrence & Bill Meade—
musicians as well as preachers!

O. W. PAYNE, PASTOR

Dec., 21, 1930.

Dear Brother Laurence and Harold:

I simply cannot refrain from letting you know the result of the campaign as measure in the light of accessions to our Church. I had the privalege of taking in, now hold your breath, only forty two people this morning. And wait a minute that is the most important thing but, with the soft pedal on, the collection plate groaned under a burden of an even $100.00 Think of it. I never in all my life have seen as happy a congregation as that of this morning, not near seats enough for t the crowd.

You remember the lady, Mrs Felthouse who came forward Thursday evening and gave us $10.00? Well bless your heart this morning when she came forward for baptismal service here her husband came and lined up with her. Talk about a happy couple that was it. Praise the lord.

May God continue to so mark your pathway through life. We will never cease to thank God for your ministry here.

Yours most sincerely,

Oscar W. Payne

389

Winnsboro,S.C.,

9/16/28.

Dr.Erwin,Pastor,

Presbyterian Church,

Pawhuska,Okla.

We,the Pastors and Evangelistic Club of Winnsboro,S.C. do heartily
commend the Meade Evangelistic Party.They have been with us for
four weeks,and have done a great work. The preaching is excellent
and is the regular gospel message. Have this read in each pulpit
to-day.

Signed: R. L. Keaton Pastor Methodist Church
C. B. Lucas, Episcopal Church
W. W. Hayes, Presbyterian Church
Oliver Johnson A.R.P.Church
H. Floyd Surles, Pastor 1st Baptist Ch.
R. T. Matthews, Pres. Evangelistic Club

390

GEORGE E. DAVIS, PASTOR
T. M. McMICHAEL, CLERK
A. C. WATSON, TREASURER
MISS DOROTHY RILEY, SECRETARY

First Baptist Church

Orangeburg, S. C.

April 25, 1920.

Mr John A. Brunson,
Sumter, S.C.

Dear Brother Brunson:-

    Replying to your letter with reference
to the Meade Brothers, I knew nothing of these brethren
until they called on me several weeks ago with regard to
holding a meeting here. They are now in their third week
and I have heard no word of unfavorable criticism with
reference either to the preaching or methods. The attendance
and interest are excellent and still growing. On account
of the Chatauqua here this week, the evening services are
held from seven to eight fifteen- the supper hour for most
of our people- but the attendance has not fallen off.

    Brother Lawrence Meade, the evangelist,
seems to me to be quite the equal of any of the evangelists
whom I have heard. He is doctrinally sound and supports his
preaching by the Scriptures. He is very thorough in dealing
with converts and inquirers in the after meetings and when
he is through with them they understand fully the plan of
salvation. I have been particularly impressed with this
phase of his work. It seems to me he goes as far as it is
humanly possible to go in leading souls to an intelligent
and definite acceptance of Christ.

    The other members of the party are
also all that could be desired and while the evidence is not
yet all in, I feel safe in commending these brethren to
you most heartily.

    With many good wishes,

GED/r   Cordially,

   C O P Y   *Geo. E. Davis*

Under the Tent, 1929

The tent held 3,000 people, and it was shipped by rail.

EVANGELISTIC CAMPAIGN SERVICES
OVERFLOW METHODIST CHURCH
Armory Secured Where Future Services Will Be Held Saturday, March 8, and Nightly at 7:30 Except Monday

MEADE EVANGELISTIC PARTY IN CHARGE

Some Startling Sermons on Present-Day Problems

Special Music   — —   Large Chorus Choir   — —   Orchestra

SATURDAY—Family Night. Sermon: "The Old-Fashioned Home."
SUNDAY, 11 A. M.—Worship in all respective cooperating churches.
SUNDAY, 11 A. M.—Union Children's Service in the Armory.
SUNDAY, 7:30 P. M.—Union Service. Sermon, "And God Said."
TUESDAY, 7:30 P. M.—Church Night. Subject, "God's Carpenter."
WEDNESDAY, State Night. Subject "How Two Preachers Got Out of Jail."
THURSDAY, Birthday Night. Subject, "The Miracle of Twice-Born Men."
FRIDAY, 7:30, Young People's Night. Subject, "The Sheik Of Dallas."
SATURDAY, 7:30, Children's Program. Subject, "The Mayor's Wife."

Morning Meetings in the Presbyterian Church at 9:30.

IN THE ARMORY ACCOMMODATION FOR EVERYBODY. — COME!

Lawrence A. & Lillian E. Meade
They were married under the tent,
in Sumter S.C., in 1928.

Santa Paula, California
August 29, 1934

The Rev. Lawrence A. Meade,
The Manse, 8th and Pleasant Sts.,
Santa Paula, California,

Dear Mr. Meade:

It is not in our power to fully express our appreciation to you for what you have done for us, both individually and as a church during the past fifteen months. But we do want by means of this letter to express to you something of our feelings.

You left your chosen work as an Evangelist and came to our assistance when Dr. Fisher's health broke and he was forced to retire. You expected to remain with us but three months, but three months lengthened into six, and six to a year and still you were here to spend your energy and enthusiasm for our blessing and the maintenance of the work here. Our lives have been richly blessed by the whole hearted, earnest, loving ministry that your have brought to us.

We especially appreciate the efficiency and energy with which you took up the uncompleted task of our building program and carried it to successful conslusion. Much of the credit for the fact that our new building was dedicated with all of the small debt covered with pledges belongs to you.

Another feature of your work which deserves special mention and which we sincerely appreciate is the splendid enlistment of the young people which you made, and the tangible program of work which you have not only planned, but successfully laid upon them as their responsibility.

There are other specific features which might be mentioned, but these more outstanding evidences of your work are enough to indicate the character and scope of your endeavors among us. With such a ministry as this we could not but profit,- spiritually and numerically. And we take this method, wholly inadequate as it is to express to you our deep and sincere appreciation of all that you and Mrs. Meade have done and all that you have meant to the Santa Paula Church.

Paul J. Leavens
Paul J. Leavens, Moderator
Ira J. Hoswell, Clerk of Session

Elders

M R Mayhew
George McCall
R C McMillan

M A Lindsay
Chas. E. Neal
R Ellick
R. J. Churchill

396

FAULKNER STREET FIRST METHODIST CHURCH. NEW SMYRNA
AND
COMMUNITY METHODIST CHURCH. CORONADO BEACH
MARTIN R. DAVIS. MINISTER

CORONADO BEACH. FLORIDA

December 20th, 1937.

Greetings:

We take pleasure in making this statement of our high evaluation of the work of the Meade Brothers evangelistic team, after having had them with us from November 28th, through December 19th, 1937. The Meade Brothers services were sponsored by the Christ Congregational Church, the First Christian Church, the First Presbyterian Church, the First Methodist Episcopal Church, South, and the Faulkner Street First Methodist Church, all of New Smyrna Beach, Florida.

Brother Harold Meade, whose part is as pianist and as children's worker, is exceptional with the children. He trained approximately 100 children in gospel songs and exercises for one program each week, which were inspirationaland entertaining. In his contacts with the children, he secured some twelve or fifteen decisions for Christ.

The Meade Brothers sang a special each night which were very much appreciated and added to the value of the service.

Brother Lawrence A. Meade does the preaching, leads the singing and conducts the morning Devotional Bible study hour each day. We have heard many comments on his preaching and Bible Studys, and all have been in praise and no adverse criticism whatever has reached us; He is genuine, sincere, earnest and deeply spiritual. His preaching is energetic, interesting, and with the whole purpose of securing decisions for Christ and of feeding the children of God in the deep things of God. His interpretation of the Scripture is orthodox and he stands by the Scripture as the Word of God, and stands behind Christ as the Son of God and the Savior of the world. He does not resort to clap-trap sensationalism, nor does he ride any doctrinal hobby horses, but in a firm, clear-cut way, preaches his definite and positive Christian convictions.

The Morning Bible Study Hour has been most helpful and inspirational, as has the entire ministry of the Meade Brothers here.

We believe the results of this Revival Service are as permanent in nature as could be achieved by any evangelist who might serve us. The churches, though five denominations were represented in the campaign, are all thoroughly satisfied with the service of the Meade Brothers. Certainly the Meade Brothers did everything that they, or any other evangelists could have for the spiritual life of our community. It has been a pleasure to have had them here and to work with them these past three weeks.

And in appreciation of them, and of their services, we the undersigned ministers, voluntarily give this unsolicited letter of appreciation.

Sincerely, yours in Christ Jesus,

Trevor Mordecai ,Minister, Christ Congregational Church,

E. M. Williamson ,Minister, First Christian Church,

B. Albertson ,Minister, First Presbyterian Church,

C. James Tyler ,Minister, First Methodist Episcopal Church, South,

Martin R. Davis ,Minister, Faulkner St. First Methodist Church,
all of New Smyrna Beach, Florida.

Our Church Hymn

x is "The House of Happiness,"
Our Church in Canoga Park,
Where old and young and rich and poor
Upon one level meet.
Then heed the summons of its call,
The sanctuary crowd,
At morning hour, and evensong
In earnest worship bowed.

"The House of Happiness"
Community Church

W. W. RALPH, Pastor
Res. 7711 Jordan Avenue
Box 176

Canoga Park, California

"The House of Happiness"

December 21, 1952.

To Whom It May Concern:

It is now my very great privilege and joy to report the "Canoga Park Cooperative Christmas Revival" which has just closed, and which was conducted under the auspices of the two Community Churches here, with Lawrence A. Mease of Detroit Michigan, leading us in the Campaign and doing the preaching.

All of us who have engaged in the Campaign are agreed that seldom, if ever have we witnessed an Evangelistic Campaign that has been more comprehensive in its scope, or more effective in every branch of the life of the Church. Many of the folks who have been here the longest say that this series of meetings have been the very finest ever held in Canoga Park.

Our Church is laboring under a very heavy financial problem, more so than any other Church in this great Valley, and yet I have heard not the slightest criticism, because of adding this item of Evangelistic Expense. Mr. Mease's financial presentations are so modest and given without any organization or guarantee whatsoever, everything is 100% Voluntary, in fact many of us thought it should presented more forcefully than it was, and yet the response was more generous than any dared to hope. In fact we are confident that one result of these meetings, is going to be increased finances for our Churches in the coming months, and this will be only a byproduct of true evangelism.

The preaching is forceful, sincere, and with a burning passion to bring people to Christ. I believe over 100 turned to Christ in a definite way during the second week of the Campaign, and we do not stress numbers for the sake of numbers. By far the greatest results have been to the Church itself.

We are rejoicing in the ministry of this man to our Community. We knew he has been greatly used of God. Our only criticism is that he did at least three man's work while he was with us, and we do not like to anticipate his becoming unable to continue in this field in which he has proven so conspicuously successful.

We pray God's rich blessing upon him during many more years of ministry in evangelism. Open your Churches to him, and your hearts to him, and you will never regret laboring with him, in God's great harvest field. Already we are looking forward to our next campaign with him.

Yours in appreciation,

W. W. Ralph.

December 28, 1932.

Rev. Lawrence A. Meade,
Los Angeles, Calif.

Dear Brother Meade: It is with a sense of deep gratitude to
God for making possible the splendid series of meetings under
your spiritual leadership, that I am writing you these lines
of appreciation. In the nearly forty years of my pastoral
work it has never been my privilege to engage in revival work
with an evangelist more nearly to my idea of true evangelistic
effort, than at this time with you.

Your intense earnestness with the spectacular left out;
your insistence upon the Holy Spirit's conviction as the
basis of decision on the part of sinners, rather than personal
solicitation by members in the congregation; your loving and
yet uncompromising presentation of the great truths of the
gospel, all together make for lasting results that are a real
benefit to the church after you have left the field.

Your morning messages were feasts that fed and inspired
the people. Some said before the meetings began. "The people
cannot get out to a morning service." But the large attendance
morning after morning, proved that hungry folks will find a way
to get to the place where food is to be obtained.

The messages to the young people were an outstanding
feature of the services, and their response will be long felt
in our midst. The children's work and the great crowd that
came out on Saturday evening when their program was given.
gives evidence of the possibilities in that department of
evangelism.

Your refusal to stress, or permit to be pressed, the
financial remuneration for your services, with such perfect
reliance upon the Holy Spirit to move the people in their
free-will offering, certainly removed that great objection
which so many have against revival efforts.

If at any time I can be of any help by a personal word
to any pastor contemplating meetings, feel free to call.

Yours in Christian fellowship,

[signature]

Pastor Christ Community Church.

Santa Barbara Ave. Methodist Episcopal Church
Corner Santa Barbara Avenue and Wilton Place

GEORGE EDWARD MONKMAN, PASTOR
Res. 1640 West 30th Street

Los Angeles, California   Oct .8th. 1932.

Dr. Lawrence A. Meade,

Los Angeles, California.

Dear Brother Meade:

I told you while you were with us how much I enjoyed working with you,
but I feel that I should drop you a line,telling you,how much we appreciate
the fine piece of work that you did in our church, and community.

I am sure that our work will be easier, as the church has been greatly
quickened, and the community stirred. I thank you for the earnest, and
untiring way in which you have given yourself to the work, in the wonderful
Bible readings, and the gripping sermons which brought under the power of
the spirit such marked conviction, and such blessed results.

We will not soon forget the fine way in which you led the music, and the
fine response that was given you.

I hear nothing but praise of your work on every hand, and I am sure that
our people will be glad to have you for another series of meetings at some
future time.   Our prayers will continue to be for your success,in this great
work,to which we feel the Lord has called you.

Your brother,

Geo. E. Monkman,

400

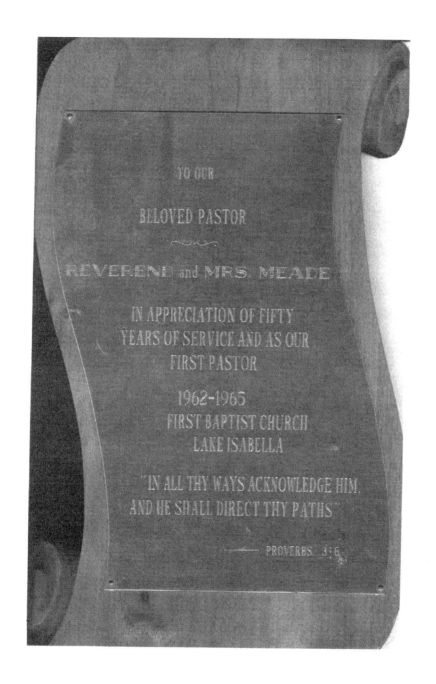

Lawrence A. Meade
1892-1971

Classic Christianity invites you to visit our website for more information!

www.classicchristianity.net

**We pray for the graces of insight and blessing as you seek a more intimate walk with Jesus.
Any glory, any praise, any blessing from this work belongs to God and God alone. Any mistake or error, we humbly acknowledge to be our own, and we apologize.**

Patricia Ediger

Cara Shelton

And our families

Made in the USA
Lexington, KY
09 January 2012